Unreasonable Behaviour

Don McCullin grew up in North London and went to work in a cartoon animation studio in Mayfair before the *Observer* newspaper bought one of his gangland pictures and set him on the road as photojournalist. He moved to the *Sunday Times*, where he worked for eighteen years. His photographs of almost every major conflict in his adult lifetime until the Falklands war, provide some of the most potent images of the twentieth century. His pictures are in major museum collections all over the world. He is the holder of many honours and awards, including the C.B.E.

ALSO BY DON McCULLIN

The Destruction Business
Is Anybody Taking Any Notice?
Homecoming
The Palestinians
(with Jonathan Dimbleby)
Hearts of Darkness
(with an introduction by John Le Carré)
Beirut: A City in Crisis
Perspectives
Skulduggery
(with Mark Shand)
Open Skies
(with an introduction by John Fowles)
Sleeping with Ghosts
(with an introduction by Mark Haworth-Booth)
India
(with an introduction by Norman Sherry)
Don McCullin
(with an introduction by Harold Evans)

Don McCullin

UNREASONABLE BEHAVIOUR

An Autobiography

with
Lewis Chester

VINTAGE BOOKS
London

First published by Vintage 1992
This edition published by Vintage 2002

15

First published in Great Britain in 1990 by
Jonathan Cape

Vintage
Random House, 20 Vauxhall Bridge Road,
London SW1V 2SA

www.vintage-books.co.uk

Addresses for companies within The Random House Group
Limited can be found at: www.randomhouse.co.uk/offices.htm

The Random House Group Limited Reg. No. 954009

A CIP catalogue record for this book
is available from the British Library

ISBN 9780099437765

The Random House Group Limited supports The Forest Stewardship
Council® (FSC®), the leading international forest-certification organisation.
Our books carrying the FSC label are printed on FSC®-certified paper.
FSC is the only forest-certification scheme supported by the leading
environmental organisations, including Greenpeace. Our
paper procurement policy can be found at
www.randomhouse.co.uk/environment

MIX
Paper from
responsible sources
FSC® C016897

Typeset by SX Composing DTP, Rayleigh, Essex
Printed and bound in Great Britain by Clays Ltd, St Ives plc

TO ALL THOSE WHO DID NOT SURVIVE

Contents

PREFACE

It has been some time since the original publication of *Unreasonable Behaviour* and I have to say that I was truly staggered by the response that it received. I thought that publishing the facts about my personal life would help to chase away some of my demons. Instead, all I was left with was the pain and guilt that I brought upon myself by betraying my beautiful wife and family. But now, twelve years on, I am extremely happy. At this moment in time I have four lovely grandchildren and a lovely new lady in my life.

I am still very much the photographer and working on all kinds of projects. I've presented three major exhibitions in France, where photography is, thankfully, still held in high regard, and last year, at the United Nations HQ in New York, I put together a major exhibition highlighting the AIDS crisis sweeping the southern continent of Africa. I have also published three new books and I am now working on a very exciting new project on the tribes of Southern Ethiopia.

So it all looks like I am, at last, beginning to pick up the pieces of my life once again. As for the future, I intend to keep working and, above all, try to be more adaptable to an ever-changing world.

Don McCullin
Somerset
March 2002

ACKNOWLEDGMENTS

Among a host of people who have opened doors for me to enlarge my life, I should like to acknowledge Bryn Campbell, the *Observer* picture editor, who first sent me to war; Philip Jones Griffiths, a freelance photo-journalist who encouraged me and taught me a great deal in the early days; Cornell Capa, who promoted my work in America; Mark Haworth-Booth for presenting my first exhibition at the Victoria and Albert Museum in London; and Mark Shand, my favourite travelling companion and friend, who has shared some dangers with me since I abandoned the world's battle fronts.

Many other colleagues and friends have been overwhelmingly generous with their help in bringing a measure of depth and accuracy to this book, going to untold trouble to jog my memory about details of events encountered together, or providing me with their own accounts of situations that I saw from only one side. With apologies to anyone I may have inadvertently omitted, I offer grateful thanks in this respect to David Blundy, Tony Clifton, Peter Crookston, Hunter Davies, Jonathan Dimbleby, Peter Dunn, Harry Evans, James Fox, Frank Hermann, Michael Herr, Ian Jack, Philip Jacobson, David King, Phillip Knightley, John le Carré, David Leitch, Norman Lewis, Magnus Linklater, Cal McCrystal, Martin Meredith, Alex Mitchell, Brian Moynahan, Eric Newby, Michael Nicholson, Edna O'Brien, Peter Pringle, Michael Rand, Murray Sayle, William Shawcross, Colin Simpson, Godfrey Smith, Sally Soames, Antony Terry, Bryan Wharton and Francis Wyndham.

Nick Wheeler, Clive Limpkin and Roger Cooper were kind

enough to let me use some of their photographs in the book, and besides my own I have taken the liberty of including a few other pictures given to me by people who sadly are no longer around to ask permission.

Above all I owe an enormous debt of gratitude to Lew Chester for his patience and dedication in bringing some order and direction to my life, and to Lyn Owen for her tireless assistance in the preparation of the script.

To Tony Colwell, my editor at Cape, go my special thanks for making it all possible.

Don McCullin
Somerset
June 1990

'They are like candles that no-one will put out, or stains that cannot be removed.'
M. Haworth-Booth on McCullin's photographs

'No se puede mirar.' ('One cannot look at this.')
'Yo lo vi.' ('I saw it.')
Goya

'To make you hear, to make you feel, to make you see.'
Conrad

PART ONE

Becoming Streetwise

I

THE BATTLEGROUND

TWO BROTHERS MET on a desert battleground on a February day in 1970. The elder was myself, covering my twentieth battle campaign as a photo-journalist; the younger, engaged in skirmishing with horse- and camel-mounted tribesmen of that remote African country, was my little brother Michael, then Sergeant, now Adjutant McCullin of the French Foreign Legion. For the short hour in which I could touch down in this arid spot, we met only to disagree.

We both spoke from too close a knowledge of war, gained in a long separation from each other. Like Legionnaires, war photographers cannot avoid the front line. In the bars of beleaguered hotels in the world's trouble spots where foreign correspondents gather there is sometimes talk of our seeing, due to modern means of communication, more of battle than anyone in history. Serving soldiers (SAS and mercenaries apart) are usually committed only to their own country's conflicts; war correspondents go to them all. And photographers, unlike reporters who can often gather better information behind the lines, are generally found in the thick of the fighting. Those who stay with the work for a long time, like the great Robert Capa and Larry Burrows, often die with it. I stayed with it for twenty years, and by some miracle survived. By the time I met my brother in Chad I had lived in the front lines of Cyprus, the Congo, Jerusalem, Biafra, and many of the campaigns in Vietnam. I was to go on to see war's depredations at Yom Kippur, in Cambodia, in Jordan, the

Lebanon, Iran, Afghanistan, even in El Salvador. Many of my good friends lost their lives on these battlegrounds.

It was perhaps the breadth of my experience that led Michael and me to differ. We had both been drawn to war by a sense of adventure, but its meaning for each of us had changed. To Michael, war was a game, a passion. Although it still held excitement for me, most of the time I could think only of its horrors. Michael's attitude was the more explicable, the more soldierly; mine was less straightforward. After all, my engagement was voluntary, for I was not under military discipline. If war had become so hateful to me, why did I not keep away? I have even been told I must have some sort of death wish – and it is true that throughout most of my life something has forced me to go out and record death and suffering. But it is not through any yearning for death for myself, or any man.

Now that I have stopped going to wars I still struggle with the meaning of all those experiences. Wars have dreadful differences, but also a dreadful sameness. You sleep with the dead, you cradle the dead, you live with the living who become the dead. Seeing, looking at what others cannot bear to see, is what my life as a war reporter is all about, and I have been criticised for forcing horrors into the view of complacent people. It has been said of my pictures of war and famine that 'we know now that our knowing makes no difference'. Yet I believe that it is not 'naive to think all that mattered'. Of course our knowing matters, and mine are far from the only photographs to have awakened to public conscience in recent years. I resent the idea – voiced more than once – that the subjects of my photography are 'matters too serious for art'. I am also deeply suspicious of any attempt to censor communication of the truth.

Even with all my years of watching, I have never been able to switch off my feelings, nor do I think it would be right to do so. Few are equipped to remain unmoved by the spectacle of what war does to people. These are sights that should, and do, bring pain, and shame, and guilt. Some sights heighten the feelings to an unbearable pitch. Once, when I was caught in a

4

forward position with American marines in Vietnam, a supply wagon bringing ammunition – a moke of the kind you might see on sea-side dunes – overshot our position in the dark. It stopped, and a sniper killed the driver, who stayed slumped in his position at the wheel, the engine droning on eerily. Through the night he was outlined by tracer flares from the other lines, unearthly in harsh yellow, orange and green. The incoming fire made it impossible for us to reach him. We watched in appalled fascination until dawn, when the battle died down and the moke's engine, finally running out of petrol, puttered to a stop.

Often in battle you think tomorrow it will be you, that you are going to be the one lying with your face to the stars. It is strange to think of a human body lying fixed in one position, staring at the stars without seeing. I remember being in a patrol when a burst of automatic fire brought down the two men ahead of me. I dived for cover, my mouth in the mud, my cameras covered with dirt, and I lay there, still, for twenty minutes during which everything in my life came back to me. At times like these, when men have died in front of you, and behind you, there is an overwhelming sense of them dying for you.

It has been said that I print my photographs too dark. How can such experiences be conveyed with a feeling of lightness? Yet, I ask myself, what has all my looking and probing done for these people, or for anyone? How many times, as the fire was closing on my position, have I thought – Is this it? Is this the day? What have I done with my life?

2

CHILDREN OF WAR

LIKE ALL MY generation in London, I am a product of Hitler. I was born in the Thirties and bombed in the Forties. Then Hollywood moved in and started showing me films about violence. At a very early age I can remember over-hearing my father telling my mother about a severed head one of his fellow air raid wardens had found during the blitz and was showing around in a box. Gruesomeness of this sort was par for the course for Londoners during and just after the Second World War, and it rubbed off on the children too.

The bombsites became our playgrounds. We went out hunting for shrapnel and the foil dropped by the Germans to deflect radar. We lived with nightly bomb terrors. Air raid shelters, like the one in our back yard, became our second homes. There was a pungent smell about those shelters – the smell of damp air trapped in that concrete shell. I lived that smell. I recall it today as fondly as other people remember the smells of summer, or of winter fires.

Children played at war because war was all there was. I remember playing toy soldiers with my little brother Michael. We would draw them up in battle-order in the yard and take their heads off by shying clods of earth. I was later to remember this battle. The play was unnervingly like the real thing.

My first home was just off the Tottenham Court Road, where my father occasionally worked as a fishmonger. The work was occasional because my father was an invalid. My mother had to make most of the decisions for us. When the family expanded, with the birth of my sister Marie, we moved to two rooms under the grille of a pavement in King's Cross. This lasted only a few months before we moved to a tenement building in Finsbury Park, then known as the worst area in north London. Again we had two damp basement rooms. Marie and I slept in one, they lived in the other. There was a scullery and a tiny lavatory, half in, half outside. It was no place for a man with chronic asthma, or kids for that matter, but it was home.

My most painful memory of the war was born of the attempt to get me away from it. When I was five, Marie and I were faced with evacuation. Michael, who was not born until a few years later, managed to escape. I remember the buses gathering at Paul's Park Primary School to take us to Paddington Station. There were many tears, and mothers waving and giving advice to their children. We all wore labels and carried little brown cardboard boxes containing our gas masks. We were told that we were going for our own protection, away from the bombs, to a rural existence.

As soon as we arrived in Norton St Philip in Somerset, Marie and I were separated. My mother had been promised that we would not be split up, but we were. My sister was taken to the wealthiest household in the village. People who had engineering companies in wartime were on to a good number. I was sent to a council house. My sister's existence and mine in that same village were from then on quite separate. Where she lived they had a maid with a black and white uniform who used to serve my sister tea. I would go round and peep through her window. Although I was her brother, I was looked upon as one of those scruffy council house children and not allowed in. Looking back, I think it may have been the beginning of something you can see in my pictures – an attempt to get as close to my subject while remaining invisible myself.

You soon became aware of, and resigned to, the position you have in society: the fact that I lived in a council house meant that somehow, for me, the die was cast. My sister was leaving us through the privilege she enjoyed in that house. My mother took the amazing decision of allowing her to stay on after the war as a permanent foster child in that rich family, who sent her to a girls' boarding school in Weston-super-Mare. So my sister went to public school. You could say – as they did in Finsbury Park – 'Adolf Hitler done her a favour.'

I felt cast out, unchosen, rather as if I were the wrong breed of dog. I remember running after my father when he set off home at the end of a visit and begging him to take me with him. My stay in Norton St Philip lasted less than a year, but I was soon evacuated again. I was always being evacuated. In my ignorance of Hitler's bombing plans, I supposed that my mother thought – Get him on the road again, give myself a breather.

In my third evacuation I hit a new low. I was sent to the north of England, to a village not far from Bolton in Lancashire. They were chicken farmers, and I got one egg a week on Sundays. Their main interest was in keeping me out of the house as much as possible by sending me to service in the morning, afternoon Sunday school, and then they would try to get me to go to the evening service as well. After tea on weekdays, they would lock me out until ten o'clock at night in all weathers.

I slept on the floor. My room had no lino or furniture, just some old chicken incubators. It was a room that was never used, and just because it was spare these people were forced to take in evacuee children they did not want.

With me in the house was a lad whose old man owned a pub in Camden town. He used to wet the bed and he got terrible hidings for it. We had landed among people who were rigid and, for all their Bible talk, very unforgiving. They found our ways alien, as we did theirs. I hated their funny way of cooking potatoes with their jackets on, and I wouldn't eat them. I would be clouted for that.

Clouting was an enduring memory from that evacuation. I was clouted by the schoolmasters, clouted by the kids in the playground, and clouted when I got home. I was building up a tidy store of resentment and mistrust.

One day I fell off a barn attempting some daredevil feat and smashed my face. That is why I have a broken nose. I crawled across a field and passed out. I woke up to see two women standing over me. They got me home, and I could see the chicken farmer was sorely tempted to bang me another one in the face for getting into trouble. He insisted on sending me to school the next day. Now that I had a huge swollen face on top of my much-mocked London voice I became an even bigger joke.

Finally, I wrote to my mother to say that I wasn't being treated well. She sent me the train fare and I made my way home. The night before I left, the chicken farmer dragged out a dustbin, emptied the chicken meal from it and filled it with hot water. I got my first bath in seventeen weeks.

That whole experience had strange after-effects. Once I got my own space, and a farmhouse, I always liked to have a few chickens about. I think they're very decorative and so, unfortunately, does the local fox. More seriously, it gave me a lifelong affinity with persecuted peoples. I know what it is like to be branded uncivilised and unclean, and to be treated as something pernicious. Except that I was ostracised and ill-treated by my own people, and not an alien race.

In the short term, though, the effects of evacuation were hardening. The loneliness and the long separations from my mothers had done for me what public school did for the boys of the middle classes. It had turned me into a tough little blighter who could stand on his own two feet. It also made me twitchy.

3

DERELICTION IN THE BUNK

BACK IN WARTIME London, I developed a variety of odd habits. I would jerk my neck out repeatedly in a convulsive way. I was terrified of stepping on cracks in the pavement – all children have a bit of a fixation about this, but mine was carried to the extremes. Above all, I liked to race the bus. I used to come out of the Tube at Finsbury Park, which slopes up like a drift-mine, see the 212 for Highgate starting up and tear along the road beside, or in front of, it for several hundred yards, past the school clinic, testing myself.

I discovered later in life that I was dyslexic, a condition that was not improved by the constant moving from school to school. By the time the evacuations were over, I could scarcely read even the simplest things, and was certainly not digesting the words I did struggle through. In those days there was only one sort of remedial teaching for slow learners and that was the cane, or a hard clip round the ear with the back of a hand. Exasperated schoolmasters seemed to think that violence would prod you forward. In my case, it simply made me violently backward. When first I got back to London I went in dread of beatings and whackings, and even punchings, that teachers had licence to administer. One master tried to speed my progress towards the Eleven Plus examination by banging my head against the school wall. Yet it has to be said that these terrifying Finsbury Park teachers were ranged against a most evil bunch of boys.

All of us returning from the country experienced great difficulty settling back into our impoverished urban homes. I know the smell of poverty as well as I know the stink of bomb-shelters and chicken houses. For me it is a compound of mildew and damp, of floor-cloths that are never clean and never get cleaned because there is no hot water, of too many bodies confined in too small a space. Even with my sister away, we would always be shifting round at home, trying to fit better into that cold, cramped basement so that my father could have the maximum warmth. I remember often sleeping in close proximity to his night-long cough. Yet the circumstances of my childhood fitted me in later years to stand before the poorest of people with humility. I would know without being told exactly what their lives were like.

Close to where we lived, in Fonthill Road, there was a notorious street known to everybody as The Bunk. It was a place beyond poverty, accurately described in a book called *The Worst Street in North London* as a home to thieves, punch-up artists and every other known type of criminal. Residents of The Bunk used to treat the police like people treat the bulls of Pamplona. And not only the police. The red alarm boxes, labelled 'Emergency, Fire', were always being punched in by the boys in The Bunk to bring round the Brigade. Often kids would set fire to one of the bombed-out buildings in order to make the call genuine. When they arrived, men of the fire brigade would be stoned, or would have their hoses cut. The children of The Bunk all went to my primary school.

Our real times were spent out of school. I spurned authority, all the boys did. We used the derelict bombed houses as our hideaway places. They were the arenas for our obnoxious behaviour. We would buy a pennyworth of chips for our lunch, ram them into a dry roll and take it into a derelict house, climbing right to the top where we would sit and discuss things, as if we were in some kind of parliament. The usual debate concerned how we were going to sabotage our school. In gutted buildings sometimes we crapped from the top floor to the bottom, pretending we were bombing Germany. It was all weird, though no doubt Desmond Morris would see it as quite normal animal behaviour. It

11

demonstrated the breaking of discipline, the breaking of authoritarian rule over us.

One of those derelict houses later played a striking role in my adult life. While still growing up, bombed houses were either a haven or a prey for vandalism. We stripped the lead and sold it to metal dealers. We ripped up the remaining floorboards and chopped the wood to sell it as kindling to old ladies for two pennies a bundle. The catacomb shells of shattered buildings gave us pleasure, and great sensations. There was nothing quite like the thrill of negotiating one dangerous level after another when all the staircases had gone. For us, it was like climbing the Eiger, and there we would bivouac for hours, in our own private places, away from the eyes of the alien adult world.

As we grew older, we went in for the pleasures of total escape from school. The school clinic was a staging-post for playing truant. It was the place to go if you had abrasions or minor injuries. I would put my name down for clinic, then go nowhere near it and abscond. I would go down into the Tube, and get out at Cockfosters, the end of the line. I would double back across the rails, to dodge the ticket collector, and then launch myself straight on to the countryside, looking for bird's eggs and snakes and things of that order. I spent a lot of time absconding, usually with a couple of mates with similarly inflated wounds.

Frequently the wounds were genuine. I got into a lot of fights. I was not a natural warrior, and usually fought other boys because I would not be pushed around by them. To this day I won't back down if I can help it, and I have had all sorts of bullies in front of me. It's a good attitude in a way, but often painful.

The boys who were most admired at school were the punch-up artists, sometimes as many as six or seven brothers in one family, and an offence against one was an offence against the lot. But it was the imaginative thieves who earned the most respect – boys who could go to Covent Garden at night and have fresh grapes for sale in the school break next day. In the centre of London there were also thousands of properties, temporarily abandoned yet undamaged by bombing, just waiting for boys to exercise their skills at breaking and entering. I was not too tempted in this area myself, less from any natural law-abiding instinct than from the sense I had that thieving was one of the surest ways of losing my liberty.

Predictably, I failed to pass the Eleven Plus, and so moved on from primary school to Tollington Park Secondary Modern School with much the same bunch of other boys. Half my class was heading for Approved School or Borstal, and I was fortunate to avoid the same fate. There was a certain code of loyalty where I lived, despite the roughness. The front door of your house was always open, and on summer evenings everything would be open. People used to sit at their windows because they never had to invert themselves, as later they did when watching television. They were used to looking outwards – and to some degree they would look out for each other.

There was also a family unity in those days. I recall that cosseted family feeling when bathing in the tin tub in front of the fire. Each of us took turns, my father first, and each had the same few saucepansful of hot water. I still think warmly of those moments, despite my brother Michael getting ahead of me in the pecking order when he was born and being apt to pee in the water.

Sometimes family unity would break down in our house when my mother lost her fiery temper. My father used to gamble on the greyhounds at Haringey. Perhaps it was a way for him to restore pride in himself when he was sick and unemployed, but it led to more than the usual problems of family finance.

My mother stretched out the family budget by leaning heavily on the tallyman and the pawn shop. I had a key role in this economy, which now seems like a sob story from Dickens, but which was only too real. I would take my father's suit on a Monday morning to the pawn shop and go again on the Friday to get it out. It was always wrapped in a bedsheet.

The whole business humiliated me. The pawnbroker was a little man called Mr Lucan, who had a bald head, wore rimless glasses, grew a little tache, and always wore a pin-stripe grey suit with a very white shirt collar. Women didn't like going to Mr Lucan because he always held on to the palms of their hands when they were exchanging tickets. I didn't like going there either. It gave me the feeling from an early age that I would rather steal than beg.

On Saturday morning I would go to pay the tallyman, then double off to pay the rent at Donaldson's in Hornsey Road. Another job of mine was to lie to those who came collecting at the front door. 'My mum's not in.' It was a poor premium to put on a kid, to start him off lying, but it was part of the old lady's constant battle to keep us clean, clothed and fed.

Our clothes came from a secondhand shop run by a woman called Jessie Chapman, which usually looked as if someone had backed up a lorry-load of spaghetti and dumped it down. In among the tangle somewhere would be something that might fit me. My mother would bring the garment home and try to knock the terrible secondhand smell out of it.

Due to my father's illness, mother became the tough character at home. She often had to go out to earn the family bread, especially in winter when my father's health was at its worse. In wartime, English women did some really heavy jobs, and the old lady worked in an aircraft factory or loading crates on to lorries at King's Cross station. She had a fearsome reputation as a fighter. My mother once took on the woman next door, who was known for her physical prowess, when she told my sister – then home for two weeks from her adoptive home in Somerset – to eff off and take her posh accent elsewhere. She pasted the woman in front of the whole street, which became an arena, all windows open and everyone watching. She did it again when another woman complained about my behaviour. My mates said they all enjoyed seeing Mrs Nash's knickers in the brawl, and my mother became something of a local hero.

I found it all rather distasteful. Maybe I had a little snobbish streak in me even then, born of an inferiority complex that took hold in Somerset when I was assigned to a lower class than my sister. I respected my mother, but my hero was my mellower father, who spent more time with me. Despite his regret that he'd been unfit for the army, he was a hero to me when I saw him carrying stretchers for the ARP. I gained a sense of gentleness from him.

In the evenings, after the remains of a bread and cheese supper and the tea cups had been cleared off the old kitchen table, my father would start making things for me and my brother – a rocking horse or a cathedral of matches. He got me making little carts and trolleys, and even a covered wagon, which Michael drove, brandishing a rubber pistol. I was the Apache Indian at the back.

I used to draw my father. I would pin up the paper on the wall and sometimes go right over the edge, so that when I took the paper away there would be a white square on the wall with lines going off it in all directions. He still encouraged me and I began to develop some skill. I loved my father, and felt the strength of his love for me. I was probably the only boy in the neighbourhood whose father never gave him a hiding. My greatest fear was his death, but I overcame it by playing a part in his survival. This often took the form of simple errands, like stealing coal from a nearby yard to keep him warm. My main service was spending time with him, and drawing was part of this. We also went to the cinema together.

By this time I had graduated from *Hopalong Cassidy* at Saturday morning children's cinema – when one boy would go in and open the fire door to let in the rest of us while the usherette wasn't looking – to the early war films. One evening, as I was getting ready to go to the pictures with my mother and father, a woman knocked at the door to tell my mother that I had been interfering with her daughter in an air raid shelter in Tollington Park. It was true, of course, but it had only been experiment on both sides.

I remember my father taking charge as my mother's voice rose an octave. 'Get yourself washed,' he said. 'We're going to the police station.'

15

I was stripped of my shirt at the sink and my mother smacked me from one side of the scullery to the other.

'If we're going, we'd better go,' I heard my father say. They're really going through with this, I thought.

He must have been stifling his laughter all the while, for we didn't go near the police station but ended up in our favourite spot in the front row of the Astoria cinema. It was as if they were taking their thirteen-year-old son out for a treat on entering manhood.

4

A SHOCKING LIBERTY

I KNEW THE war was over for good when my mother launched her attack on the air raid shelter in the back yard. She and I demolished it together with ordinary household hammers. It took months, and it transformed the level of the ground. When it was done, my mother started a little garden.

I was less ready for peaceful pursuits. As the real soldiers were being demobbed, I joined up. A little group of us twelve- and thirteen-year-olds organised pitched battles on Hampstead Heath. We made our own weapons. I used to fashion Bren guns – the English automatic weapon of the day, and very accurate it was. I would provide 'first aid' from my father's old ARP kits. These ferocious bush wars took place in our imaginary Killing Fields behind Kenwood House. There we would welcome death, and took pride in giving a good performance. I doubt if any of us knew of Robert Capa's amazing picture of the falling soldier in the Spanish Civil War but that was our most cherished way to die.

The end of hostilities against Germany and Japan left a whole generation of urban kids unable to think in any terms other than those of war. I was mad about it, and the movies fed my madness. The Astoria cinema was showing little else but John Wayne or Errol Flynn in films like *Back to Bataan*.

I also had access to the best of British toy soldiers. Some of the local housewives used to take in lead soldiers – a gross on a tray – and do what they called home work. They would paint them at home to earn extra money, the way some people take in typing today. So there was always a constant supply of fresh soldiers for my war games with young Michael in the back yard.

By the time I joined the real cadets, with their proper uniforms, at the age of thirteen, I was already a veteran. My outfit was the Royal Fusiliers, and I remember the enthusiasm with which I would buff its badge – a blazing cannonball. We assembled in a drill hall near Brunswick Square in Bloomsbury and spent weekends in camp at Osterley Park, where proper training was carried out with blank cartridges and thunder-flashes. It was like simulated war. I thought it was great.

Even so, my army career did not last long. My father and one of my teachers helped to turn me towards a gentler interest. Drawing was the only talent that was not assiduously beaten out of me in my schooling. It also was one of the few skills that the boys at Tollington Park were prepared to tolerate – even to admire. Being good at English or maths could get you branded as a teacher's pet or bright spark. Drawing was all right. It was extraordinary, like magic. I am not sure how extraordinary my talent was but it led to Mr Cooper steering me into a trade art scholarship and attendance at the Hammersmith School of Arts and Crafts and Building – a school for bricklayers as well as budding artists, opposite Lime Grove television studios.

It was hardly the Slade, yet I felt as if someone had given me a passport, a key to a locked garden full of colour and light. For one thing, there were girls at Hammersmith, and I had never been in a classroom with girls before. Of course I displayed no breeding, kept up my disdain for anything female, and so gained no quick favours with the girls, but I was among people with expectations altogether different from those of the boys in The Bunk. It was as if a wand had been waved over Finsbury Park and I had been spared for a much nicer life.

Then suddenly the bottom dropped out of my world. My father, who of all the family had been most thrilled to see his lad win a scholarship, became critically ill. As the attacks grew worse, and he began rapidly to lose weight, I would stay awake at night willing him to live. But the odds – with a million coal fires in those days pouring smoke into the winter air – were against him. One night he was taken away to St Mary's Hospital in Highgate, which looked like an old workhouse. My brother and I were sent to a neighbour's house where the family was quite posh, the man having a job at Harrod's. I sat stiffly in their parlour leafing through something called the *National Geographic Magazine*. At home we sometimes saw the *News of the World*, and I would glance through *Picture Post* and a magazine called *Illustrated* while waiting my turn in the barber's shop, but I had never before seen photography of the sort that was displayed in the pages of the *National Geographic*. I became absorbed and forgot the dread of my father's sickbed until the policeman called at the door. (There were no telephones in our houses in Finsbury Park in those days.) I remember the hushed conversation with the adults and knowing without being told that the worst had happened.

My father, once a well set up man of 5ft 10in., weighed little more than six stone when he died. He was forty years old. A friend once said to me in later life, 'It doesn't matter how old you are, the day your father dies it's like being kicked in the balls.' That is a pretty accurate description of how I felt. The scene of my father laid out, the burning candles and the smell, is one I shall never forget.

I was fourteen, and there was no question now of staying on at art school. The elder son was expected to take over the role of father and start to carn the family keep. At least finding a job in those days was not a problem, though few of them led anywhere. My mother's mates on the railway soon had me working as a pantry-boy on the LMS dining cars. I used to go from London to Manchester on a train called the 'Comet', the 9.45 am special for businessmen, which would return from Manchester in the early evening. It was interesting to see those grimy satanic northern cities, with their tall factory chimneys belching dark smoke, before the Clean Air Act which might have kept my father alive if it had arrived much sooner. Besides, I had freedom. I was leaving Finsbury Park every day and travelling all over England. I would make the best of it.

Internally, I was angry with God – if He existed. He had taken a liberty in removing my father from me, the one person in my life who had made the misery of poverty seem irrelevant. I would disown God. A strength arose in the midst of the pity I was beginning to feel for myself. On the surface I kept up the flippancy, slinging plates out of the train window as we passed over a viaduct, to see what effect they would have. I was Jack the Lad, with thirty shillings in my pocket, and sometimes double that in tips. But the buried resentment burned, not very deep down.

5
HUNTING DOGS

I SPENT MY first savings on a Teddy Boy suit. It was navy blue hopsack, and it cost £7.7.6 in Stoke Newington High Street. With it went the obligatory suedes with thick spongy soles, brothel-creepers blue of course, and a black bootlace tie. I wore the outfit on my first date, with a girl in Hornsey, and it poured with rain. My hair hung down and the suit was shrinking on my back as we made our way to a dance in Highgate at a place called Holy Joe's, or St Joseph's Church, near where my father had died.

This was sophistication, though the kid in me was not buried far beneath the surface. On evenings when the old lady had to work late, I would be Michael's protector. Despite my age, we still shared the same bed, and we would lie there and listen to Valentine Dyall, 'The Man in Black', reading a series of radio horror stories, with the blankets pulled over our heads to keep out the bogeyman.

At the same time, I was trying to train myself in all things that interested men. The bridge between boyhood and manhood for me was motorbikes. There was a boy down the road who kept his bike in the bedroom. He had trays for the oil laid out across the floor – he could, so he said, do an oil change and have his girl at the same time. To the rest of us in Finsbury Park this seemed to be the essence of cool. I swore that one day I too would own one of these machines. In the meantime I rode pillion.

I left the railway when I got a job at the cartoon animation studio W.M. Larkins, with a fashionable address in Mayfair.

I had shown some of my art school drawings to the boss, Peter Sachs, a Jew who had escaped from Nazi Germany, and he let me in on the ground floor as a messenger boy. If things turned out well, he said, he would allow me to mix colours.

Colour mixing was not to last long, for it turned out that I was partially colour blind, and certainly not up to the subtlety of animation. I was all right when I stuck to blues, reds and yellows, but my browns, beiges and greens were less secure. I went back to running messages, too inexperienced in their eyes to be taken into the dark room. The only photography I had ever encountered was sitting with my sister in Jerome's in the Holloway Road, having out portraits taken for the family.

Mayfair touched me in other ways. I became very conscious of my appearance. I was not conceited, but I fretted about not having enough money to buy clothes. Walking from work from the Underground at Piccadilly, I would catch sight of myself in the window of the Rolls-Royce showroom as I turned into Charles Street and go to work on the arrangement of my collar and cuffs. I also remember swinging round into Berkeley Square and smelling the scent of that wonderful shop Moyses Stevens, looking at the orchids in the window with water running down it. It made me aware of a different world, a world far removed from my biking mates and the boys from The Bunk, who were now emerging from their first confinements in corrective or penal institutions. Mayfair held out the promise of escape from Finsbury Park and all that.

But not yet. I bought a Velocette 250, with a fish tail and girder forks, which would throb along at 50 miles an hour. I felt like an ace at Brooklands, with no such things as crash helmets in those days. We would drive out in formation on Sundays, down the A10 to Collier's End, where we would dive off an old survival dinghy from the war into the ice-cold river. We would eat some continental food at a cafe on the way home and then bomb the rest of the way up the arterial road to Finsbury Park. We were no Hell's Angels, and they were great days of freedom, with friendships quite different from the relationship I had with my old Bunk boys, the hunting dogs, who were now hanging out in packs looking for trouble.

Despite my biking friends, I still needed the mad dogs. Intimidation was always strong in Finsbury Park, and there was a force-field all the time trying to draw you into something mischievous. I avoided thieving, but gang warfare was a stronger temptation. There was suppressed aggression and a lot of resentment in me. I wanted the respect given to those serious street fighters – the swaggering elite of the Seven Sisters Road, where the tribe had a name: The Guvnors. In a corralled car, the tribe would strut their stuff at dance-halls or harry the whores in Shaftesbury Avenue. One or two did become ponces, but the sexual level then was little more than a flick through the carefully censored nudes in *Health and Efficiency*. On Saturday nights the tribe would turn up in force at the Royal dance-hall in Tottenham. A refusal to dance from a girl was hard to bear in front of this mob, and you'd hope for salvation in the rumbling sound at the start of a good punch-up. That would make the evening and set up an electric air when you walked in next week.

With The Guvnors, though they were predators themselves, you felt safe from other predators, like the bigger, older criminals who lurked in the background of our neighbourhood, and the police. The police were our natural enemies. If you were caught in a cul-de-sac by the coppers, as I was on one occasion, you could be sure to be on light duties for the next week. All this, of course, was just before the first wave of coloured immigration in Britain. In some ways we were like white negroes, the out groups. Though we were a funny kind of negro, since most of us were as bigoted and racist as they come.

When it came to the time for national service, I was a pretty fractured personality. I had come to like my job in Mayfair, and the people there were kind to me, but I felt as if they could see 'Finsbury Park' indelibly written across my forehead and 'working class' on the other side of my head. I couldn't see how I was ever going to be much more than a messenger in the world. I was sure of one thing. I didn't want to go into the army and be pushed around. A few years of Bill Haley had shaken all enthusiasm for the soldier's life out of me. So I smarmed my way into the air force.

6

TANK WARFARE

'THERE YOU ARE!' we were told. 'One of the wonders of the world, so you'd better wonder at it.'

We had been marched up to an RAF bus, ordered on board and driven into the desert to see the Pyramids. To us recruits the Pyramids seemed dull and expressionless heaps of stone. The highlight of our day was the barney that erupted as we were getting ready to take the bus out. Some Arabs (or wogs, as with shameless lack of concern for ethnic sensibilities thugs like us called them in the Fifties) had been pressing us to buy some glass jars. Few objects were less suited to the needs of people on 27 shillings a week and living under canvas. Some of the lads had resorted to direct action by snapping down the bus windows, sharpish, on the vendors' fingers. Jars would be tumbling in and no money would be going out. The Arabs then mounted a spirited counterattack.

At eighteen I wasn't really ready for civilised behaviour, much less the Pyramids, but I was slowly beginning to get the hang of service life. They had said to me: 'Right, McCullin. You're in films. We've got a whole load of tins of film at Queen's Flight, RAF Benson, in Oxfordshire. They need numbers painting on them. There's a million of them.' It was an underestimation. They had mountains of Second World War air reconnaissance film. Painting numbers on the cans was a long way behind whitewashing coal in terms of interest. I thought, I'm not going to do this, and there was wide support for this view in my little group. We mounted a guard on the ridge, to keep lookout for the sergeant who periodically wobbled our way on his bike, stowing the playing cards and grabbing the paint brushes only when he hove into view. We controlled our output by our sightings, as they say in the RAF.

My thoughts turned to foreign parts. I had been told that the Canal Zone was a God-awful posting – this was two years before Suez – so I applied for Hong Kong. Naturally, I got the Canal Zone. Those who had applied for the Canal Zone landed as inevitably among the sky-scrapers, junks, and almond-eyed ladies in slit-skirts of the Far East.

I was posted to a barbed wire compound in Ismailia, close to the spot where Lake Timsah turns into the Suez Canal. The heat hit you like a hammer.

As soon as I arrived they put me in a tank. It bore no resemblance to the glamorous army machine of the same name, but resembled a vat, the size of a large room, with deep rusty sides, full of acid crystals. My tank was the most inglorious part of the process of aerial photo-reconnaissance. It was where the films got developed, in bulk. My film cartoon experience amply qualified me to clean it out.

Every morning I was lowered into this object for the day's work. As a treat, I would later be allowed to stir the noxious chemicals, or even get a go on the map photostat machine.

We had to do guard duty three nights a week, for which we were issued with a Sten gun, a most ill-conceived weapon which could fail to hit a London bus at ten paces. Occasionally I would catch people coming into the camp to steal and hand them over to the RAF police who would then phone the local police. You'd see this Egyptian policeman coming along the side of the Canal, complete with fez and cane. We would drive up, salute, and perform the usual courtesies. The offending detainee would sometimes protest that he was only trying to retrieve something that had gone on to the wrong side of the wire, and the policeman would fetch him a clout round the earhole; much to my pleasure, for I would be thinking that if it weren't for him I would be in bed. I had a pretty ignorant attitude.

One of the photographers urged me to take the

photographic trade test. It would mean more interesting work, and more money. So I took the written test, and failed. Suddenly my life improved. I was still a photo-assistant but the RAF decided I should have a better posting. I was let loose on the Mau Mau in Kenya. It amounted to exchanging the inside of one large tank-like structure for another, this time a huge aircraft hangar housing bombers, where we slept. It was overrun with rats. At least the army performed the guard duties.

My elevated role in the Kenya emergency was to work what was called a bulk-processing machine for Bomber Command, Nairobi. The bombers came back daily with 3,000 or more pictures of Mau Mau country, or bombing patterns, or both, to be developed at speed. I was the speed. The Canberras were the worst, from my point of view. They could take pictures from six camera mountings simultaneously. The intelligence people used these pictures for the next day's offensive against the rebels. For me the work was hectic, and not very interesting.

I was more appreciative of Kenya itself. Nairobi was a charming colonial town in those days, with Great White Hunters in safari hats trooping in and out of the Stanley Hotel. In my time off I made a new sortie into the high life, persuading the daughter of a Dutch farmer to teach me how to sit on a horse. My horizons widened still further when I made friends with some of the bomber crews in our hangar.

They would let me fly with them as supercargo on their raids on the Kinangop plateau, then a Mau Mau stronghold. I enjoyed the raffish, Dambusters air about the whole proceeding: these chaps in helmets and goggles with stuff all over their noses saying Bravo, Wingco. In fact the Lincoln bombers, with my illicit extra weight, were a bit unnerving. You realised what a struggle they had to get off the ground and stay in the air when they leapt what seemed 1,000 feet after they had released the bomb load.

Sometimes, on the way back, they would fly in low by Kilimanjaro, so we could get a sight of the zebra herds and elephant and wildebeest on the plains of Amboseli. On occasion, I managed to go up with Harvards, the little fighter escort planes. They used to strafe the jungle in true Hollywood war-movie fashion and lark about in the sky on the way home.

In all this, at such a callow age, I never gave a thought to the damage being done to the villages below, or to the rights and wrongs of the colonial situation. To us, the Mau Mau were monster baddie Indians, well-known from the blood-curdling tales in the Other Ranks' Mess of atrocities and unspeakable oath-taking ceremonies. As to Great Britain's right to throw its weight around on another continent, that went without question. We were all Labour of course in Finsbury Park, but when it came to anything foreign, I was a super patriot, well to the right of Alf Garnett. My country could do no wrong.

It was an outlook commonplace then, but being overtaken by events. My service career was a kind of extended Cook's tour of the end of the Empire. I was posted to Cyprus. In Nicosia, Eoka terrorists, in the name of *enosis*, freedom, were gunning down unarmed British soldiers as they shopped with their families on Ledra Street. Ledra Street would acquire the name Murder Mile. But, away from the capital, at RAF Episcopi, near Akrotiri, we were in another world. We emerged from our tents in the morning to crags soaring in clean air, a blue sea directly below, and the stones of the site of the Temple of Apollo glowing in the Mediterranean light. In off-duty hours we learned scuba diving.

Sometimes we would ride shotgun, or more precisely sten gun, with the escort cart that went into Nicosia. This was not too dangerous as Eoka rarely attacked armed soldiers. It gave us a chance to see the city and to gain some insight into the deep instability of the island: the smouldering animosity between the Greek and Turkish Cypriots. The only thing that seemed to unite them was the pleasure of blasting songbirds on Sunday mornings.

A more lunatic, but to us enjoyable, way of travelling round the island was as part of a football team which used to play the other bases. On the dangerous mountain roads we would always be coming up on trucks heavily laden with grapes, heading for the factory. As we passed it would be like Clouzot's film *The Wages of Fear* – hair-raising. The lads would all be reaching out and trying to make instant wine as we inched past. And the truck driver would be trying to bawl us out while not plunging into the ravine at the same time.

Civilised encounters with the local population did not figure large on our agenda. One evening we had a supervised night out, under guard, at a bar in Limassol. It was some PR exercise connected with the fact that there were visiting MPs on the island who wanted to be assured that the servicemen and the local population were getting on famously. We simply were not ready for mixed society. On this rare human opportunity, I seized the chance to make eyes at a pretty Cypriot bar girl. It cost me an arm and a leg in purchased drinks just to make the eyes. I tried to consolidate my advance by manoeuvring the chairs for a closer encounter. My proffered chair missed its target, her descending and shapely rear end, and the poor girl landed in a heap on the floor. It led to a brisk end to the cavalier career of this particular Virgin Airman.

I emerged from the RAF with the dizzying – and complimentary – rank of Leading Aircraftsman and an African General Service medal, which was a bit of a laugh. I had also, in theory, seen the world. As well as my postings in Egypt, Kenya and Cyprus, I had made flying visits to Aden and to Khartoum, where I caught a breathtaking glimpse of the Nile. But aside from such glimpses, I had mainly seen a world I didn't want to know – a world bounded by a barbed wire perimeter fence.

If I failed to become an RAF photographer, I did make an important acquisition: my first camera. Someone had said they could get marvellous bargain ones on the milk run to Aden. I decided that this was a better destination for my life's savings of £30 than a pair of lionskin drums. So I became the owner of a brand new Rolleicord. It was one of those twin reflex cameras that you hold up to your chest and look down into. I had no notion then that that was the camera used by the great photographers of the Thirties, Bill Brandt and Brassaï.

I recouped some of the outlay almost immediately by taking aerial photographs of RAF Eastleigh on one of my Harvard rides. I made 150 postcards to sell off in the camp at a shilling each. The sergeant of the photographic section came in just as another batch was going through the developing fluid, and he started to create. 'Someone's on a bloody good racket here,' he said, 'and I want to get to the bottom of it.' He didn't mind my having a racket of course, he was just narked that I hadn't cut him in.

I ran short of cash when I got back to Finsbury Park. And I came across this object that didn't seem to have purpose or place with me. I couldn't think of anything I could use it for. So I made £5 by pawning the Rolleicord.

My mother said to me one day, 'What happened to that lovely camera?' I told her. She said. 'That's terrible,' and she went off and used her own money to redeem the pledge. What happened as a result of that generous act was to have a dramatic effect on my life.

7

THE MURDER

IT TOOK A remarkable set of circumstances to put me back on the road to photography, and they revolved tragically round a murder.

At first, when I returned from national service, I felt as if I had never been away. The world of Finsbury Park had not changed, neither had its characters. In my absence my mother had had a difference with the man who lived upstairs. He was in the habit of coming home drunk around midnight and taking the belt to his little boy. One night my mother took the law into her own hands and broke a large chalk ornament (won at the Hampstead Fair) over the man's head. There was blood and chalk all down the stairs. She had gone off in the police Wolseley with the bells ringing and was later bound over to keep the peace. I think the child was glad of her intervention.

One notable event had taken place in Fonthill Road – the first West Indians had set up home in Finsbury Park and many of the locals were not pleased. I found them to be nice, gentle people.

Larkins in Mayfair took me back and decided to make some use of my smattering of photographic knowledge by setting me up in a little dark room to copy line drawings. I learned to process the film in my own way, and got to know the artists and animators much better. They were a delightful crowd. The kick or be kicked attitudes that had got me through national service satisfactorily seemed less convincing here. What I am describing of course is the slow beginning of a liberal education for a person who had no recourse to books. Trying to read only made me feel foolish. At the age of twenty-one my entire library consisted of two little books my mother had bought for a shilling each when I had been in short pants – one on painting, the other on wildlife.

The Guvnors were still lolling round in greasy-spoon cafes, feet on the tables weaving their fantasies. The only visible change was the new taste in Dillinger-style hats. Once I had got my camera out of pawn, they were only too keen for me to produce glossy cinema-still photos of them in their new images. Then I ventured more ambitious pictures of them in different locations. I enjoyed handling the camera but had no thought of what to do with the photographs beyond entertaining their subjects.

The favourite hangout was a little cafe in Blackstock Road run by a stout Italian woman with a pretty daughter called Maria. 'Can we have Maria's tits on toast?' the boys would ask, and the mother would say, 'Come on boys, be serious, be nice, don't be naughty.' The popularity of this exchange straddled my service career.

Gray's Dancing Academy in the Seven Sisters Road was now the Saturday night venue. Anything less like its name was hard to imagine. Ex-wrestling champion Bert Aserati, with ears like clenched fists, was the bouncer who could block the door with his huge bulk. The gang paid lip-service to him because they respected him, though even Bert could not be everywhere at once. The place acquired a reputation for drawing George Raft and James Cagney types from all over north London, who came with the sole intention of taking on the local hard nuts. Often they would end up laid out like dead bandits in one of those old-fashioned American photographs. Gray's was in fact rather like a speakeasy, the obelisk revolving lights at your feet incessantly, as if there were a thousand mice trying to get out of the building.

The girls would come there thinking they were meeting Humphrey Bogart at the Kasbah. I too was allured by that atmosphere. I was also allured by the girls. It was at Gray's that I met the prettiest girl I had seen in my life. She was blonde, with huge eyes, and her name was Christine. She had come on a tentative expedition with friends, from Muswell Hill, which was considered a rather upper-class area by our standards.

I knew she was my girl straight away. I nearly had a brawl with another bloke who also liked her. He was quite good-looking and kept taunting me: 'I can have her any time.' He didn't. I wound up with her and I found she was a lovely girl. We didn't have a lot in common. She was very bright, with eight O-levels, and could have gone to university if she had been pushed. She worked in an office at London Bridge which imported ground nuts and other things from Africa. She understood French and could work a telex machine, but her origins were not intimidating. Her father was a postman, and she lived in a council flat with its own bathroom. I persuaded her that I loved her, and I became her steady boyfriend.

In those days there was a firmly set out path for a young man to follow. First he got the violence out of his system, then he went out with a girl for a two-year period before he married her and settled down. To my surprise, Christine's parents accepted me as her regular chap, deceived perhaps by the wholesome effects of my mother's garden hose. Yet, despite her civilising influence, I had not reached the end of my wild youth. I went for a bloke one day who started pestering me at a bus stop and at the end of the fight fox-trotted with Christine and a broken lip round Hornsey Town Hall. But the most bizarre fight was my last in Finsbury Park.

We were on our way home from the funeral of a girl who had committed suicide over one of the local boys, and were in an emotional state, when one of the hard nuts in the back of my old Ford Consul demanded a pee in the Holloway Road. In his haste to run off up an alleyway, he broke the wing mirror. I got out of the car and called a name after him. I should have gone for him while he was peeing for that is when it is most difficult to carry on a fight, but I was not fighting mad, only annoyed. The next thing I knew was him standing before me, flourishing a brick in front of my face. I managed to hit him in the ribs, and then I grabbed the brick and hit him across the head with it. I kept on hitting him as the blood oozed from his head. I felt it was either him or me.

Then I said, 'Have you had enough now?' His reply was to smash his head into my face. As we stood there, both pouring blood, he said calmly, 'I think that's about even.'

We got back into the car, and I drove him to the Royal Northern Hospital to get his head stitched up. I didn't know him well but he always had a friendly greeting for me after that. Christine was unnerved by this sort of violence, but she remained loyal to me. Arriving home at Fonthill Road from one of our regular dates at the cinema, we found my mother, unusually, still up. She had news.

'That gang you hang around with at Gray's,' she said. 'They're in trouble. A policeman's been killed up there.'

It turned out that a man older than was usual in the gangs had been at the centre of the barney. Ronald Marwood, a 25-year-old scaffolder from Islington, had gone to the Academy with a knife to settle some vengeful argument, though knuckle-dusters were as far as things went usually. He had probably thought only of intimidation, but when the gangs took sides and fought on the pavement outside, a policeman tried to wedge himself between the opposing sides and had been stabbed in the back. He died from loss of blood. Marwood fled, but his father persuaded him to give himself up.

Those of us who lived in Finsbury Park spoke of little else but the killing in the next few weeks. It also focused national thinking on the growing phenomenon of delinquent youth and gang violence. At Larkins I was pumped for what I knew. I told them that many in the gangs lived in the streets around me, and that I had gone to school with them. The Guvnors hadn't been directly involved in the murder, as it happened, but I took some photographs of them into the office, where I was told I should try and get them published. Someone suggested taking them to the *Observer*, a liberal, socially concerned quality Sunday newspaper which I had never read.

In those days there was none of the sophisticated security apparatus that now bars newspaper doors. In my hopsack suit and suedes, I was able to walk straight into the *Observer* offices in Tudor Street and be directed to the picture desk without prior appointment. The picture editor, a man called Cliff Hopkinson, looked carefully through my folder, then swung back in his chair and gave me a long inquisitive look.

'Did you take these?' he said at last.

'Yes,' was all I replied.

He said, 'I like this picture, and I'm going to use it. Would you do some more for me?'

I left, full of excitement, with a formal commission for more pictures, and a writer by the name of Clancy Sigal was asked to produce the story. Yet Finsbury Park was still to have its say in the matter.

Even as I was leaving the cafe in Blackstock Road, at the end of a session photographing the boys, I saw the familiar Wolseley waiting. As I approached, the car door opened and I heard the friendly invitation from the law.

'Get in.'

I said, 'No.'

'Get in if you know what's good for you.'

I got in. Always resist the first time, but never take it too far. That was the game around here.

'We've reason to believe that you have been in that cafe with a stolen camera.'

I told them it was not stolen. They asked to see the purchase receipt, which of course I didn't have with me. They suggested a short drive to where I lived to find the receipt, otherwise I'd be heading straight for the police station.

'Okay,' I said, 'but do me a favour – don't park outside my house. If my mother sees you, you'll be in terrible trouble.'

That broke them up: 'So your mother is tough, eh?' but they did as I asked. I went in the house, rummaged through my little chest of drawers and found the receipt. When the old lady asked what I was doing I just said that I was tidying up. When I nipped out to show the receipt to the police they went all oily.

'Can we drop you back to where we first found you, sir?'

It was a wonderful moment, refusing a copper's favour and

seeing them off. And of course I really had been of assistance to the law. If my mother had come across them harassing me over the camera, there is no question, she would have brained them with the heaviest available ornament.

The pictures were published as a half page in the *Observer* on 15 February 1959. I was twenty-three years old. The big picture was one I had taken before the killing. It showed the lads in their best suits posed in a burned-out house in The Bunk, though it had been renamed Wadcote Street to improve its image. I had got them together as they were setting off for an afternoon at the Astoria cinema.

Now, much more than then, I can recognise that it was a strong picture. It shows an awareness of structure that must have been instinctive because I would not have known what the term meant at the time. It was also brilliantly exposed, which must have been a fluke, for I did not possess a light meter.

That one picture changed my life. People have told me that if I had not made a breakthrough with that photograph, then I would have done so with another. I don't think that would necessarily have been the case. I had a low tolerance of rejection, and no burning desire to be a photographer. If I had been obliged to battle my way into Fleet Street, I would never have got there.

8

A FASTER SIDEWALK

IT WAS NOT only the policeman who lost his life at Gray's Dancing Academy; Marwood also died. After standing trial he was hanged, according to the ruthless law of capital punishment. For these two men, the events that night in Seven Sisters Road led to tragedy. For me, they led to the start of a new life.

When those pictures appeared in the *Observer*, I was described as a stills photographer in the film industry, which was pushing it a bit. My job only involved copying animation drawings, but suddenly everyone seemed to be offering me assignments. *Life* magazine phoned, so did the BBC. A West End theatre company wanted me to photograph their show. The *New Chronicle* and the *Sunday Graphic* came on the line. The *Observer* also asked for more work from me. At Larkins the phone kept ringing until they became mildly annoyed by it.

Although it was a most rewarding time, I had no experience of being in demand nor of the kind of money that was being thrust my way. When £10 a week was a good wage, the *Observer* had paid me £50 for my pictures. It was the largest sum I had ever possessed, and it led to my next social leap – opening a bank account. Home life at Fonthill Road also underwent a transformation. My mother took to searching for the *Observer* on Sundays, not a big seller in those parts. A telephone was installed, so that my new career wouldn't interfere with Larkins.

Christine was working in an office in Bond Street and we

used to meet for lunch most days in Lyons Corner House, like Trevor Howard and Celia Johnson in *Brief Encounter*. We started making plans to marry over an economy bowl of soup and a roll. I would then dart off to photograph down-and-outs in Whitechapel or outbreaks of teenage rebellion wherever they might occur. I even took a portrait of the young V.S. Naipaul for his first book jacket.

The sense of being at a disadvantage for lack of education was still strong in me. In a letter from *Photography* magazine, commenting on some of my pictures, the editor said among a lot of nice things that something in particular was 'very mundane'. I thought this must be high praise, until I found the word in a dictionary. Even so, I did summon up the courage to leave Larkins and strike out on my own.

I worked freelance mainly for the *News Chronicle*, for a magazine called *Town*, and for the *Observer*. I felt more pride walking down Fleet Street to the old *Observer* building than I had ever done in my life. In truth it was a strange place, where everything seemed to be done on a shoestring. The pigeonholes and windows looked as if they hadn't seen an office cleaners for years. The whole building looked as if Rembrandt had a hand in lighting it. Yet in the gloom I bumped into loveable but eccentric *Observer* characters, like the affable editor David Astor, and Jane Brown, who I swear was no taller than my elbow and who carried her Rolleiflex and her Leica in a shopping basket.

During that period I started travelling all over England for stories, staying at railway hotels, watching men in those gloomy breakfast parlours where everyone was afraid to clink knife and fork. I began to sense a certain dignity coming over me, that a national newspaper should be trusting me, Don McCullin, to go and take a picture of some significant event which would then appear with my name under it.

I was learning quickly. In Fleet Street you stepped on to a much faster sidewalk. You acquire a much quicker perception because speed is important. You are always trying to go faster than the man next to you. It's a tempo, not a training, and I always thought it amazing how Fleet Street could pick an ungroomed person like me and make me see and do things I wouldn't have believed possible, simply by plugging me into a much higher voltage.

Our improved financial position at home meant that my mother was able to buy the house where we lived, and shortly afterwards to sell it again, taking Michael away to the cleaner air of Wisbech in Cambridgeshire. Before leaving she made arrangements for me to rent the top two floors, and Christine and I were married.

It was not the most stylish occasion. How uncomfortable and conspicuous we felt in our new clothes as we left Liverpool Street station in a train taking a crowd of soldiers back to barracks in Colchester, and us to an unimaginative honeymoon on the East Coast. When we returned to our fifty-shillings-a-week flat I put up some wallpaper and magnolia gloss, which I thought took Fonthill Road upmarket a bit, and decked out one room to serve as darkroom, kitchen and bathroom. The tin bath was kept by the stove, to be handy for transferring hot water. All we had besides were a few sticks of furniture and a dubious television; a visitor would get the chair while we sat on the bed. Christine's parents thought that their daughter had gone down terribly in the world. The people living beneath us were too lazy to put out their empty milk bottles and we would hear them breaking them up with a hammer in the kitchen sink.

I started looking over my shoulder at Finsbury Park with some suspicion, though not without affection. I didn't feel disloyal to my roots but knew I was in a precarious situation, neither wholly in one world or the other. Both could be unforgiving. I was frightened of mixing with intellectual journalists and was becoming aware that a photographer's status was well below that of a writer. I instinctively rebelled against such attitudes, and despite a strong sense of widening horizons my feelings were confused.

Two newspapermen did a great deal for my confidence in those early days. Philip Jones Griffiths, himself a great photo-journalist, introduced me to the Pentax camera, and I bought one secondhand, downgrading the Rolleicord which rested tranquilly on the chest. The new toy was light, could be held at eye-level, and would take different lenses. The *Observer* writer John Gale teased me to live as close to the edge as he did. One stormy night we were together covering a Channel swim when he dared me to join him in the water that had been declared too dangerous for the competitors to enter. I can hear his great booming voice now – Guards and Sandhurst – urging me to follow him as he was lifted up and down by that vast, billowing sea, like some Wagnerian apparition bellowing into the night: 'Come on in, McCullin, you fucking coward!'

For me, the real decision to live dangerously was taken in Paris, where I had gone with Christine to make up for our mundane honeymoon. Paris, after all, was the home of serious photo-journalism, with *Paris-Match* and the great agencies like Magnum, and so Paris could not be ignored if I was at all serious about my work. It all started with a Frenchman making a pass at my very pretty wife and receiving from me – as he would have done at Gray's Academy in Finsbury Park – the offer of my fist and a mouthful of obscene threats, incomprehensible as they were to him. The scene reduced my poor wife to tears, and afterwards we sat in a cafe while I leafed glumly through the magazines. In one I came across a striking picture of Vopos (East German military) jumping over some barbed wire. It was the beginning of the Berlin crisis and the Wall. Suddenly I saw the direction in which my photography had to go. I said out loud: 'I have absolutely GOT to go to Berlin.'

She did not flinch or complain, that wife of mine. Indeed I owe her an enormous debt of gratitude for encouraging my ideas. She always supported me – although she had no inkling as yet of how much her tolerance would be expected to bear in the coming years as I travelled further and further into danger, when often it must have seemed as if I were trying to commit suicide.

We cut short the second honeymoon and returned to London. I raced over to the *Observer*, to be told they were not interested in my going to Berlin. 'Okay,' I said to Denis

Hackett, the editor on the desk, 'but I'm going anyway. Tomorrow.' My blood was up.

It took everything I had – £42 (a month's earnings) for the ticket alone. I arrived in the divided city with a letter of introduction from a slightly relenting Hackett to the *Observer*'s correspondent and soon found myself in a grand ornate hotel in Berlin's artist quarter, face to face with the flamboyant and vibrantly arrogant Patrick O'Donovan. He always wore a carnation and had a remarkable scar across his face, acquired (he later told me) when as a Guards officer in wartime he had unwisely stood up in his tank as it approached a wire strung across the road.

'I'm going to show you Berlin,' he said. 'Are you interested?'

I was more than interested. I wasn't about to refuse to hit the celebrated night spots of Berlin with one of the great newspapermen of the day, even if (as was then true) one pint of beer and I would be rocky. Besides, this was still le Carrés Berlin, before the reconstruction, and still, underground, the Berlin of the Thirties. In one bar we found a naked lady riding round on a horse in a sawdust arena. We were asked to leave by a man in an ankle-length overcoat when Patrick became too eager to mount the same horse. So the night progressed – out of one bar and into the next.

When I collected Patrick next morning, he looked utterly untouched by the previous night's debauch and sported a fresh carnation. We headed for the Friedrichstrasse, where the Wall was being built up, with breeze blocks. American soldiers, their machine guns at the ready, lurked in doorways, looking tense. I got out my Rolleicord and the little 35 mm Pentax and started using them.

It was on the strength of those photographs of the Berlin Wall that I made my real breakthrough in Fleet Street, the *Observer* giving me a regular contract for two days a week at 15 guineas. With this untold wealth I managed to buy for £1,300 a tiny cottage in Colney Hatch Lane, where my first son, Paul, was born a year later. Those Berlin pictures also won a British Press Award for the best series. I could feel ambition growing, the blood raging in a torrent round my body. I was like a prize-fighter, trained and on his toes, waiting only for the day of of the big contest, wanting worldwide recognition. At the age of twenty-eight, and in a mood of macho exuberance, having been extravagantly puffed by the *Observer*'s picture editor in *Camera* magazine, I was ready for a big international assignment. When it came, shortly afterwards, I little knew how powerful an experience it would be.

9

THE FIRST CONTEST

CYPRUS WAS THE contest I wanted. Though I felt less than sure of myself when I arrived at the Ledra Palace Hotel in Nicosia and walked into the bar. I hadn't encountered before the crowd who considered themselves the elite, the international press corps, and they certainly didn't seem eager to encounter me. A few faces turned towards me expectantly and then abruptly turned away again. They were on the lookout for old cronies; newcomer nobodies with cameras round their necks were of no interest at all. I was relieved and grateful when one chap came over and said, 'Just arrived?' and started nannying me. Since I had been in Cyprus as a national serviceman a lot had happened and I was only dimly aware of most of it. Cyprus had got its independence and the Greek archbishop, Makarios, had become president. Relations between the Greeks and Turks had gone from bad to abysmal. British soldiers were still on the scene in large numbers, no longer as an arm of the imperial power but as mediators in the civil war. There had been many atrocities in the outlying Turkish villages and, my new friend thought, events were about to take an even nastier turn.

We chatted on for a bit before it suddenly became clear to me that my adviser had more than a professional interest in my welfare. He was homosexual. Nothing had prepared me for the possibility that such a masculine professional as that of war correspondent could harbour what, in those blinkered days, was regarded as sexual weakness. I would learn later that heterosexuals had no monopoly on ability, or courage, but at the time I cut our conversation short and sought other company.

I found it in a beanpole of a man called Donald Wise, a photographer for the *Daily Mirror*, and another nice chap called Ivan Yates from the *Observer*. Yates had been doing some articles on the Greek Orthodox Church when the conflict suddenly interrupted his pious researches and made him the man-on-the-spot. So it came about that I eventually rode into my first battle with an ecclesiastical correspondent.

The real war correspondents were all led off – as I was later to discover real war correspondents often are – for a guided tour of the island by air, all laid on by the RAF.

Ivan and I were left to our own devices. Nothing much seemed to be going on, which again I would learn often seems to be the case in trouble spots. There didn't seem to be anything better to do than go and look up my old haunts around RAF Episcopi and Larnaca. Ivan had to be back for a dinner appointment, but he was keen to come along if only to see the Temple of Apollo.

Around Limassol and Episcopi little could be seen except a lot of British paras on roofs keeping their eyes open. They had spotted Greeks mobilising and were worried that something might happen, but didn't know what. We were on our way back through the suburbs of Limassol, on schedule for Ivan's dinner appointment, when it happened.

We were going through the Turkish quarter when we heard this terrific 'braaaap, braaaap.'

'The bloody exhaust has fallen off,' I said, annoyed.

We got out of the car and went round the back, but the exhaust was in perfect condition. The noise I had heard was of two Bren guns firing across the top of the car.

'Christ, Ivan, we're in the middle of it.'

It was late afternoon, and we were deep in the Turkish quarter. I said to Ivan, 'I want to stay here because it looks as if this is going to be it.'

I drove out to get Ivan a cab, and then came back to the same spot. As I parked the car, I saw a group of men with weapons crouched in the road. They wore old long British greatcoats and balaclava helmets. I went up and asked for the police station. They jumped on me, and I reached the police station under close arrest, with Turkish escort. After some hours of questioning the police released me and in the middle of the night took me to what had been a community centre and was now converted, because of the hostilities, into a hospital.

After some fitful sleep, I was woken early by a clanging noise. It proved to be a bullet hitting the iron grille of the window behind which I had been sleeping. Then it started in earnest and the firing grew heavier and heavier. The intensity of that hail of bullets was greater than anything I was prepared for. The reality of firepower exceeds almost anything that Hollywood dares to offer.

I was shaking with a combination of awe, fear and a kind of excitement. Though it wasn't clear at the time, what had happened was that some 5,000 armed Greek irregulars had furtively surrounded this small Turkish quarter of Limassol and opened fire from corners and rooftops. The Turkish community had withdrawn for safety into communal buildings, and the Turks were mounting a counter-attack.

I went out into the middle of this gun battle and took shelter behind an armoured car, wrongly thinking it would give me protection. From this vantage point I took the picture that later aroused so much comment – of a Turkish gunman emerging at a run, his shadow sharply defined on a wall. I took risks that later I would never have taken. I was determined to face up to fear and defy it. As the battle moved I ran here, there and everywhere. I was wound up to an extreme pitch, feeling completely surrounded by this onslaught and weighted down with the responsibility of being the only pressman there to record what was going on and to convey it to the world. I ran from street to street, trying not to miss one significant thing, trying to get as close as possible, to carry myself into situations where reporters, and especially reporters with cameras, were never meant to be. Some shots I took when I was in the direct firing line of snipers.

It was a kind of madness. The battle lasted all day, and I felt

I had lived a lifetime. In one street I saw a cinema, into which families had been put for safety, come under heavy fire. I saw people stumbling into the battle as you and I might do, going round the corner to the local shops. Some couldn't register what was going on. An old woman got caught up in the crossfire, and fell. An old man, I suppose her husband, came out to help her, as though she had slipped with her shopping basket. She lay in a pool of her own blood, and he fell beside her from the same sniper bullets.

I saw women running with mattresses over their heads for protection from the bullets, as they might put on scarves to keep off rain.

I watched horrified as, under the duress of fire, one of the buildings disgorged its Turkish defenders and its occupants. Women and children also began to appear. I remember putting my cameras down and belting across the fire-field to retrieve a three-year-old whose mother was screaming, and carrying it to safety. In later years I would develop a principle about trying to put back into a situation from which I was taking. But there was no theory at work that day. It was all instinct.

Part of the cause of the Cyprus conflict, I sensed – and tried to capture it in that picture of the gunman – was nothing more than the Eastern Mediterranean, moustachioed, half-bandit undercurrent of vendetta, or what people called machismo. This touchy masculine pride and honour, pride in aggression and revenge, instantaneous reaction to a situation in which there were for the combatants only black and white, only emotional certainties, no grey questionable areas or matters calling for deliberation or understanding, was all acted out in the fierce heat of the sun.

Yet what remains with me even more strongly than that gun battle is my first quiet encounter with the carnage of war. It took place in a little Turkish village of stone and mud called Ayios Sozomenos, about 15 miles from Nicosia. It was very still as I got out of my car on the village outskirts and saw shepherds herding their flocks away. I photographed an attractive young girl of about eighteen wearing a headscarf and carrying a double-barrelled shotgun. She held her head high as she was solemnly walking away. I could hear distant crying. And I could smell burning. I could sense there was death around. I heard voices and went towards them up a rise in the ground. Some British soldiers were standing by an armoured vehicle. I went up and said 'Aye, aye' as if I'd seen them after a country walk in Somerset.

'Morning,' one of the soldiers said. 'Want to see a dead body, mate? There's one over there. Been hit in the face with a shotgun. Not very pleasant.'

I thought, O Christ, am I going to be able to handle it?

I came to this man's feet, which were splayed, and my eyes travelled up the length of his body to the face – what was left of it. I could see the dark brown eyes fixed in a stare, as if looking at the sky. I thought back to my father's death. I thought, This is what it's like. I thought, It is bad, but it's not too bad for me to bear.

As I walked away the soldier said, 'Oh, there's two more in that house.'

I went to the stone house and knocked on the window. There was silence. I turned the handle and opened the door. The early morning cold syphoned out warm sticky air. It was a sticky carnage that I saw. The floor was covered with blood. A man was lying on his face, another flat on his back. There wasn't a mark on him, or seemed to be none. There was no sound. I let myself in and closed the door. I could smell something burning. In another room I found a third man dead. Three men dead, a father and two sons, one in his early twenties, the other slightly older.

Suddenly the door opened and people came in led by what I later learned was the wife of the youngest man. They had been married only a few days. All the presents were laid out in the front room, all shot up in the gun battle. Broken cups and saucers, glass objects and ornaments, brought as gifts to the wedding.

I'm in serious trouble now, I thought. They will think I have trespassed in their house. I had already taken photographs. It wasn't just trespass in the legal sense I had been guilty of, for

I had trespassed on death, and emotion too. The woman picked up a towel to cover her husband's face and started to cry.

I remember saying something awkward like – forgive me, I'm from a newspaper, and I cannot believe what I am looking at.

I pointed to my hand with the camera in it, asking for an invitation to record the tragedy. An older man said, 'Take your pictures, take your pictures.' They *wanted* me to do it. I was to discover that all Middle Eastern people want to express and record their grief. Grief is something they express very vividly. It's not just the Turks and Greeks, but a Mediterranean thing, a very outward display of mourning.

When I realised I had been given the go-ahead to photograph, I started composing my pictures in a very serious and dignified way. It was the first time I had pictured something of this immense significance and I felt as if I had a canvas in front of me and I was, stroke by stroke, applying the composition to a story that was telling itself. I was, I realised later, trying to photograph in a way that Goya painted or did his war sketches.

Eventually, the woman knelt down by the side of her young husband and cradled his head. I was very young then, and I knew that pain, and I found it hard not to burst into tears. When I walked out of the house I was shattered. I was dehydrated. My mouth was glued together.

I think I grew up that day. I took a step away from my personal resentments, my feeling that life had been uniquely tough on me, giving me evacuation and Finsbury Park, and taking away my father when I was young. That day in Cyprus, when I saw somebody else losing their father, somebody else losing their son, I felt I could somehow assimilate this experience so that my own pity could cease to be personal and instead become general. And I could just say 'OK. I'm not the only one.'

The next day, in another village, I photographed the family of a Turkish shepherd who had been shot in the hills. The poor shepherds were the soft targets of course. They were preparing a makeshift coffin and the dead shepherd's son was looking on, a young boy about the age I was when they brought my own father's body back from the hospital. With a curious ceremonial dignity they offered me the bullet that had passed through the shepherd's body. Experiences like this were an ordeal, but I also felt as if they were a privilege. In an inexplicable way they were teaching me how to become a human being.

Cyprus left me with the beginnings of a self-knowledge, and the very beginning of what they call empathy. I found I was able to share other people's emotional experiences, live with them silently, transmit them. I felt I had a particular vision that isolated and homed in on the essence of what was happening, and could see that essence in light, in tones, in details. That I had a powerful ability to communicate.

What I hoped I had captured in my pictures was an enduring image that would imprint itself on the world's memory. I was looking for a symbol – though I could not then have put it that way – that could stand for the whole story and would have the impact of ritual or religious imagery.

I soon knew that my first war pictures had some impact. By syndicating my early photographs successfully, the *Observer* was able to send me back to Cyprus twice more in the following weeks.

10

DELINQUENT PHOTOGRAPHER

I WAS TOO young and disrespectful for the Fleet Street old guard. They criticised everything, from my low standards in dress to the size of my cameras. They deplored my total lack of appreciation as to where and when it was proper to take photographs. I would take a shotgun in the boot of my car when going out of town, so that I would always be prepared for some good poaching, a habit which raised eyebrows and fed a mildly delinquent image.

Others, closer to my own age, looked upon me with some curiosity. They could see that I had a certain talent but wondered how I had derived it from such an ignorant and bigoted mind. They tried to educate me. 'No, no, Don, you've got it all wrong! No, you mustn't say that . . .' Eventually I began listening to them and slowly became aware of the appalling things that would come out of my mouth. Some things I could never learn. I could not tolerate being called 'my photographer', as if I were the reporter's very own personal possession. I was also allergic to all forms of regimentation, and this often led to trouble. I once found the photographers covering the Commonwealth Prime Ministers' Conference at Marlborough House all lined up like greyhounds in the slips. Some of them with old-fashioned plate cameras sneered at my little 35 mm job and instructed me to keep to my place and not run out in front and spoil their pictures. Why should I take orders from these people, or be ridiculed like a guttersnipe? When the pack of Prime Ministers arrived, I started to dart here, there and everywhere for close-ups. I broke all their rules and earned their opprobrium.

Yet I was to step out of line once too often, and nearly got the sack for it. I had been sent to photograph Harold Wilson soon after the Labour government came to power in 1964 and arrived at the House of Commons where *Observer* columnist Kenneth Harris was to interview the new Prime Minister on the verandah. I got the details of a pre-arranged plan from the PM's Political Private Secretary, Marcia Falkender. While the two men talked, looking out over the River Thames, I was to station myself on Westminster Bridge and give a signal when I was ready to take photographs. As I got into position, a gust of wind blew the Prime Minister's hair all over the place. Kenneth Harris took out his comb and deftly flicked Wilson's hair back in place while I was snapping off pictures at a furious pace in some glee.

When I got back to the *Observer* office I handed in everything to the dark room for processing. The boys in the dark room grinned as they racked off some 20 × 16 prints of Kenneth Harris combing Harold Wilson's hair. Far too large for any paper to use, the 20 × 16s would nevertheless make wonderfully outrageous posters. Unfortunately one of these huge prints found its way into the hands of the paper's managing editor, Ken Obank, and I was summoned to his office for an explanation.

'While I admire your timing,' Obank said, 'and your perception as a photographer, I deplore the fact that you have taken advantage of a situation given to the *Observer* in complete confidence. I'm therefore going to cut up the negatives in your presence. Really I should fire you. Had these pictures become public, the consequences would have fallen on this newspaper.'

I wasn't blamed for actually taking the photographs, but they were angry about the large prints lying around where anyone could pick them up. If they had left the building it would have been undermining to the Wilson government and to the *Observer*'s reputation as a newspaper of trust. I was properly reprimanded, and the whole matter was quickly hushed up.

My scrapes were small when compared with those of my brother. While I was photographing Prime Ministers, he was getting into a spot of bother. Michael was seven years younger than me and grew up with a more internationally-minded generation in Finsbury Park. After a brief forced exile in Wisbech, he found his way back into his old London gang which blazed the trail in Europe for the football hooligans of later years. One day he returned from the continent covered in bruises and one eye closed. The Belgian police had caught him and some of his mates turning over a deux chevaux outside a café in Ostend. Michael had run for it and dashed into the reinforcements round the corner as they were drawing their truncheons. He managed to escape but only after considerable damage had been inflicted on him.

I didn't take seriously his flippant suggestion that he could always escape retribution, like a latter-day Beau Geste, by enlisting in the French Foreign Legion. People in deprived Finsbury Park were not accustomed to making gallant gestures of that sort. Yet that is precisely what he did. Not long afterwards, I received an official letter from the Foreign Office asking if I knew of my brother's whereabouts. It appeared that the Belgian authorities were anxious to extradite him. I put the letter straight in the fire.

At least he kept a kind of liberty while many of my Finsbury Park mates were in jail. They would write to me for books – one at a time because that was all the authorities would allow. I could not shake off the feeling of being uneasily suspended between two worlds, and still not at ease in the self-consciously highbrow atmosphere of the *Observer* office. I was glad when a call came to send me again into what I was beginning to regard as my own territory – war. This time, in Africa.

PART TWO

Going to the Wars

II

WITH THE MERCENARIES

I FLEW INTO the Congo with a great deal of nervous apprehension. I had heard much that was sinister about this once cannibal area. Joseph Conrad called it the Heart of Darkness. Now, in November 1964, the story was that some rebel warriors of evil repute, supporters of the murdered President Lumumba, were committing atrocities on whites and holding missionaries hostage. White mercenaries were going to their rescue. All this was going on many hundreds of miles up-country and I was expected to get there somehow. The place had a name that was later to become notorious – Stanleyville.

I landed at the only place from which Stanleyville was accessible – a streaming hell-hole then known as Leopoldville, the capital of the Congo. (It is now known as Kinshasa.) Almost a thousand miles of roadless, impenetrable jungle and crocodile-infested river, I discovered, still lay between me and my goal. Like other journalists I plugged into Leopoldville's sleazy, steam-bath bars, wondering how on earth to get out, and whether this end-of-the-world situation wasn't also the end of the road.

The bars alone told the whole dismal Congo story, for those lucky enough to be writers. Arms-dealers, dodgy minerals prospectors, experimenting pharmaceuticalists, Belgian plantation owners of the type who chopped off the arms of troublesome workers, drunken mercenaries, stranded air crews and some of the most devilish misfits of the world congregated here, occasionally approached by humble

African 'missionary boys' telling them how well they knew their Bible and asking if they could have something to eat.

For photographers, who couldn't use this telling materials, the news was dire. Joseph Désiré Mobutu, the man who controlled the army and the security apparatus, and who was already developing an alarming reputation, had put a ban on any journalist leaving Leopoldville. One journalist, it was said, had already been killed.

In the meantime, matters up-country were becoming critical. Rumours abounded that the rebel tribesmen – Simbas, or lions – were eating the livers of public officials in the main square of Stanleyville. President Tshombe had ordered an army to the rescue – of Belgian paratroops, Mobutu's men in the Congolese army, and mercenaries of a motley of nationalities. These were led by an Irishman, known as 'Mad' Mike Hoare. While this operation was in progress, all ordinary traffic of Stanleyville stopped. The only free movement out of Leopoldville was of military traffic, and this gave me an idea.

My eye fell on one of the mercenaries who drank in the bar at my hotel. He was a stealthy looking, muscular, short man with a sergeant's stripes and strange eyes, eyes which said the person could be unfriendly, if rubbed the wrong way.

'Are you English?' I asked.

'Yes, I'm from London.'

I told him I was from the *Observer* newspaper, which was not strictly true. I was actually on assignment for a German magazine called *Quick*, but I reckoned the name of the *Observer* would carry more clout with an Englishman in Africa. 'What are my chances of going to Stan?'

'None at all, as far as you're concerned,' replied the sergeant. He didn't seem hostile, so I went on questioning him.

'When do you go, and how?' I asked.

'We fly up in two days, by Hercules transports, American planes, with American pilots.'

'Any chance of me getting some khaki?'

He looked at me and smiled. He had conceived, I think, a

bit of a liking for this bloke with a mad idea. Like mercenaries often turned out to be, he was a bit mad-brained himself.

'Can you fill me in? Where do you sleep? How many are you? Can I get boots?'

I kept pumping him with questions, and before I knew it not only was my scheme shaping up but my sergeant friend – whose name was Alan Murphy – was giving me help.

At the appointed time, the night before departure, I sneaked into the mercenary barracks, a fleapit hotel on the other side of the Congo river where they had converted the dining room into a dormitory. I was clad in the clothes that Murphy had found me, jungle boots and khaki and the green beret of what they called the Fifth Commando. Silently I lay down beside a mass of snoring bodies, but didn't sleep much. It was raining and thundering outside.

'If this thing falls apart,' Murphy had told me, 'you're on your own. I'll help all I can, but if it comes unstuck, I don't know you.'

This drifted through my head as I awoke from drowsing at 5 am to a half-lit world of crashing rain, muffled voices and men scratching their heads and getting on the boots. The thought of going to Stanleyville suddenly seemed thoroughly undesirable.

Murphy approached, using his strange eyes to monitor me out, like a dog fox leaving a trail. He didn't speak.

Outside there was a truck ticking over. One of the mercenaries who clambered aboard was wearing the German Iron Cross. We were driven briskly to the military airstrip, and as we dropped off the end of the truck I thought my legs wouldn't bear me up.

A man with a short-sleeved shirt and a button-down collar called, 'Line up, you guys, line up.' He was short but had a very commanding manner. I felt sure I was looking at my first CIA man, taking part in America's big clandestine involvement in the Congo.

He snapped out names, read out from a clipboard. The only one I recognised was Murphy. At each name, someone left the line and climbed into the plane – a giant Hercules transport.

Soon there were only three men left, of whom I was the quaking one. I could feel myself shrinking while my little military bag (no bigger than a school satchel) holding my cameras seemed to be swelling to enormous size. This is it, the game's over, I thought to myself. Gloomily I recalled the reputation of Mobutu's security men, and wondered what you had to do to be sure you got deported.

'What's your name?'

Gruffly and militarily, I hoped, my name somehow came out of my mouth. He scanned down the list, and looked down it again. Any moment now, I thought, there's going to be an explosion. He looked up and hard at me.

'It's not here.'

'It should be,' I barked.

'Howdya spell it?'

Spelling it out must have given full force to this wild Irish/Scottish sounding name, a trouble-making mercenary's kind of name, because he said suddenly, 'Okay, get in.'

My physical tension was such that for a moment I could barely stand or walk. Then I was almost too buoyant. As I climbed into the aircraft, I was ablaze inside, smothered by internal laughter. I had pulled a stroke against not only the Congo government, but against the CIA as well.

The mood didn't survive the flight. As the engines changed down for the descent to Stanleyville, my mood changed gear with them and the apprehension started again. Then the big doors came down on the C130 and the first thing that struck me – the thing I knew the meaning of from Cyprus – was the pungent smell of death.

The Belgian paras had reached Stanleyville before us and had shot up a lot of human beings. Hideous bloated corpses lay in the sun, while men in white masks were still levering them from the long grass. Even before we had got off, the stench of death in Stanleyville was being sucked into that plane.

I knew now, emerging into the searing heat, that this was worse, far worse, than anything I had witnessed in Cyprus. I could hear a crackling noise, which was the sound of small arms fire, and an occasional heavy thump and crunch: mortar bombs going in. The battle was still in progress. The killing was still going on. In Africa it is difficult to stop it.

Free beer was dispensed in quantity at the Stanley Hotel where we detrucked. Dutch courage figured prominently in the mercenaries' plans, and I needed a drink. As I downed my beer, a jeep arrived, and I could hear doors slamming, orders being shouted, to a background of gunfire. Men started hurrying out. Murphy was acting as if he didn't know me.

'What's your outfit?' an officer called to me as I hung back.

'I'm from Katima,' I improvised.

I sat in a jeep with a helmet that had been thrust at me along with a rifle that I wasn't keen on touching. We were said to be heading for what they called mopping-up operations on the other side of the river. Mopping-up operations had been part of the explanation for the bloated corpses around the airport. I began to reflect on what I had got myself into – a most hideous large-scale set-up, with no rights or rules or immunities, with some of the most violent, cruel people in the world.

At the dock, mercenaries were grouping to cross the river near a large pile of logging timber waiting to float downstream. By this timber there were twenty young Africans, all sitting, all bleeding; some were as young as seventeen, some perhaps even younger. All of them had been beaten. Some of them looked as if they had been skinned alive. These I learned were what in Leopoldville they called the Simbas – lion men. Here they were just called the youth – the Jeunesse. I didn't behave too professionally in a photographic way. I just went up and hurriedly started taking pictures, then quickly put my cameras away.

'What's this all about?' I asked a mercenary.

'Oh, they're killing these guys. You'll see them in a minute. There's a really nasty black gendarmerie chief, a really evil bastard. He's doing away with that lot. He's been shooting them all morning. He takes them to the river bank and shoots them in the back of the head, then kicks them into the water for the crocs.'

I felt overwhelmingly moved by this little bunch of human misery, sitting there, waiting to be killed.

I realised too how vulnerable my own position was as an inconvenient witness. As the crackle of small arms intensified, I could see Africans streaming in haste off the ferry, faces drawn, eyes rolling, urgently making as much distance as possible from the other side. Mercenaries started to lumber on board in their place for the trip back, carrying heavy machine guns and Brownings. My eyes kept darting to the little group of Jeunesse, some tied, some not, waiting to be shot. I had learned an awful new fact about war and killing – that people build themselves up for atrocity. They suppress their humanity by humiliating, torturing, tormenting their victims first. And the victims wait to be killed.

While we were standing on the dockside, someone said, 'The boss wants you lot on the other side of the river.' And he asked me, 'Have you got a gun?' I said I had and got back into the jeep and sank low into it. I could see all the other mercenaries knocking back looted whisky to build up their courage and kill off their fear.

The English officer then asked me, 'Where did you say you came from before you got to Leopoldville?' Again I told him Katima.

'No, you couldn't have done.'

I thought then that I had better come clean, or as clean as possible. I told him I worked for the *Observer* newspaper.

He got on the radio to Mike Hoare. Then he turned back to me, very seriously, and said: 'You're in trouble, old son. We're going to hand you over to the gendarmerie, to those black guys killing all these people.'

I felt panic. Though I had all the cockiness and fearlessness of the inexperienced war correspondent, behind it all there was a nasty shadow saying: 'Hang about, if they can do this to those poor bastards, and nobody knows you're here, there's no reason why you shouldn't disappear too.'

Half an hour later word came through that 'the old man' wanted me on the other side. I was shipped across the river on a pontoon ferry with the jeeps, the Browning machine guns and the mercenaries, but without the rifle. I was so concerned about the gendarmerie threat, I hardly noticed the river being raked with fire.

On the other bank there was total confusion. The mercenaries had rounded up hundreds of people. They were sorting out those they thought were Simba warriors. It didn't look to me as if they were very particular in their choice.

I was taken to a clearing, which was part of a mission where, I learned, eight Belgian nuns had been murdered by the Simbas in the previous week. There were a lot of exhausted mercenaries, who had obviously been fighting, lying around. In a little hospital there I later found a doctor's microscope with thousands of smashed glass testing sheets, suggesting a painstaking level of destruction.

I was led up to Hoare, who said, 'I've got no time to talk to you. You will stay here overnight and then I'll be handing you over to the Congolese authorities in the morning. I have no alternative.'

It was growing dark and I was hungry and tired. I was also thirsty and I was nervous. I had no water nor any canteen food. I had the cameras but the film I'd taken of the young lion warriors had been confiscated. I had nothing to show for my efforts, even if the most merciful thing happened and I was just booted out of the Congo.

A mercenary came by and offered me food. But before I could get a word out, an officer interrupted to say, 'Don't give this man any food. He doesn't deserve it, coming in here, using our unit, disguising himself. Give him fuck all.'

'You can fucking stick your food,' I said.

I slept on the ground, in a foetus position, wrapped around my cameras. Next morning the fighting had died down and I could see some of the mercenaries shipping back to the other side of the river. After what seemed an eternity, but was probably only a couple of hours, I was taken to see Hoare again. This time he seemed more relaxed.

'Much against my better judgment,' he said, 'I am going to let you come with us. We're going downstream. The Simbas have abducted thirty or forty nuns and missionaries and we're going to see if we can retrieve them, and save their lives. But I must say, you took a bit of a risk, and if you had been dealt with by anyone else, it could have gone against you, and gone against you dangerously. But I admire a bit of spirit, and so you're welcome to come with us.'

Relief and elation struggled for the upper hand. The deal Hoare proposed was that I should consider myself a soldier first and a photographer second. I would have a weapon but I was not to fire it unless specifically instructed. Fortunately, no instruction ever came. The missionaries we were looking for were mainly Belgians and Canadians. It was known that the chief missionary, a man called Carlsson, had been shot in the crossfire when the Belgian paras had retaken the town. There were another fifty missionaries and nuns still unaccounted for – either abducted or dead.

We recrossed the river. By the timber pile another group of Simba 'Jeunes' was being brutally groomed for execution. I photographed them and their persecutors.

We went about twenty miles downriver in a little convoy – two big trucks and a couple of Landrovers. I didn't expect that we would find any missionaries alive, or even dead, given the methods of river disposal.

Alan Murphy and I could now talk to each other openly. The thought of being friendly with some of the other guys sent a chill through me. A South African Nazi claiming to be a doctor took a leading role in cooking the meal that night – chickens freshly slaughtered – and I decided to make do with biscuits.

The mercenaries were not over-fastidious in their methods of interrogating villagers *en route*. All the information they were getting pointed to a place called Asanti, about fifty miles on, where there was known to be a mission building that had been overrun by the Simbas. To get there meant another river crossing in the light assault craft. During the passage the mercenaries frightened off a dug-out canoe, deemed hostile, with a burst from the Browning gun.

We got to Asanti and surrounded the mission, meeting no resistance. Indeed, we met with no one. Then a trembling

Belgian missionary appeared and told us there were some black sisters hiding in a building behind the mission. At first they were too frightened to open the doors to us, but eventually they came out crying, laughing and bringing several sick Congolese children with them.

Outside the mission there was a makeshift shrine to Patrice Lumumba with a glass front and gold tinsel round it. It had been built by the Simba rebels and, according to the sisters, had been the scene of daily sacrifices of their enemies. Two mercenaries kicked in the shrine and set the thing ablaze with a drum of palm oil.

In the middle of this conflagration, an Irish mercenary sidled up to me to ask if I could take a picture of him with the Belgian missionary. 'I'm not very religious,' he said, 'but it will keep my mother happy.'

We heard that the bulk of the missing hostages were being held by the rebels further down the road in a long, low building we had missed on our way from the river. We doubled back, half suspecting an ambush. Any suggestion of cover was machine-gunned, to be on the safe side, but it proved unnecessary. The Simbas had gone.

We could hear wailing when we got to the building, then screams which turned into screams of delight. The white nuns and missionaries came pouring out, scarcely able to believe that their ordeal was over. Not all were found. Some had been raped and hacked to death on the journey downriver.

The rescue of the missionaries gave the mercenaries a little hour of glory, but in reality they were a rough crowd. I got on relatively easy terms with Hoare, and even with the hard nut officer who refused me food, but I had no illusions about the people I was with. Back in Stanleyville, I roomed in a commandeered house with a Rhodesian mercenary called Peter, a compulsive looter of jewellery who had joined up after shooting his wife's lover. And Peter was one of the most human. Their nightly diversion was to work themselves up with an old blue movie before they went to work on the local women, whom they would first bath and douse in Old Spice.

Racism was not a qualification for the job but they seemed to be racist to a man.

One night I woke up in a cold sweat to hear a burst of gunfire that sounded as if it was in the room.

'What on earth's that, Peter?' I said.

'It's OK mate, go back to sleep. It's just some silly bastard letting off firearms.'

Unable to sleep, I crept down to the kitchen in the early hours to get something to eat. There, in a great pool of blood on the floor, were the two young African boys who helped cook and keep the place tidy. Both were dead, riddled with bullets.

When I checked the thing out it appeared that they had been killed by a rather shifty South African junior officer as part of a drunken bloodlust. His story was that the two boys, who had accompanied the mercenaries on the march to Stanleyville, had been stealing weapons. Whether or not they had been doing this, there didn't seem any case for blasting them at three o'clock in the morning without any suggestion of a legal proceeding. I made myself unpopular by reporting the matter to a more senior officer, saying that the South African should be disciplined. I was not so politely asked to leave.

After delivering my pictures on the German commission, I took my Congo experiences to the *Observer*, where they were written up by my friend John Gale, under the title 'Climb Aboard for Stanleyville'. It had a formidable impact though, for obvious reasons, I had to conceal the role of Alan Murphy in my adventures.

I was to hear of Alan again in tragic circumstances fifteen years later. He died in a struggle with two policemen, one of whom was shot, in the East End of London. At the inquest his mother told a crime reporter friend of mine that her son had 'once saved the life of Don McCullin', and I suppose in a way he had.

I went back to the Congo twice more, soon after Mobutu had overthrown Tshombe and established himself as one of the most evil men of Africa, responsible for a lot of killing.

The restrictions placed on my movements made it almost impossible for me to operate, though I did have the experience of a drunken mercenary trying to hold me hostage at gunpoint in a town called Paulus. The second time, in 1967, I entered illegally across the Rwanda border to join a group of renegade mercenaries led by Colonel Jean 'Black Jack' Schramme, who were bottled up in the town of Bukavu, surrounded by the Congolese army. They were trying to build an airstrip with their bare hands in order to get out. A sort of phoney heroism grew up over their stand. It circled the world in news form as a sort of small-scale Dien Bien Phu. I spent ten days in Bukavu with the mercenaries, sharing their fears of sudden attack and being strafed in the streets, but it was hard to admire them even in adversity.

I shared a billet with a mercenary called Alex, who had recently served a nineteen-day sentence in a Congolese jail. He told me tensely that he intended killing an African for every day he spent inside. He became more relaxed when after a few days he reached his target.

I was told by John St Jorré, another correspondent who had come in with me, of a 'drinks party' organised for some Indians who had returned to their looted homes. The mercenaries were lying in wait and forced the Indians to drink whisky to reveal the whereabouts of their hidden gold. One of the Indians protested that there was no hidden treasure and was cold-bloodedly gunned down.

The mercenaries did get out. Some deal involving the Red Cross and, I suspect, the CIA was stitched together to ensure their safe departure. They walked away from the siege in a little blaze of glory. But they could never be heroes to me.

12

SEARCH AND DESTROY

WHEN I RETURNED to London after my first visit to the Congo I discovered that my Cyprus pictures, taken earlier in the year, had won the World Press Photo Award, the top award for a photographer, and I was the first Englishman to win the £500 prize. I was delighted, not just by the money but because I thought it would increase the opportunities to do the work I wanted to do. At the same time I felt the beginnings of uneasiness, which would become much more pronounced in later years, at the idea of receiving a prize for depicting the misery and suffering of other human beings.

The award did help me professionally, without a doubt. I was now recognised as an international photo-journalist, among the first to be sent for when any conflict suddenly hit the news. This soon took me to the war that was already usurping the world's headlines and would continue to do so for the next ten years – Vietnam.

In Vietnam I would learn a lot about the technical difficulties of photography under fire. One of the greatest dangers lay in taking light readings. Pictures can be rattled off at speed, but when it comes to making a correct appraisal of the light there is no substitute for a few moments of immobility and deliberation, thus becoming a still target. Loading film was another high-risk business. On my early trips to Vietnam I had a camera called a Nikon F, which did not have a hinged back. You could only load the camera by taking the back off and having a good fiddle around. Under fire, I used to lie flat on the ground with the camera on my chest, and do it blind. If I had put my head up to look at it, I would probably have been a dead man.

Vietnam killed a lot of newspapermen. Forty-five lost their lives there and another eighteen were listed missing, almost certainly dead. Both journalists and photographers were involved, but the photographers got the worst of it. Photographers had to get out in the field where the risks were infinitely greater. There was no security in any of the different methods of covering war. Sean Flynn, the son of Errol, was said to go flamboyantly into combat on a Honda, toting a pearl-handled pistol, while Larry Burrows, the brilliant English photographer who worked for *Life* magazine, was the model of professionalism and polite diffidence. Both joined the list of the missing, presumed dead.

You could take all the precautions, like wearing your tin hat, buttoning your flak-jacket and loading your cameras horizontally, but ultimately there was no defence against the worst. If you stepped on a landmine, or on to the wrong helicopter, that was it. Yet Vietnam was the war that attracted newspapermen more than any other. This was partly a reflection of the appetite for news, but it was more than that. The war had an addictive quality for those who covered it. Michael Herr, in his book *Dispatches*, would later suggest, 'Vietnam was what we had instead of happy childhoods.'

I first went there early in 1965, dispatched by the *Illustrated London News*, a classy old magazine that was short of money. They wanted me to do the pictures and the words, and were apologetic about it, but it suited me very well. On the flight over I conquered my aversion to reading to the extent of dipping into Graham Greene's *The Quiet American*.

It was good preparation though not sufficient warning of the incredible heat and humidity or the notices at the airport referring to what the Americans called 'an in-country plague situation'. In Saigon I checked in at a hotel that was pure Graham Greene, the Hotel Royale, run by Monsieur Octavie, an ex-Legionnaire who had stayed on after the country was partitioned. They showed me up to a room and a double bed that looked as if it had seen a lot of screwing, but this may have been my inflamed imagination. Though there were no prostitutes in the bar below, M. Octavie, quirkily by Saigon standards, never allowed women into the men's rooms. He just had very old beds, and very old everything else. At least the company was good. After the war was over, I heard that the building had been converted into a factory making flags for the new Vietnamese nation.

The presence was nothing to what it later became but it was already conspicuous. For a correspondent wanting to work in South Vietnam there was no way around it. If you went into the field of combat you went in an American helicopter. You had to get your MAC V accreditation from the American military and they were the people who determined where you could go. Your full accreditation card would give you the honorary rank of major – handy for getting around the US bases but not, I thought, a very comforting document to have on you if you happened to be captured.

I was attached to what was called an Eagle Operation, directed at suspected hideouts and villages under the control of the Viet Cong. There was a savage procedure to these operations. It would start with heavily armed helicopters flying over the suspected VC territory with the main purpose of goading sniper fire from the ground. Once enemy positions had been identified by this method, the search-and-destroy operation would begin. This consisted of concentrated bombing of the area, then sending in the Vietnamese Ranger troops at lightning speed. Their task was to flush out the rebels.

I went in by helicopter with the Rangers to the town of Kan Tow in the Mekong Delta, where VC activity was suspected. The flight crew were all American.

It was my first time into a battle by helicopter and I was really fired up as we skimmed low over the trees. Not as much as the Rangers though. They almost knocked me out of the helicopter in their haste to disembark.

They came to a mangrove swamp and started to make their way with infinitely more care. We had been warned to look out for a Viet Cong device called the punge stick, which could pierce a boot with ease. The sticks were notched bamboo, needle-sharp and almost impossible to withdraw once embedded in a foot.

We gathered speed again as Kan Tow came into view. About fifty yards from the village the Rangers battalion, urged on by its three American advisers, broke into a trot. They commenced firing from the hip and emitting blood-curdling yells. Anything that moved – from a dog to a chicken – provoked a hail of bullets.

At first the village seemed to be deserted, apart from the bodies of dead water buffalo, unfortunate victims of the air strafing. Then a soldier shouted and produced a soaking wet man, shaking with terror and clutching a year-old baby. He had been hiding up to his neck in the slimy village stream.

The soldiers started poking around on the ground and came across holes covered in palm leaves. Out of these holes emerged whole families, though mainly women and children. I learned later that this village used to dig slit trenches, but these were automatically bombed by the government forces.

The soldiers started poking further afield. More men were found. They were promptly taken prisoner, their hands tied behind their backs with their own shorts. Two men darted out of a bamboo shack just ahead of me and plunged into the river. I saw one blown to pieces by a hand grenade. The other tried to claw his way up the far bank only to be caught by the concentrated fire of twenty rifles.

Without a common language it was hard for me to determine on what basis the South Vietnamese troops chose their targets. It seemed to me they were simply trigger-happy. I also felt that what I was witnessing was not likely to achieve the avowed aim of American policy – winning Vietnamese hearts and minds.

All the men of the village, without exception, were treated as suspects, as clandestine members of the Viet Cong. No arms were found in Kan Tow, but I was assured that the VC were expert at plunging them in the inaccessible muddy ooze of the rice fields.

We took off with a load of prisoners and as the helicopter banked I thought how easily some of them could fall out. When the war grew even uglier, some did.

By dusk we were all back at the Soctrang base with another score of new VC suspects. The interrogation of prisoners was not something I was invited to photograph.

On later trips I would find myself photographing more Americans than Vietnamese. As the US President Lyndon Johnson poured in ever more combat troops to shore up his South Vietnamese ally, the fiction of the 'adviser' melted away. The images of war became unmistakably American. I was there on the bizarre day when the Marines hit the beach at Da Nang. They came charging up, M-16 rifles at the ready, as if to take and give heavy casualties in a sort of replay of Iwo Jima. They were then met by a South Vietnamese welcoming committee of almond-eyed girls in ao dais who insisted on adorning the would-be combat heroes with pink and white orchids. But combat for these soldiers was merely deferred. At places like Khe Sanh and Hue, the Marines would take the most appalling casualties.

Vietnam bred its own species of gallows humour and black farce. One of my more ludicrous experiences occurred in 1966 when *Quick* magazine sent me out with a German reporter called Horst, who kept clicking his heels and bowing, making me want to hide.

Horst and I went into the jungle as part of an army patrol probing for VC. The day, aside from sleeting with rain, had been uneventful, but come the night, when we were camped in slimy mud with the rain still bucketing down, we heard another noise – *Shwam*, the sound of an incoming shell. I found myself locked in Horst's sogging embrace with him saying to me, 'Dear Christ, what was that?' The shelling went on with Horst grabbing me each time for comfort and begging me to tell him when it would end. As if I had any idea. Then a gruff drill-sergeant's voice came through the night.

'Hey, you guys, quieten down sharp over there.'

It had some effect but that was the tour on which my image of the iron German soldier collapsed.

70

Like most correspondents on the road I would eat in the officers' mess of whichever American stockade I was passing through. These were dour places – plastic seating and red lights, with the bar as the main focus, but not a cheerful one. Human troughs of self-pity, these were the places to go if you wanted insight into the belligerence born of booze and firepower. You would see other officers holding maudlin, sad, peculiar conversations with imported Vietnamese women whom they called 'hooch' girls or 'slopes'. These women would come in to serve them beers, and do their washing and possibly other things. They were widely believed also to report back to the Viet Cong.

Faith in firepower made the Americans oddly immune to the lessons of the past, and led them consistently to underrate the enemy. Dien Bien Phu, if it was recalled at all, was remembered as a French failure rather than as an extraordinary achievement of Vietminh arms, under General Giap's leadership. The French artillery officer at Dien Bien Phu committed suicide in despair – he had said it was impossible for the enemy to bring such a weight of artillery through the jungle.

The scale of US presence reinforced overconfidence. Everything about the Americans in Vietnam, from the size of their soldiers to the mountainous contours of their ammo and garbage dumps, seemed to dwarf anything Asian. To those who wanted to believe in America's global mission against Communism, it gave an impression of immovable solidity. To the doubters it increasingly spelt waste on a mega scale, waste of country, waste of lives and waste of spirit.

I read somewhere that Americans throw away enough food to feed 50 million people, and a fair bit was being pitched out in South-East Asia. Shortly after my third trip to Vietnam, I went to Bihar in North India and the contradictions in human society were inescapable. I moved from a situation where resources were being used on a massive scale to kill people to one where no resources were being put into keeping people alive.

Almost the entire province of Bihar – some 50 million

people – was afflicted with famine. A failure of the monsoon rains had wiped out most of the rice harvest and all the late crops – wheat, barley, vegetables – had simply not appeared. I did my work in Monaghyr, a village inhabited only by untouchables, where the autumn harvest had produced a tenth of its normal yield and the well had dried up.

No heroics are possible when you are photographing people who are starving. All I could do was to try give the people caught up in this terrible disaster as much dignity as possible. There is a problem inside yourself, a sense of your own powerlessness, but it doesn't do to let it take hold, when your job is to stir the conscience of others who can help.

13

FIRST THE LION, THEN VULTURES

I FOUND IT hard to settle back into life at the *Observer* after my first trips to the wars. A kind of restlessness swept over me, as if it were time to move on. Though I thought of the *Observer* as my newspaper, my home, its shoestring budget prevented the paper sending me on any but the rare foreign assignments. Usually I would go as a freelance for other publications, and once the main job was done, I would then produce more reports and pictures for the *Observer*. In this way the newspaper would benefit from inexpensive foreign coverage and I could do the kind of photo-journalism I wanted. The situation was hardly ideal.

Most of my *Observer* stories were domestics. I remember being despatched to Dartmoor, not for a study in landscape but for pictures of the grim, remote penal settlement built there originally to house prisoners from the Napoleonic wars. While I was photographing the spectacle of too many of Britain's most dangerous and hardened criminals locked up in one place, I noticed a young man waving at me furiously. I lowered the camera and saw that it was one of my old mates from Finsbury Park. If he was resentful at seeing me there as a visitor, rather than an inmate, he didn't show it.

Other stories I found less rewarding, though triviality sometimes provided memorable moments. I was given a very firm and precise briefing for an assignment at a nudist camp near Sunningdale. This was in the days before the *Sun* page three pictures, so you could say I was breaking fresh ground, though my pictures had to be decent enough for breakfast tables in quality newspaper homes.

I was greeted on arrival by a voluble and voluptuous woman without a stitch on who kept saying in a very posh voice, 'Why don't you take your things off, you'll feel much more comfortable.' My excuse for staying clothed was that the *Observer* wanted these pictures very quickly. She became suddenly highly co-operative. 'Now where would you like me?' she called as she leapt up and down in the water, splashing it eagerly across her breasts. A line of naked bottoms, bosoms and protruding stomachs, and heads with baseball caps on, were queuing for the naked lunch. Beyond them people were playing volleyball, a most uncomfortable game when you haven't got yourself strapped down. One persistent young man trailed me round the camp with the repeated advice of 'Come on, get 'em off'. Getting a usable picture of a man poling a punt, as I had been asked, was something of an achievement I thought. The volunteer kept his sandals on but was less adept at shielding the area that I knew could not be flaunted in a family newspaper. You couldn't take the job any more seriously than a McGill postcard, and I felt I could do more important stories at far less personal risk.

My dissatisfaction with the *Observer* came to a head with the arrival of the colour magazine. There had been no great enthusiasm for it in the paper, but as the *Sunday Times* was beginning to taste success with theirs, after a bumpy start some while earlier, both the *Observer* and the *Telegraph* decided they had to bring out their own magazines to stay in the running. I was not among those who welcomed the development. I was happy with black and white: it was easier to use and often, to my mind, produced pictures with greater impact, though later I was to do some of my best work for a colour magazine.

Once the decision was taken, the *Observer* was faced with the need to import people who were good with colour – rare birds in those days, and mostly to be found in the fields of fashion or advertising, or else working for geographical magazines. Some of the assignments that I thought should have been mine went to this new crew. At the same time, my early patrons on the picture desk had moved on and the new picture editors tended to treat me as if I were some kid street photographer, only to be used in narrow circumstances. I left quietly at the end of 1965 and teamed up with the people on the *Telegraph* magazine. It was a terrible mistake. I left the slight assignments of the *Observer* for even slighter ones at the new paper. The only project I enjoyed was an exploration of the legend of King Arthur. This involved spending a lot of time in the West country, an area I had come to love. I shot much of the wild forest material near Glastonbury in a sombre, haunting colour that seemed suited to legends. The feature was well received and repeatedly syndicated.

The *Telegraph*'s main contribution to my development was to cast me away on a desert island. The late John Anstey, the *Telegraph*'s reclusive magazine editor, thought it an amusing idea to abandon me and a young writer called Andrew Alexander on a tiny island in the Caribbean and to see how long it would take before we cried for help. They chose Necker, in the British Virgin Islands. It was an island about three-quarters of a mile long and half a mile wide, with a long hill running down the middle. It was inhabited by snakes, scorpions and tarantulas. The nearest outpost of civilisation was three miles away on Mosquito Island, where some Americans were building a hotel. We were allowed the clothes we stood up in, a pocket knife, a machete, fishing line and hooks, a limited supply of matches, iodine, a canvas sail (to catch rain) – all things a shipwrecked sailor might possess. A red flag was given to us to hoist should rescue be required. We also took two gallons of water to get started; the local doctor said we would need at least four pints a day.

We made ourselves a shack and called it, with rare premonition, the Chamber of Horrors. We suffered severe heatstroke through building it energetically in the midday sun on the first day marooned. Word of this ludicrous adventure got round the islands and, after a couple of days, an American senator appeared in his speedboat and yelled, 'Hi, you guys, how's it going? Can I get you any goodies?' It was the kind of encouragement we could have done without at that stage.

Andrew, who is well read and can play the piano, was at the opposite end of the personality spectrum to myself, but we got along all right, for a time at least. In the evenings we used to talk about great restaurants in Soho which, allied to the thirst, would make our tongues swell up to enormous size. Sleep was always a difficulty. The mosquitoes and other insects were more venomous and persistent than any I had encountered in Vietnam or the Congo. We often caught angel fish and trigger fish, which we would cook, wrapped in leaves, at the bottom of the fire. We supplemented this with prickly pears – lethal, as their name suggests, but at least moistening the mouth.

Water, indeed any kind of moisture, was the big problem. By the time we decided that coconuts were the answer, we were too weak to climb up the trees to get them. Cutting the trees down – there were only three coconut trees on the island – was against the rules. By the ninth day, we were down to half a pint of water between us. By the twelfth, there was just a mouthful each. Andrew tried chewing the inside of a cactus for moisture, but without any great success. After eight days he had written in his log, 'We are getting sorry for ourselves and resolve to stop it. Don has all the Cockney's special capacity for grumbling and I have a morbid taciturnity in these conditions which he must find very trying.' More difficult for me to cope with was Andrew's slight asthma. Stress would make him frighteningly breathless. While I griped, he became tense and short-tempered. Yet everything was done in slow motion because of our gathering weakness. All that accelerated was our squabbling, which we conducted through cracked lips that could barely move.

Out of temper, and out of water, we hoisted the red flag and were taken off in the early hours of the fifteenth day.

It was a phoney ordeal, but an ordeal none the less. We had each lost two stone in weight, and my medical report said: 'He was in an extremely dehydrated condition . . . Mentally he was lethargic and depressed.' We had disappointed ourselves:

the newspaper thought we might be good for three weeks while we had it in mind to do four.

Then something happened to lift our spirits. Alex Low, the picture editor, decided he could do better. He cabled to London to the effect: 'Pathetic show, Alexander and McCullin. Myself and local beachcomber willing to re-enact.' These two jokers went out to the island, lost their cameras in the sea, chopped down one of the sacrosanct palm trees, and ran up the red flag – all in the space of three days. But no lasting damage was done by the enterprise. Andrew went on to become a distinguished political columnist, and I was eventually rescued by three old mates from the *Observer* who had since gone to the *Sunday Times*. One of the trio was the illustrator Roger Law, who later created the television series 'Spitting Image', but it was the designer Dave King who arranged for me to meet *Sunday Times* magazine art editor Michael Rand, and he who paired me with my old reporter friend Peter Dunn for my first assignment with the *Sunday Times*.

The *Sunday Times* had money, and was ready to spend it. Peter and I were despatched on a slow swing through North America that would take us at least five weeks. Rarely before, even in war zones, had I been away for more than two. It is true the paper wanted value for money – four stories in all: a piece about the lives of merchant seamen, another about Cuban exiles in Miami, a big colour story on the Mississippi, and a gritty look at the Chicago police. Yet it showed confidence in the people they were sending. I liked that.

I had been to the States only briefly once before. I had been sent to New York by a German magazine to cover the Harlem riots of 1964 but arrived too late for a single rioter to be seen. This trip was to be different.

We left Glasgow on a 10,000-ton cargo ship on which I discovered long-distance drinking and seasickness. I remember Peter coming down to the cabin where I was lying uncertain if I was alive or dead and saying: 'Where're my new boots? I'm going to sort that little bugger out.' Mercifully, we docked in Charleston before he found them. In any case, new boots would have been of little use in a fight with the Cuban exiles we met in Miami, where I got striking pictures of car boots full of machine-guns. It was all said to be for the freedom struggle, but we weren't so sure. I developed some respect for Fidel Castro, for the people he had chucked out all seemed to be hardened crooks.

New Orleans was a great town for hitting the jazz joints. From there we took a barge to Baton Rouge, in Louisiana, where Peter fell sick for a couple of days, giving me longer to respond to the Mississippi, a wonderful river – massive, cantankerous and uncontrollable. I photographed an old negro by the riverside who said, 'Come down into the water, boy, and let me baptise you.' A few miles upriver I spent the night photographing the Ku Klux Klan, with their white hoods and flaming crosses. Then we went to a cotton plantation where the big-bellied boss told us, 'I do believe we treat our niggers very well on this estate.'

In Chicago the two detectives assigned as our escort took us to a basement area where the man in charge of the city morgue conducted us round the 'Stink Room'. He showed us unclaimed derelicts – some fire victims, some killed in road accidents, and the corpses of many just found dead on the pavement. He lamented our missing a woman who had gone through a few days earlier. 'You should have seen the tits on this dame.' I did not regard it as a time for taking pictures. Whether it was the Chicago morgue, or the relief of finishing the assignment, or simply applying a new-found skill, I don't know, but I arrived back at Heathrow somewhat pissed. I couldn't even stand up, and some ambulance men came to prise me off the plane. I spent the next twelve hours sleeping it off in the airport sick bay.

For me the *Sunday Times* was an opening into what became known later as the Swinging Sixties. Some of my friends became celebrities and celebrities became my collaborators and subjects, and sometimes my friends. I had moved the family to a semi-detached house of some style in Hampstead Garden Suburb, where one day I received a posse of Italian film makers who arrived in two large limos with expensive coats slung over their shoulders. In their midst was an older distinguished man with crinkly grey hair who turned out to be the great director Antonioni. He seemed a little surprised to find that fashionable London photographers lived modest lives with their families around them. I could see why when he outlined the plot of a film he was planning to make in England about a photographer who by chance finds evidence of a murder on one of his negatives. What little of it was true to life seemed to have little connection with mine. Style had become everything now that we had left the social realism of the angry young man behind. One sequence had the photographer-hero mobbed by teeny-boppers wrenching off their coloured tights for an orgy. Yet I was flattered when Antonioni told me he admired my reportage, which he had seen in European magazines. What exactly he wanted from me I was unsure, but I went around with him while he was looking for locations. He transformed one dreary park in South London by having everything in it painted, including the grass. I produced the blow ups for his film *Blow Up*, which became a cult movie.

The success of the *Sunday Times* was a Sixties phenomenon in itself. It had transformed itself from a deadly dull Tory rag into probably the most exciting newspaper in the world, and most of the transforming was done by people in their twenties and thirties under a brilliant and enlightened young editor from Yorkshire called Harry Evans. The Delinquent Generation of the war years had come into its own, with a drive, commitment, scepticism and rebellion peculiar to that age. I felt safe and happy with these people. Harry had great enthusiasm for photo-journalism, and that made a big difference to me. He was always interested and friendly without interfering, and under him photographers gained a new status, helped no doubt by the photographic staff having in their midst a member of the Royal Family, Anthony Armstrong-Jones.

The editor of the magazine, for which I did most of my work, was Godfrey Smith, a thoughtful man who knew how to get the best out of people with the minimum of fuss. When

I left for the war front in Biafra the day after our third child was born, Godfrey sent my wife a massive bunch of flowers. You pulled out a little bit more for someone who showed he cared in this way. Godfrey's free-wheeling think-tank – which included Dave King and Peter Crookston, whom I had know at the *Observer*, Francis Wyndham and fashion editor Meriel McCooey, as well as art editor Michael Rand – turned the Sunday colour magazine from a frivolous optional extra into a force to be reckoned with.

I was allowed to edit all my own pictures at the *Sunday Times*, a privilege that was not extended to any other photographer in Fleet Street, nor I think in the world. In exchange I would go away two or three times a year and risk my life. But I was also allowed some relaxation away from the world's wars with interesting projects like the Beatles or Fidel Castro's Cuba. I photographed the Beatles on two occasions, and was instantly engaged by the personality of Paul McCartney. It was harder to warm to John Lennon, who tended to sneer about passers-by who recognised him. As well as enormous talent, he had an abrasive, aggressive quality that was ironic in an apostle of Peace and Love. It was no easier to hit it off with Yoko Ono, who fussed around while I was trying to take pictures on a studio set (designed by Snowdon) on the top floor of the *Sunday Times* building in Gray's Inn Road. It was an all-day session the Beatles had asked me to do for them when they got tired of people asking them for pictures they did not possess. I had come in from taking some location shots and did not want to hear her talking not to me but to others about where I was stationing myself to take the interiors.

'Why is he standing *there*? Surely he should be *here*,' she would say as she came up behind me, making as if to lift me along. Needless to say, I didn't move.

One of the most unlikely matches of the time was an excursion I made with Edna O'Brien to Cuba after the missile crisis. I arrived in Havana before Edna but not before the film of her novel *The Girl with Green Eyes* was showing in the cinema opposite my downtown hotel. Photographically, it was not a good omen. I failed to get any interesting pictures at the prison where Castro and his revolutionaries had once been held, now a technological university, and I felt decidedly uncomfortable with the surveillance I was given by two North Vietnamese diplomats who seemed fixated by my United States Army battle jacket. I found the long tannoyed public addresses given by President Castro as tiresome as all the queuing up for meals. Dinner on the lawn of the British Embassy in honour of the celebrated Irish novelist, with the sea as a backdrop and men in white coats continually providing drinks, was much more my style. Had I come too far from Finsbury Park?

I had a birthday in Cuba which Edna marked with the presentation of a sombre poem, *First the Lion, then Vultures*. Edna, who is a very kind and considerate person, was never put off by the difficulties in Cuba. Maybe she saw parallels to her own Irish people's struggle against the English. Anyway, she came away from Cuba with a deep love for the place and its spirit. I came away just loving Edna.

14

JERUSALEM

The period of phoney war before the onset of six days of vicious fighting between the Arabs and the Israelis in June 1967 proved an unusually languid time for me. Under the misguided impression that Egypt would be a key listening-post for rumours of war, the *Sunday Times* had sent me to Cairo. My partner there was Phillip Knightley, one of the many Australians to attach themselves to the paper and enlarge its fun factors. As day succeeded day, and the Egyptian High Command resolutely kept us away from any zone that might be remotely warlike, we established a routine stroll from Semiramis Hotel down to the Gezira Sport Club, where Phillip spent time improving his backhand on the tennis court while I swam. Lunch and dinner were long, leisurely affairs by the poolside.

It was one of those gilded but all too infrequent periods in journalism where there is nothing to be done apart from spending the proprietor's money in the most relaxing and dignified manner possible. Not that we made no effort at all. In an attempt to outflank the military machine one day we took a taxi to Sinai, where we had heard there was a considerable arms build-up. Arriving in the Canal Zone, the taxi driver made an unscheduled stop at the office of the field security police, at which we were greeted with warmth by a colonel who appeared to be Peter Ustinov's double.

'Welcome to Suez, English gentlemen,' he beamed at us before steering us straight back to Cairo.

After a fortnight in Cairo Phillip decided the war rhetoric

(*Previous page*) Don McCullin in Vietnam, by Nick Wheeler.

Don and his brother Michael.

Embryo existence in Finsbury
Park – Don as a baby; his father
and mother; playing with brother
Michael in the back yard; dressed
up in Trafalgar Square; at school
with the kids from The Bunk;
as the biker.

The North of England before the Clean Air Act, as the young McCullin saw it.

Self-portrait in RAF uniform, taken at home in Finsbury Park with his first Rolleicord camera.

The Guvnors in a bombed house in The Bunk – the picture that started McCullin's career as a photographer appeared in the *Observer* in February 1959.

Don at twenty-one, Christine at
nineteen, 1956.

Sunday morning in
Chapel Street market,
Islington – the victim of
Don's assault with a
brick chats in a relaxed
social setting.

Before the Berlin Wall was built – East German 'Vopos' and American soldiers at demarcation lines in Friedrichstrasse and near the Brandenburg Gate.

(*Overleaf*) Exercise in realism – early morning for the homeless of Spitalfields Market, London.

would blow over. This was an opinion shared by the British Foreign Office and by Frank Giles, the foreign editor of the *Sunday Times*. We were both recalled from the Cairo duty. The very next morning Israeli Mystere and Mirage jets struck the Egyptian airfields in the Western Desert. The war had begun.

The Cairo experience had been negative but not futile. When it came to the business of launching correspondents and photographers off to the war, everyone was directed to the Israeli side where there was at least a possibility of access. Had I stayed in Egypt I would have missed the war in photographic terms altogether. As it was, after one night's sleep at home, I found myself at Heathrow again with a tribe of other newsmen *en route* for Cyprus, the nearest jumping off point for the conflict.

The next move was not obvious. Some correspondents rushed to sign up fishing boats which generally proved to be a mistake. One of their number was to spend the war marooned in Lebanon. Eventually he cabled home, 'Am I in doghouse query', and received the reply, 'Return Kennel-wards soonest'. Those of us who hung on at the airport were rewarded with the news that the Israelis were planning to send in an aeroplane to take off journalists.

Undoubtedly the Israelis felt they had more to gain from press attention. All the chest-beating by the Arabs about 100 million co-religionists being ready to smite an isolated Israel had had an effect. At that stage the Israelis were considered very much the underdogs in the conflict.

The Israeli plane that flew us into Tel Aviv that night was a De Haviland Rapide of elderly vintage. When we sorted ourselves out at the Dan Hotel it appeared that there were four *Sunday Times* survivors in the first wave – myself and another photographer, Neil Libbert, and two writers I had not worked with before. Murray Sayle, another Aussie, had a talent for being first. Colin Simpson was a stealthier character altogether, best known for his cunning in exposing bent antique dealers and insurance fraudsters. He was not a regular war correspondent, though he had nothing he needed to prove in this area. He had seen action as a regular army officer during the Malay emergency.

Our immediate problem was deciding how to divide up the war effort. We had no crystal ball, much less orders on how to go about it. Though we were all agreed that we were not going to wait on the services of a conducting officer, Murray seemed determined to go to Sinai, where a tank battle was raging. I had no intention of being deflected from the one place that I was sure would yield the greatest war pictures – Jerusalem. Neil Libbert teamed up with Murray to go South, while Colin and I headed for the Holy City in a hire car.

Driving towards Jerusalem in the early morning was oddly peaceful. So peaceful, in fact, that we thought we might have missed the war altogether. A BBC news report on the car radio indicated that the old city had been taken. We drove carefully towards the Jaffa Gate along the Bethlehem Road only to find it firmly in the hands of the Arab Legion. Colin backed the car at high speed, narrowly avoiding an unexploded mortar bomb in our path. Unknowingly, we had got ahead of the Israeli troops.

We noticed that beside the road through the valley there was a deep communications trench that led from the Israeli forward positions up into the gardens of the Dormition Monastery on Mount Zion. Through our glasses we could make out Israeli troops entering what looked like a tunnel. We decided to risk the valley road again, abandon our car near the monastery, and take our chance with the Israeli soldiers.

Within minutes we were explaining to the forward company commander that if he was set upon making Jewish history, it was only fit and proper that the *Sunday Times* should be with him to record it. We were accepted right away, and moved off with them through the olive groves.

The assault battalion we joined was called the 1st Jerusalem Regiment. We were with the point platoon, moving in single-file and bent double behind the scanty cover. There was no time to crawl. The Israelis behind us kept up a constant fire, directed at the walls of the old city. At first the only opposition came from isolated bursts of automatic fire – usually the reassuring crack of bullets well over our heads but occasionally the chilling, sucking 'whup' of one too close. Our objective was the Dung Gate, though we paused briefly on the way to check out a tented camp recently abandoned at the Arab Legion, their gear still neatly folded on their beds.

Eventually Colin decided to hitch a lift on a friendly tank while I stayed with the point section that would be first through the gate. Colin raised a laugh among the soldiers as he moved off when an officer said that I was the brave one, getting so close to the front of the assault.

'Him? He's a Scotsman called McCullin, and just too mean to buy a telephoto lens, that's all.'

This was certainly a period when I felt that I had a charmed life, that danger could not touch me.

It was Colin who took the first fall. As we were going for the gate, his tank fired its gun and so surprised Colin that he tumbled off into a clump of prickly pear. I was too absorbed to be aware of this at the time. Colin and I were not to meet up again until the battle for the city was over.

We came through the Dung Gate at a rush. I was on a high, swiftly tempered by the need to concentrate in order to stay alive.

We took a lot of casualties in that first hundred yards inside the gate, coming under heavy sniper fire, bullets ricocheting in all directions as we fanned out. I found myself in a section lined with low walls, only two or three feet high, but cover of a sort, and there I got one of my better known pictures of Israeli soldiers firing over these walls. So exposed were we that if the Arabs had used mortars we would not have stood a chance.

As the Israelis increased their fire we edged forward into an area of little stone houses in very narrow streets, some barely more than a yard wide and obvious death traps. We took the widest we could find. Suddenly a Jordanian soldier ran out in front of us with his hands up. He did not appear to be armed, but everyone was jittery because of the snipers, and we all hit the ground. The Jordanian was blown to bits. The officer told them to cease firing, and soon after another young Jordanian and an old man came out of a house to be taken prisoner. The unit was moving further down the street when the lead man was shot dead, and a few yards later the next man received a bullet through his chest. A doctor came up to me and started screaming for a knife to cut away the man's clothing, though I failed to understand the torrent of Hebrew until someone said 'knife' in English and I fumbled for mine while the man died. Then the soldier just behind me was shot by a sniper behind a wall. He was stretchered off with a handkerchief over his face.

The weight and speed of the Israeli attack was beginning to tell. More people started to surrender, among them a large number of men in pyjama suits. Jordanian soldiers wore them instead of uniform, hoping to be mistaken for civilians. The Israelis were laughing and making fun of them, but I saw no Israeli soldier mistreat anyone. They all seemed to venerate the city, and there was no looting or desecration. On more than one occasion I watched Israelis hold their fire when sniped at from the roofs of religious buildings of any persuasion.

Outside the city walls a tank battle could be heard raging. The Jordanians had taken their tanks to high ground and were pouring shells into the city as Israeli armour moved forward to engage them. It was soon all over.

I slumped down, immobile after all the hectic action. I had no thought of what to do now.

'Why are you sitting there?' an Israeli soldier called to me. 'History is being made, my friend. You must go to the Wailing Wall.'

'What's the Wailing Wall?' I asked.

I found the Wall through a series of back alleys that today are cleared, leaving the wall exposed on an open plateau. In this warren of medieval streets Jordanian snipers had exacted a heavy price from incoming Israelis, who now stood with their faces screwed up before the Wall against which they appeared to be banging their heads. I took a picture of those soldiers paying homage.

'We've waited a thousand years for this,' one man said to me as soldiers were hugging and kissing each other around me, lifting each other off the ground while snipers' bullets ricocheted off the Wall itself.

I spent time in the Dome of the Rock, where Mohammed was said to have risen into heaven. Now it was being used as a casualty station and a holding area for prisoners. I took more pictures of the victors jesting over the vanquished.

That evening I went back to the Wailing Wall, where Israeli soldiers were standing around listening to news of their victory on radios borrowed from Jordanian cars whose number plates were prized as souvenirs. Between newscasts the Israelis sang patriotic songs until they were told to pipe down because they were making life easy for the few remaining snipers. I saw two Israelis killed by their own men. They were running to the Wall in the dark and were shot by nervous sentries.

As the night wore on it grew very cold. While the battle lasted we had been infernos, stoked with adrenalin; now we were drained and lifeless. I checked into the King David Hotel, scene of the 1946 atrocity when an Irgun bomb had killed ninety, mostly British military personnel. I was told I could choose from any of several hundred empty rooms. I was too tired to take a bath before falling into bed. I slept like a dead man, and awoke next morning to see the sheets covered with red dust. I remember thinking guiltily that I would be in trouble for that, and then made the mistake of asking for ham and eggs for breakfast!

Unless I did something really flagrant, like asking for ham at breakfast or expressing ignorance of the Wailing Wall, people seemed naturally to assume that I was Jewish. On the other hand, in Israel you realise that there is no such thing as a typically Jewish look. Several of the soldiers with whom I entered the city had blue eyes and fair hair.

I had time for one social occasion – morning coffee with Cornell Capa, brother of the legendary photographer Robert Capa, who was killed in Indo China while covering the war for *Life* magazine. Then, as I had already decided that I wanted to get my pictures back as fast as possible, I hitched a lift back to Tel Aviv, where I found Colin Simpson in the Dan Hotel, knee-deep in maps of Jerusalem. It turned out that he had managed to climb back on his tank and had entered the city through the St Stephen's Gate. He thought that I might have been shot in the first assault and was relieved to see me. He had spent part of his day in Jerusalem looking for my remains, even peering under the shrouds of the Dome of the Rock.

I had been worried about censorship at the airport but in the event just walked through. I was going so soon that they didn't realise I was a newspaperman. They thought I was just another scared visitor baling out.

'Why are you leaving?' the man at the passport control asked me. 'There is so much to see. We are victorious.'

The whole airport was in an exuberant state. We now know, of course, that the great victories of that war in Jerusalem, on the West Bank, in Sinai and on the Golan Heights would provide the seeds of anguish in later years, but there was no hint of this at the time. All was rejoicing.

15

ANOTHER DESERT WAR

I FIRST ENCOUNTERED Viscount Montgomery of Alamein in Egypt shortly before the Six Days War, and I'd had a bit of a desert war with him myself. We were thrown together by a *Sunday Times* stunt designed to steer him back into the limelight so that he could redirect all his old desert battles of the Second World War in print. The problem arose when I was asked to take a picture of him. Monty had backed off with a pained look on his face. He got into a lengthy discussion with the *Sunday Times* top brass escorting him and word came down the chain of command that my appearance was in some way not fitting for taking photographs of the Field Marshal. It seemed that the length of my side-burns were the chief cause of offence.

I put in a special request to return home. In no way was I going to cut my hair to suit an old martinet, however legendary. I stuck to my guns and ended up snapping away, side-burns intact. He liked people who stood up to him.

I had gone on the trip expecting something of a holiday. It was my first visit since I had been to Egypt on national service, and instead of employment as a 27-shillings-a-week skivvy I was going back as part of an international VIP junket. I was to be back-up to the official photographer, Ian Yeomans. Also in the party for the twenty-fifth Alamein anniversary was the magazine's art editor, Michael Rand, and the *Sunday Times* editor-in-chief, Denis Hamilton, a quiet and formal but nice man who had been a junior officer on Monty's wartime staff. It was he who had unloaded a

89

succession of Monty's memoirs on the readership in serial form with tremendous success. For us, therefore, Monty had a double aura – not only was he a revered national hero, he was also good for circulation.

I saw a different Egypt. We stayed initially at the luxurious old Mena House hotel by the pyramids, to which I was inclined to give better marks than on my first sighting twelve years earlier. In my room, courtesy of the management, was a transistor radio, a bottle of eau de cologne, and a huge chocolate cake with 'Welcome to the United Arab Republic' piped on the top. In the morning, I discovered that there was an Egyptian paratrooper standing on guard duty outside each of our bedrooms. Even President Nasser seemed to regard Monty as an honoured guest, and most of the top Egyptian brass paid court to him at one time or another.

We moved on to Alexandria, to a riot of red carpets and bands, in a marvellous old piece of Hungarian rolling stock. We were enjoying an almost royal procession, though there was one rather awkward situation when a reporter and photographer on the *Daily Express* tried to penetrate the enterprise. It was Fleet Street at its most wily, attempting to get a slice of the action – not unreasonably perhaps, for Monty was considered national property. I could see myself in their place and felt sorry for them, but it was a Times Newspapers deal and that was that. The Egyptian authorities saw them off, protesting loudly.

This stately progress continued until we reached El Alamein. One morning a Russian helicopter descended from the sky and out on the dunes emerged a man in full dinner jacket balancing a tray of cold drinks for the party. Mike Rand almost choked. All laughter had to be stifled because of the presence of his military highness. Nobody could be seen to be ridiculing the main event.

I had begun to think it was going to be nothing but suppressed mirth all the way when suddenly the number one photographer, Ian Yeomans, took sick. That was the moment when my side-burns came under the scrutiny of the eye of history, and I found myself peering through the viewfinder at this wiry little man with the amazing translucent blue eyes that gazed back at you from a skull-like head.

Monty, of course, was the entertainment. For much of the time he went around with General Sir Oliver Leese, whose main passion was digging up cacti in the desert for transshipment back to England. Leese was a giant of a man with a dreadful war wound which came on exhibition when he tried to negotiate his bathing trunks. He was also a very charming man, which is more than could be said for Monty. 'Come on, Oliver,' Monty would say. 'Let's have a talk away from these dreadful press people.' When it was arranged for Monty to pay a visit to Nasser, we all gathered to give him a good send-off. His parting words were, 'Now I'm going to see General Nasser and you press people are not allowed.' He was a great one for pulling rank, and liked to rub it in, did Monty. I learned only later the story about Winston Churchill saying to the King, 'Sometimes I think Monty's after my job,' to which the King replied, 'What a relief. I thought he was after mine.'

When we got to the battleground where Monty and the Eighth Army had thrown back Rommel's tanks, it was an anti-climax. Most of the remnants of war had long since been removed, though there were still dodgy bits of German S-mines around, still perfectly capable of blowing off your leg. We were warned not to pick up anything. There had been many serious accidents among the civilian population in an area that had been sown with millions of anti-tank and anti-personnel mines. They gave Egypt its legacy of amputees.

After Monty had delivered a few lectures we started back in much the same stately manner, despite unwelcome events taking place in the real world, one of which was the Colonels' seizure of power in Greece. A telex arrived from the *Sunday Times* in London telling me to proceed to Athens immediately. Monty would have none of it.

'Donald will not go to Athens,' he stated with an air of finality. 'He will remain with my party. Nobody leaves my party.' I stayed with his party.

One morning I was showing off on the beach doing a handstand in front of the house cleaners in a hotel complex and I fell into a table full of drinks and cups. There was a lot of merriment. Oliver Leese must have told Monty that I was making the ladies laugh. 'You must go home and cosset your wife,' Monty said to me sternly. 'You must have nothing to do with ladies.'

When we were talking about women one evening, Monty came in with his wicked gleam. 'You know Oliver's got a lady.' It was true, Oliver had a very nice lady whom he had known for many years, but Monty managed to cast a red light district glow over the enterprise.

Jesting complaint was all part of Monty's funny way. He must have said we were taking two years off his life at least a dozen times, and he was obviously having a whale of a time for a man of seventy-nine. Great men must be allowed their share of oddities, though I think Monty had more than most. One of the more inexplicable foibles was the shine he took to me, and not just in the desert. When I returned from the Six Day War, he telephoned to invite me to his home. It was Christine who took the call. 'Are you the housekeeper?' the piping voice demanded briskly. Once assured that he was through to the right number, he issued his request for my presence at Isington Mill in the wilds of Hampshire. It would be a difficult journey, I figured, but there was no dodging it. This was like a royal command.

He met me at the station. The staff almost came to attention as he led me out into the station yard where stood a lovely old Rover car. To my astonishment, he himself was to be my chauffeur.

'Are you quite comfortable?' he asked before he let in the gear and began the slow, stately drive – at all of seven miles an hour. At one moment he dared to lift a hand off the steering wheel and pat the dashboard.

'This is real wood, this,' he said with pleasure. 'Two-thousand-pound job, this vehicle.'

Lunch – a rather meagre meal – was served by a little house-keeping lady in a room furnished in light oak. Afterwards I was escorted to an identical room upstairs – it even had the same books on the coffee table.

'Winston Churchill gave me that painting,' Monty said, pointing to one of the framed pictures on the wall. 'I shall probably sell it one day.'

He always had a wicked little kick-back in his remarks. Referring to the consequences of the Six Day War he said, 'Most of our friends of the desert pilgrimage seem to have got the sack.'

'Would you like a beer?' I think it was a very large concession on his part – a non-drinking, non-smoking man – to pour a beer for me.

At four o'clock – 'not a minute before, nor a minute after' said Monty – the housekeeper brought in tea. A huge iced cake was placed beside the pot of tea and cups on a tray. Monty said nothing, just watched her intently come and go. He seemed to have little time for women. He was like an old tomcat watching that programmed servant. He handed me a huge wedge of cake, and scarcely before I had finished was asking if I would like some more.

'If you don't have it the rats will get it,' he said, dangling the implication that the 'rats' might not have four legs.

I visited Lord Montgomery at least half a dozen times over the next three years. He would usually get in touch through Denis Hamilton, and the ceremonial of the visits was always much the same. On one occasion, however, he had me photographing his flower beds, giving particular prominence to the red and white astilbe. Another time he honoured me with a visit to his garage, where he opened the huge doors to reveal Rommel's caravan captured at the battle of Alamein.

Usually we talked about whichever war I had just returned from, and he was always knowledgeable and precise. I remember at the removal of General Westmoreland at the time of Tet gave him particular satisfaction. He was the only person I called 'Sir', but I felt that this man had earned respect. As my view of him began to mellow, I saw the reality beneath all the honours as that of a very lonely old man.

16

THE BATTLE OF HUE

FROM MY FIRST visit to Vietnam I always felt that the Americans could never win the war, for all their power. That sense was never stronger than at their victorious battle for Hue.

It was one of those occasions when the timing of my arriving in Vietnam went wrong – or maybe too exactly right. As the Air France jet approached Bangkok I heard over the pilot's radio of the Tet offensive, the synchronised Viet Cong invasion, in the lull of the New Year holiday, of a hundred South Vietnamese towns and cities, including Saigon itself. Astonishing things were happening. A Viet Cong 'kamikaze' volunteer had leapt out of a taxi at the US Embassy in Saigon and fired the first rounds in the battle for the American citadel. Diplomats were said to be returning fire from the Embassy windows. Four thousand guerrillas, smuggled in disguised as family visitors for the Lunar New Year, had materialised at the same time inside the city defences. The South Vietnamese HQ was under siege, so was the Presidential palace and Tan Son Nhut airport, where we were supposed to land. We were diverted instead of Hong Kong, and there I sat, waiting, when the news came through that Saigon had been reclaimed. The symbolic Embassy battle had lasted six hours and left 26 dead. I felt I should have been there to cover it. Some 37,000 people died in Vietnam in the aftermath of Tet.

In that aftermath my friend Eddie Adams, an American photographer, took the decisive picture – of the police chief, in public, shooting a bound Viet Cong prisoner in the head.

More even than the My Lai massacre, that picture was to create a turning point in the heart of the American people. No longer were they in a war that they found to be honourable.

When finally I got to Vietnam, I headed north, to Khe Sanh. There, in a dustbowl in the hills of north-west Vietnam, close to the North Vietnamese and Laos borders, a replay of the French disaster at Dien Bien Phu thirteen years before was taking place.

Two crack North Viet divisions – directed from Hanoi by General Giap, the victor of Dien Bien Phu – had approached the big American base in Khe Sanh down the Ho Chi Minh trail. One was the 304th, the very same that had led the assault on the French. Linking up with 60,000 troops already in the area, the NVA had surrounded Khe Sanh and its small strategic airfield, a key to north-south movement. The American Marines in the base – outnumbered eight to one – were virtual sitting ducks as their enemy tunnelled to within a hundred yards of the camp wire. Their lifeline was air support, on a scale the French could never have conceived. The massive B-52 bombers dropped 5,000 bombs a day on the besieging North Vietnamese army and thousands of tons of napalm.

I flew up to Da Nang, the huge US military base on the coast, still intending to go to Khe Sanh, though I was daunted by the amount of coverage it had received already. Reporters and cameramen were being flown in on the planes which came to bring out the wounded. They were using American air superiority to get their own job done. I had the same thought in mind when I saw in the press centre a bone-weary David Douglas Duncan, an ex-Marine Colonel from Korea, and a very, very good photographer. He had rolls and rolls of film from Khe Sanh. It tipped my decision. What was the point in doubling up on David?

There was talk of a US counter-offensive to reclaim the chief South Vietnamese city still in Northern hands – the Imperial City of Hue. This sounded a subject for me.

Hue, an ancient mandarin walled city, stood on the banks of the Perfumed River up near the demilitarised zone. It was the cultural capital of Vietnam, Oxford and Cambridge combined. It had fallen in Tet to a force of 5,000 Viet Cong and NVA regulars, and their flag now flew above its battlements. There was a large civilian population and some horror was expressed that such a place should become a battleground of war. If the Americans were to recapture it, the action was bound to involve heroic assault and close street fighting for the Marines. As with Jerusalem, I was drawn to the idea of covering a battle in an ancient city.

Under a heavy overcast sky, I joined the convoy of the Fifth Marine Commando as it started rolling up to Hue. It ploughed through heavy mud and rain, past houses collapsed and pitted by artillery, and columns of fleeing refugees. It was very cold.

We trucked to the southern tip of Hue. The news was that the Marine force ahead of us had liberated the southern half of the city. The task of the Fifth Commando now was to free the Citadel, the walled city on the north bank of the Perfumed River.

A vast bridge complex running down into the river had been blown. Big spans of it were broken in the middle. Ahead of me lay the northern city of Hue, apparently dead, crawling with North Vietnamese regulars, they said, a formidable and tenacious foe. Though not my foe. I never felt that the Viet Cong and the North Vietnamese were my enemy. Although I arrived in Hue looking indistinguishable from an American Marine, I was not on an American mission. I was, what I always tried to be, an independent witness – though not an unemotional one.

Waiting to cross the Perfumed River, I went out with a Marine patrol probing the firefights around the edge of the city, and checking out the seemingly deserted houses near the battle area. They went round the houses in a very macho fashion, throwing their weight around, rattling and banging their equipment. I hung behind, waiting at the back.

They entered and emerged from a house. I heard one say to another, 'There's nothing in there but a dead Gook.'

I went in the house, to a dark room, and saw a mosquito

net draped over the bed. There was a candle burning. As I moved closer to the mosquito net, I saw a corpse lying behind it, lying in a dignified way. I looked and thought, That's a very small person. As I lifted the gauze, I saw that it was a small child in a grubby shirt. I let the mosquito net down and took stock. For the first time I pressed the emotional buttons that sooner or later got pressed in war. I left that patrol thinking about that small boy, that curtailed small life, which didn't amount to anything to these men except as 'another dead Gook'.

I went back to the command centre and found another patrol. They were detailed to routine mopping-up. Bunkers and air raid shelters were approached with the warning cry 'Fire in the hole!' before a grenade was lobbed in. From one such fired hole emerged a family of wounded Vietnamese civilians.

When finally I reached the water's edge I found a very tall US Naval Commander in charge of operations. He smoked a big cigar.

'Good morning,' I called. 'I'm from the Sunday Times in London and I've come into Hue with the Marines. Could you tell me when I could board for crossing the river?'

He looked down at me with utmost contempt. 'Excuse me,' he said flatly, 'you will not board any of my boats. You will leave this compound.'

'Well, I'm sorry, but I do have authorisation,' I said, 'and I have accreditation to cross, and I'm part of this set-up.'

'I don't give a damn. You will leave my compound. You will not board my boats.'

I knew I would get nowhere with this man. He was one of those John Wayne types you sometimes came across, too busy admiring their own performance to take anything in. As I was walking away, thoroughly dejected, my eye fell on some Vietnamese soldiers boarding a pontoon assault landing craft further up the river, out of this man's clear sight.

I darted through trees and gardens and surfaced close to the pontoon. With a bit of sign language, I got a friendly invitation to come aboard. I dropped my height, bent my knees and waddled on at the end of the queue. The gate went up, the boat backed out, it turned and set off downriver. I could see the huge, enthralled-with-himself Naval Commander, standing with his legs apart, still smoking the stogie, surveying the scene. As we put-putted past him I stood up to my full height and put up two fingers and gave him my best smile.

On the other side, I was getting ahead of the phase-lines, the plans of advance into battle, though I didn't know it then. I left the Viets and found myself walking through mandarin gardens and waterparks, and by miniature lakes, within the confines of a medieval wall. It was peaceful. Then I heard small arms fire, and the crunch of incoming mortar. I had to jerk myself out of this mood of pleasant strolling and remind myself of the war.

I spotted some men taking cover in a roadside by the gardens. I could see bandages, bloody bandages, and bloody flesh. I ran over to them – they were Americans – and lay down in the same ditch. The crack of AK-47 rounds could be heard above our heads.

'What's happening?' I asked.

'There's a hell of a lot of VC ahead. We've got casualties already, and we're waiting for the medics to come.'

At a distance, I saw a man sitting by a wall with a corpsman (as they called the medics) close to the Citadel walls. I pointed out this scene to the man who had spoken. 'What's going on over there?'

'That's a man who'll surely get a Congressional. He's just taken two rounds in the face.'

I crawled along until I found this soldier sitting with his back to the low wall. There was blood and saliva running down his face, and the huge personal dressing he was applying was turning red as I watched. His eyes were like infernos, pleading with the pain. I raised my camera as he turned his head from left to right, requesting me not to do it. I backed off.

Later, in a lull in the fighting, I crawled over to another group of Marines who found me a tin helmet. One soldier, who had never met an Englishman before, said, 'Let me do something special for you.' He conjured up a magnificent fruit cocktail out of nowhere. I was lying in a ditch, sipping this gift, when there came a most tremendous escalation in the noise of battle. The incoming mortars were terrifying but so was our own back-up effort. The American fleet, fifteen miles away in the China Sea, were dropping shells in front of us in a co-ordinated pattern and, I later discovered, soldiers would spend sleepless nights worrying about them dropping short.

They were also bringing in Phantoms, just over our heads, to drop napalm. The actual canisters were released behind us to hit the Citadel in front of us. So your imagination gazed upon this huge delivery of canisters with a lot of apprehension.

Suddenly it grew dark. The Orientals believe that all sorts of demons are let loose at night, and sometimes they would prove to be the Viet Cong and the NVA, turning people's fear of the dark to their own advantage. I was too exhausted to be scared. Exhilaration and adrenalin exhaust you. Your nerve-ends, your antennae, are raw, hanging out. Normally they tell you everything, and they make you feel everything. I was exhausted, but still excited and, above all, hungry.

In the fading light, I hunted for food. The soldiers were issued with what they called C-rats, a personal pack with some tinned food. I knew that even after a long time in the field, there were some C-rats that the soldiers couldn't stomach. I soon came across plenty of discards of a concoction called ham and lima beans.

Spooning into my lima beans, I registered that, for the first time in my life, I was in a battle on a gigantic scale. My previous Vietnam battles, and the battle for Jerusalem, were skirmishes compared to this. Only a few months earlier, in the euphoria after the Six Day War, I had said that I would like to do war photography every day of the week. Hue was to teach me a terrible lesson.

The Americans had told me they were going in for a 24-hour operation. As the days turned into a week, and then a second week, I suddenly became an old man. I had a beard.

My eyes were sunken. I was sleeping under tables in tin shacks, on the floor, shivering with the cold at night. I never took off my clothes, and I kept my helmet close by me, and a flak jacket for a blanket. I had acquired the jacket from the first field casualty station, where they cut the stuff off the wounded and the dead, and threw it on a big pile.

One morning I emerged from my little hut and went in a new direction, to the right instead of the left. On the other side of the corrugated iron sheet which made up the side wall of this little Vietnamese house I found a dead North Vietnamese soldier. He had been lying almost head to head with me for days; shot in the mouth. The bullet had ripped its way through the back of his head. Such macabre sights were almost commonplace. You would find corpses or detached limbs. I went to retrieve an object by the roadside once and found it was a foot that had been run over by a tank. The human mutilation was matched by the physical mutilation. Hue, that beautiful city, was becoming a city of rubble.

I heard some heavy incoming shells one morning when I was out with a Marine close to the Citadel wall. We both jumped into a foxhole by the wall, one that the NVA had dug for themselves for the impending Marine invasion. We were cowering under our helmets when the American said, 'Goddammit, there's an awful smell here.' I noticed that this hole was not firm underfoot. Even though we were in sand, it was too soft. I looked down and saw a row of fly buttons by my boots. We were both crouched on the stomach of a dead North Vietnamese soldier and our weight had caused the stomach to excrete. Despite the shelling, we both leapt out and ran off in different directions, to find other bunkers.

In this kind of war you are on a schizophrenic trip. You cannot equate what is going on with anything else in life. If you have known white sheets, and comfort, and peace in the real world, and then you find yourself living like a sewer rat, not knowing day from night, you cannot put the two worlds together. None of the real world judgments seem to apply. What's peace, what's war, what's dead, what's living, what's right, what's wrong? You don't know the answers. You just live, if you can, from day to day.

I was with some Marines one evening, probing below the Wall, when someone said 'Tsai Kong', the name for the Chinese stick grenade, a small grenade like a lollipop. I saw the grenade lying between me and all the other soldiers except one, a tall gangling marine who was standing behind me. I dived into the dip in the ground. There was a colossal muffled explosion, followed by a rush of fragmentation. I felt a lot of stuff hitting my legs, and my waist. My lower half went numb. This is it, I thought, I've been wounded. I tried to recall what I'd read about being wounded and remembered Robert Graves saying it was like someone hitting you with a forceful blow. There had been forceful thumps all over my body. I thought, Any minute now I'm going to feel blood. I put my hand down to my crotch . . . I had already called out, I suppose like a child would call for its mother. There was a shout of 'Corpsman'.

Then I felt down my legs. There was no blood, and there were no holes, just the numbness. I had been struck by all the debris and stones but not by the fragmentation. The gangling man had taken the whole lot in the back of his head, under his helmet. He was down, with blood oozing from his head and neck. The other soldiers were all firing in the direction from which the grenade had come because that meant close proximity. Very close. Then the back-up came and they poured all kinds of M60 into the area, heavy machine-gun rounds.

We pulled back to the compound where Myron Harrington, the commander of Delta company, was based. Harrington was now looking with dismay at every new casualty. This was no mopping-up operation. His company was fast being whittled away by the Wall. And only at the Wall. One day I had stood chatting in a courtyard, and had just stepped into an adjacent courtyard for a moment, when a mortar shell landed just where I had been standing, seriously injuring the two soldiers with whom I had been talking.

The Marines have a tradition; they don't abandon their

wounded or their dead. Harrington would send out details at night to bring back anyone unaccounted for. I went on one of these night missions and felt as if I was intruding on something very private. They were bringing two bodies in and it was the first time I had seen a Western soldier weeping. He was black and was crying over a dead white comrade.

I took a picture of another black Marine hurling a grenade at the Citadel. He looked like an Olympic javelin thrower. Five minutes later this man's throwing hand was like a stumpy cauliflower, completely deformed by the impact of a bullet. The man who took his place in the throwing position was killed instantly. One day I took a picture that was not of soldiers in action but of a dead Vietnamese with all his scattered possessions arranged around him in a sort of collage. It was composed, contrived even, but it seems to say something about the human cost of this war.

17

LESSONS OF WAR

SOMETIMES I CRAWLED ahead of the phase-line in order to be in position to photograph the Marines advancing towards me. On one such occasion the advance was suddenly blocked and two men were killed right next to me, where I lay eating dirt in a foxhole. The platoon commander had his throat clipped by a round from an AK-47, and I saw him trying to get his finger into his throat to stem the bleeding. A muscle in his leg had been lifted right back. I crawled over to him after most of the others had crawled away, leaving us extended. The officer began talking heroically about bringing fire down on us, for a diversion.

'Listen, let's not be irrational now,' I said.

Suddenly the remaining men were looking to me for leadership. With the officer out of action, I was easily the oldest there. The fire was too intense to entertain any immediate thoughts of carrying the officer to safety, so we held on until the old M60 came up again and gave us covering fire.

To my way of thinking, the battle plan of these Marines lacked sophistication. There was altogether too much charging straight down the line, like American cavalry shooting from the hip. With the benefit of raised positions, NVA snipers were just picking men off. Through sheer force of numbers and firepower, it seemed that the marines must eventually win, but at what cost? You could see that they were losing faith in the war. The swing of public opinion against the war at home in the States was also manifesting itself here in the front line as it was being fought. Several soldiers had told me that if they got out of Hue alive they would be writing to their Congressmen, opposing American involvement in the war. Most American soldiers were openly contemptuous of the South Vietnamese troops who operated in the rear. Even in Hue you could see ARVN looting the possessions of the people they had come to liberate.

One day a child appeared suddenly in the thick of the battle. Thousands of civilians still hid in Hue, though they tried to flee from the front lines, and this child just appeared, an unexplained presence so far forward in the battle. Everyone's attention turned to it. Soldiers became human beings again instead of warriors. It hurt these 19- to 22-year-olds to see this lost infant. Gently they shepherded him to a corpsman, who took him into a house and dressed the nasty gash on his head. I photographed this being done by candle-light, and the soldier who carried the child away from the sniping and the mortar fire, did so as if he was making the most important delivery of his life.

A Marine arrived one night with the resupply ammunition, driving up to our position in what they called a mule. It was a little, open-topped, moke used for ammo and taking out the wounded. He overshot our position, and the phase-line. Out in no man's land, a sniper killed him. He stayed slumped over the wheel with the engine ticking on. We were all watching this dead soldier, lying over the wheel, with the engine ticking on through the night. Star-shells were going off, those huge 50-dollar star shells, all night long. They gave an eerie, fluorescent yellow light by which we watched that dead soldier till dawn, when the petrol ran out and the moke's engine died.

The Citadel was eventually taken. It took such a torrent of shells to do it that there wasn't much worth having. Hue was devastated. The wooden houses had been blown away, the city centre was rubble. They had destroyed the city in order to save it. Almost 6,000 civilians were killed in Hue, more than the military dead on either side. At Khe Sanh, where the siege lasted 77 days, the bombing and shelling exceeded five Hiroshimas.

Yet this was not the whole cost. The minds of the living were being mutilated as much as the bodies of the dead. On one of my last days in Hue i heard some whimpering behind a shack. Two Marines, real old Rednecks, had got a little Vietnamese with a rope round his neck and were leading him around as if he was some kind of pet billy-goat. They blindfolded and gagged him and made him kneel and lie down in the dirt. They put him through misery and torment. It was the same cowardly, murderous sequence I had seen in the Congo, now being practised by apostles of freedom in Asia.

Eleven days I had spent in Hue . . . I am not sure what it taught me. I don't know if it taught me anything beyond a new appreciation of how terrible war can be. It certainly made me ashamed of what human beings are capable of doing to each other. In a grim way I suppose it taught me to survive, and part of that new knowledge was knowing when to leave.

Very early in the battle, a Marine chaplain had come up and offered me the last rites. He had frightened me, and I had said firmly, 'No, I don't want that.' Somehow he put the fear in me, offering me the sacrament, and the flesh of Christ. I thought, this man is offering me a very pessimistic ending here. He spooked me. I thought, I've got to put some distance between me and this man.

That night I mentioned the incident to a friend. I must have displayed great emotion, because he urged me to take it easy. There are people at home, he reminded me, thinking of you. I was touched by what he said at the time, but it wasn't until I got back to England that I felt its full force. While I had been courting death in Hue, my little boy Paul had almost died at home. He had been playing with a bow and arrows, the ones with rubber suckers, and he had put one in his mouth. It stuck to his throat, and he very nearly suffocated.

Before I left Hue I thanked Myron Harrington for what the Marines had given me – camaraderie to one who didn't bear arms. He told me he would see me in London. Wrongly, I didn't believe him, and took my leave.

I went down to the casualty clearing station where they kept the body-bags, the plastic body-bags, and the living bones. I saw the priest who had spooked me before, and he smiled.

He said, 'Are you going to Da Nang?' I told him that I was, and he said, 'Well, I'm going to Da Nang too.'

When the helicopter arrived they said there was room only for one person. The priest suggested I should take it.

I said, 'No, no, it's your place, Father. You take it.'

'Don't argue, I'm your senior.'

I said, 'Listen, I'm sorry about back there. It just frightened me.'

'You don't have to explain,' he said, 'go.'

I got in that helicopter and flew down the coastline of Vietnam. I couldn't speak, and felt as if I had aged twenty-five years. Another photographer aboard that helicopter, a very courageous Frenchwoman, Catherine Leroy, who had been among the Viet Cong in Hue on the other side of the battle, later astonished the world with her pictures of the war. She sat opposite and looked at me, and I gazed at her. I didn't want to talk to her. I didn't want to speak to anyone. I had a screaming in my mind, as if the shell explosions and the fire were still raging there. Images of blood and death and dying. It was all still there in my head. I was totally shell-shocked.

In Da Nang I thought I could start to restore myself with a hot bath and a bed. Then, in the press centre, I met Fred Emery from *The Times*.

'Listen,' he said, 'they want something in London urgently about what it is like up here. Could you talk it through with me? Would you do that?'

'Can I have a bath first, Fred,' I said.

My sleep was a long series of linked battle nightmares. To get home I had to fly first to Saigon, and then to Paris, where I found myself on stand-by at Orly. At ten o'clock there were still 100 people missing from the plane. Then I heard some of them coming, English rugby fans who had been to the France versus England international. They were singing through

Orly, peeing in the pot plants, dragging fallen comrades. Fallen from drink, not war.

Years later I went back to Hue and walked through that battleground, where I had been so close to death, where I felt I was death's permanent companion. It seemed so inconsequential, the whole thing. Those men who died, and those men who were maimed for life, went through all that, and it was totally futile, as all wars are known to be. Without profit, without horizons, without joy. I remember there was a street in Da Nang called the Street without Joy. They could have called the whole country after that street.

18

CHILDREN OF BIAFRA

FIVE MINUTES AFTER setting foot on Biafran soil I was in jail. I had made the journey after hearing reports that a woman had reached Iboland with the severed head of her child in a bowl you would normally eat your rice meal from. My *Time-Life* reporter colleague, George de Cavala, on the plane to Port Harcourt, had been diligently typing up his notes. They thought we were spies. Five hours later we had talked our way out. I was free to embark on one of the most emotional assignments of my life. As a nation Biafra survived for no more than three years. In each of these years I recorded its fragile existence, its struggle and its decline.

The feelings around by the Biafran conflict are now hard for Europeans to recall. But in 1967 intense emotion seized not only Africa, but the whole world. At one stage it threatened to split even my paper, the *Sunday Times*.

The breakaway fragment of Nigeria had become a separate country on 30 May 1967, when Lieutenant-Colonel Odumegwu Ojukwu proclaimed its secession from the Nigerian Federation. The Ibo, the dominant tribe of the new nation, had a prime motive for declaring independence – fear of genocide.

George and I had just returned from the North of Nigeria, home of the hereditary enemy of the Ibo, the Hausa. It was from here that the woman with her gruesome rice bowl had fled. Here, in medieval mud-walled cities, Muslim emirs presided in feudal fashion. In the Strangers' Quarters of places like Kano, which we had just left, migrant Ibos had been savaged, looted and murdered by Hausa and fanatic Muslim extremists. Almost 50,000 were said to have died.

The Ibos, intelligent and resourceful, seemed fitted to escape their oppression and to declare the secession of their eastern territory. They had the wealth of Nigeria's oil and mineral resources in their lands. It later became apparent that some foreigners with oil and mineral interests were not averse to seeing the Ibo free of the uncertain politics of the Nigerian Federation, where Britain still exerted a strong influence. Most of these outside interests were French. But Biafra's fatal weakness lay in its inability to defend itself. All the heavy equipment and most of the military organisation was on the Nigerian side. After a few weeks' pause, the Federation, under the leadership of General Gowon, decided to invade.

Totally outgunned, Biafra seemed likely to collapse in a matter of weeks but its resistance was fierce, and enduring. As the bitter conflict dragged on opinion polarised. While the French gave covert support to the Biafrans, the British Government, behind a public pretence of neutrality, pumped large amounts of arms into Nigeria. The Soviet Union did the same, only more openly.

Popular opinion in Britain was split, and this split was reflected by my own newspaper, where the Foreign Department took to pro-Nigerian line, fearing 'Balkanisation' – one breakaway state in Africa leading to many more – while the magazine (with which I worked) strongly sympathised with the Ibo. We were influenced by the magazine's guru figure, Francis Wyndham, a brilliant writer and a friend of mine. He was closer to the fray than most. He knew Ojukwu. Harry Evans leaned to the Nigerian side but he was much too good an editor to suppress honestly held alternative views. Throughout the conflict, the magazine ran Biafra-sympathetic pieces totally at odds with the view in the paper as a whole.

Such subtleties of British feeling of course had not penetrated to the Biafran police who arrested me at Port Harcourt. In their eyes I was suspect, merely by being British. And our wanderings in the north of enemy heartland could only make us more suspect. We had seen the army in Kano trying to contain anti-Ibo feeling there, by patrolling the streets with staves and punishing looters – the same army that was trying to bring Biafra to its knees. We did have some explaining to do, but the Wyndham connection worked. One hour after our release I was taking tea with Ojukwu.

He was a noble and dignified man – a gentleman, I thought, and well-equipped to handle the English-speaking press. He had been brought up in Epsom and educated at Oxford. He was thoroughly at home fielding our questions. Only one gave him pause – my request to go to the front.

I got permission, though the circumstances were ironic. I went with a French photographer, an ex-para called Gilles Caron. In terms of nationality we should have been on opposite sides. In fact, we were very good friends. The other irony was that, given the size of Britain's undercover contribution to the war, any bullet I encountered in this fray would have been paid for out of my own taxes.

Two days later we joined a Biafran battalion which planned to cross the Niger river and hit the Nigerian army from the rear. They had to go behind enemy lines and creep up to attack and seize a strategic bridge, the key central crossing from Nigeria to the new Biafra, at a place called Onitsha.

We had qualms when we saw the troops. It was a rag-tail outfit, 600-strong, many with the backsides out of their trousers. Some had equipment and a uniform, some had not. Many had no shoes for this sortie into the bush. Winkle-pickers had high status. On some bearers' heads, cushioned on banana leaves, were borne very modern rockets. They also carried – to my astonishment and pleasure, though I thought more important things should have come instead – many crates of beer.

Silently we crossed the River Niger into enemy territory. It was no smoking, no lights, and all very clandestinely exciting. I knew this was the real thing. Not just a charade laid on for the benefit of pressmen, as sometimes happens. We found a village in which to stay over night and then set off through swamplands with the soldiers.

Progress was painfully slow. It took four days to cover little more than 30 miles. And we were getting weaker by the day. Our provisions ran out long before we reached our destination. By the end Gilles and I were chewing on coconuts to stem the hunger and dehydration. Still, there were limits to what I could be persuaded to regard as food.

On the night before the attack, one of the bearers brought me a meal just as I had taken off into the bush for a pee. I was conscious of a patient but irritated presence behind me while I performed and turned to see a man standing with a bowl which he held out for me to take. I could not identify the large round substance in it.

'What's that?' I asked in some alarm.

'It is your meal, Sir. It is Congo meat. No blood, no bones.' It turned out to be a giant snail, the size of a small goldfish bowl.

'I can't eat that. You have it.'

The man was delighted, and dug out the insipid flesh with great relish. He wouldn't otherwise have eaten that night. This was a meal prepared specially for the visitors. The troops, it seems, were going into battle on empty stomachs.

Before long I worked up a powerful dislike to the colonel in charge of operations, who went by the name of Hannibal. He spoke English, strangely enough, with a Yorkshire accent and was married to an Englishwoman, though this did nothing to soften his scorn for the British position over the war. As a result he didn't like me. Gilles was altogether different and much in favour. By the fifth day friendliness between Gilles and Hannibal had waned, and it finally disappeared when some deserters were spotted and rounded up. What happened to them was quite unexpected.

At a clearing in the bush Hannibal drew the men up into a square, like the quarter-basse employed at the time of Napoleon. After orders were given for the attack on the morrow, the men caught trying to run away were brought forward to be disciplined. Three rag-tag people were made to lie down while soldiers of some rank (displayed by their better uniforms) went off to cut staves six feet long which they were flexing as they returned. Punishment was 25 strokes of the rod. Gilles' sense of military honour was affronted by the spectacle of the victims rolling around in the dirt, biting their knuckles and trying not to scream.

Parched and in need of fortification after the caning, I asked Gilles if he thought we could plunder some of those crates of beer we had seen. I went up to the man standing on guard by the crates.

'Any chance of one of those beers, my friend?' I asked in all innocence.

The man giggled, and then they all started laughing, eyes rolling hysterically as the camp became engulfed with laughter on the night before the attack. I stood looking from one to the other with no understanding of what they all found so funny. Eventually one of them explained after wiping his arm across his face. 'It is not beer for drinking, Sir. It's enemy beer.'

Still in the dark, I said, 'What do you mean, enemy beer?'

'It is for . . . we take a light, and we throw it at the enemy.'

I went back to Gilles more disturbed than usual.

'This operation's mad,' I said. 'That's not beer at all, they're Molotov cocktails. They're going up against Nato rifles with beer bottles filled with petrol.'

Next morning the silence of fear was in the air. I said to Gilles, 'This lot are definitely going over today.'

'I hope so. I want to get this over and get back.'

Around nine o'clock in the morning, rather late in the African day which usually starts in the cool of dawn, the first mortars started dropping. There was a lot of running about, a lot of confusion. Men were already returning wounded from the front. One, with his intestines bubbling out from between his fingers, was trying to incarcerate his stomach with the palms of his two hands while he walked. I moved on to the Front.

There, in the dense smoke and noise of small arms fire, I met a horrific sight. It was a jeep on fire, a Nigerian army jeep in the back of which sat a woman engulfed in flames. She was alight, burning from head to foot. I was harrowed by this sight of a human torch, slowly moving backwards and

112

forwards, mouth open, emitting sounds, beyond all help.

'For Christ's sake!' I said to one of the officers. 'Do something. Do anything. Put her out of her agony.'

And he said, in a drawly Sandhurst voice, 'Why should I? She's only a tart.'

I ran round the front of the jeep, and there was a Biafran struggling furiously to get the clothes off the dead driver before blood and fire ruined them.

Ahead of us some men were being pushed in our direction. They were prisoners: Nigerian soldiers who, like the occupants of the jeep, had been caught off-guard.

Rapidly men started stripping the clothes off the soldiers' backs and blindfolding them. Hannibal was taking map co-ordinates. Someone came over and said, 'What shall we do with the prisoners?' Without looking up, he replied, 'Shoot them.'

Gilles said to me, 'I don't believe this. I had thought this was an honourable man.' But Hannibal repeated the order. The Biafran soldiers looked at each other a bit perturbed and very gingerly pulled back the bolts of their AK-47s. Then they looked at each other again.

The prisoners started weeping, and their legs were shivering: they were breaking out into uncontrollable crying and shaking. Then someone opened up with an AK-47. And then there were more shots.

One of the prisoners seemed to have become the main target of all the shots. He slumped to the ground with a dreadful thumping of the body and a terrible heart-rending sound. This was followed by an exhalation of air. It was like a beast in an abattoir. I was rigid with shock. I couldn't move. The other man, who had been missed, was in full flood of tears, vainly pleading and begging. I stood there incapable of speech, incapable of movement. Gilles was also rooted to the spot.

It was a long time before we could speak a word to one another after that.

The bridge was taken, or rather our end of it. We moved on to the bridge. Up to this point the assault had been going according to plan, but the Nigerians had managed to regroup themselves and were counter-attacking. In the space of an hour they dropped some 300 mortar shells around and on the bridge. I remember to this day the sound of the mortar shells as they were hitting the huge bailey-type iron construction, the clattering echoes, and the ricochet of bullets coming off the ironwork.

Things were becoming critical. It was soon clear that our new position was not tenable. There was a general with-drawal fast. We started moving away, aware that the operation had failed totally, retreating as fast as we could. I was very anxious not to be left behind in a headlong flight. The sight of two Westerners in Vietnam camouflage could easily have given rise to the interpretation we were mercenaries. Most of the mercenaries involved in the conflict were on the Biafran side, though the Nigerians had Russian and English mercenary pilots.

Once the retreat had begun there was general terror of being captured. Fears of reprisals for Hannibal's methods of dealing with Nigerian prisoners were now added to the fears of genocide. It became a rout.

The walking wounded, and the too severely wounded, the crawling wounded, started grabbing desperately at us, saying 'Please Sir, do not leave me. Take me. Take me with you, Sir. Please carry me, Sir.' They were grabbing at my legs as I was crashing through the bush.

There were men lying with their eyes hanging out, the socket gone; men lying with mortar wounds in their legs, unable to move and desperate with the fear of being captured by the Nigerian army.

The fire and the mortars kept coming.

Leaving these wounded behind made it a terrible retreat. We were all, every man who could run or walk, intent on saving our own skins. We just crashed on and on, putting as much distance between ourselves and the bridge as we possibly could.

We were still in enemy territory. And there was still the Niger to cross, and at least thirty miles to go before we reached the crossing point. We got to a village and a Biafran officer commandeered every bicycle in it. Gilles and I, and a *Telegraph* journalist who'd arrived, were given bikes, and with a guide ahead of us who knew the dry tracks we pedalled furiously through the bush and the jungle footpaths. We made tremendous speed until we reached the Niger river where big boats were waiting to take us to the comparative safety of the other side. We reached the boats soaked in sweat, utterly exhausted. It was dark.

We got into the boats and crossed the river. The relief at having kept our lives made it one of the greatest river crossings we could remember. It was totally still. A galaxy of stars hung in the sky but the air over what was left of this hopelessly outmatched little Biafran battalion was heavy with disappointment and failure.

There were epilogues to this day's events, both happy and tragic. I was not able to find out what happened to the wounded we had abandoned, but the Nigerians were in general far more merciful in victory than they had been reputed to be. They did not go in for vicious reprisals, or bloodbaths or genocide. They behaved well. Hannibal, in contrast, became a wanted war criminal. Gilles was to die tragically, in similar circumstances to the atrocity we had witnessed, as a prisoner, in another dark jungle a long way from Africa.

I went back to Biafra as often as I could. My access was due to the offices of a strange public relations firm called Markpress, which operated out of Geneva. They used to vet people who were trying to go to Biafra. Unless you were wholly pro-Biafran you didn't get in. I became a so-called trusty of this organisation. At that time the machinations behind the scenes in this war still hadn't become apparent, but with each visit my own belief in the soundness of the Biafran cause dwindled.

I went back in 1969 to work on my own. My plan was go west up to the Okpala front where the 52nd battalion of the 63rd brigade of the Biafran army was reported to be trying to break through the encircling Nigerians. I made it to the front but, on getting out of the Landrover, my legs buckled under me in the sand. I had gone down with malaria, or something very like it.

I woke up in a grass hut with a Biafran woman tenderly bathing me with lukewarm water. It was part of a field hospital. A doctor injected me with what, he apologised, was not a virgin needle. I lay in a feverish daze for two days until I was strong enough to fulfil an engagement to eat breakfast at the Army commander's house.

Some fried plantains had been placed before me. I was politely trying to dig into them with the commander urging me to eat, because the attack was to take place today, when renewed waves of fever and nausea overcame me. I hastily excused myself and collapsed vomiting in the sand outside, with my eyes, I'm told, rolling all over the place. I passed out again and woke to find a woman wiping my face with a leaf.

I doused myself with water and was rescued by one of the Biafran officers. He was very pukka, right down to the Sandhurst swagger-stick, except for a large pair of wellington boots. He fed me some palatable rice to strengthen me for the two o'clock push.

At noon they started bringing in ammunition. They brought in mortars: huge French ones, 120s. To go with them were precisely two shells. Then they started dishing out two rounds of ammunition to each soldier. I must have been looking askance, because my rescuer – Captain Steven Osadebe – explained, 'I'm sorry Donald but we do not have much ammunition. We give each man two rounds. Then when we go forward, we capture Nigerian weapons and get more ammunition that way.'

Then the boys were paraded. I remember one, of about sixteen. He was wearing an ill-fitting, old-fashioned pin-striped suit. His feet were bare. Some of these boys were ferociously disciplined for trying to run away, they were beaten about the shoulders with the swagger-stick, or shaken and knocked about the head. All were lectured. The officer stood on his toes and sprang around using his hands, much like Jonathan Miller at the National Theatre. A whistle blew, and we went forward – myself still deliriously feverish – into the most fearful barrage of Nigerian small arms fire.

It was as if someone had a huge whip and was striking the trees. The bullets were zipping through and cutting trees, cutting leaves. It was like music. A whipping mistral of firepower. Then the mortars started coming in. Soon men could be seen running with hands clutching at ripped bellies, men running with bloody faces.

A man next to me was thrashing about in the undergrowth. When he tried to stand I could see that a bullet had gone through his mouth and taken out the side of his cheek. Another next to me was lifeless. I was trying to load my camera and shoot pictures. Some casualties were coming in so fast that I slightly got the willies. I saw the commander bent over one of the dead soldiers and talking to him as if he were still alive. He was praising the man's courage, and thanking him on behalf of the Biafran nation. It was moving and alarming at the same time.

I went back to the front line to where the wounded were being sent and saw again the pin-striped suit, now with a bullet hole in its shoulder. I saw men carrying other men on litters, home-made litters. There was an old truck, which looked like a Dormobile van with the windows gone and the doors off. It was in an ill state of repair. Men were sitting in the truck and holding their wounded arms and legs. One was lying with his intestines dribbling out of his hands.

The Biafrans didn't have the medical facilities you see in other wars. These people were pared down to the bone. A man with a huge gaping hole in the side of his face could not be spared any morphine. Head wounds are less painful than other wounds, but they are still dire. Most of the wounds in this battle were to shoulders, upper arms and the face, because the men were crawling forward on their arms and knees.

I asked the driver with his load of wounded why he didn't move off.

'We cannot leave until we are completely full, Sir. We cannot spare the petrol.'

In the rear of the battle I saw Captain Osadebe again, in an agitated state. He had taken a Nigerian army round, a Nato rifle wound, in his right leg. They'd pumped some morphine into him and taken him into the house. He was becoming delirious. He said, 'Donald, Donald, I'm worried. Please Donald, promise me you will go and tell the men to move forward. They will listen to you.'

I couldn't face sending men further to die, crawling on their stomachs against insuperable odds and firepower, with their non-existent ammunition. Clearly, what I had been told was not true, there was no general advance on a 20-mile front. I also knew Steven needed some reassurance to still his agitation.

I said, 'Okay, Steven.'

I went outside the house and lurked about, and then went back in again. He said, 'Did you do that?' I said, 'Yes, Steven, they're moving forward.'

I was suffering from the after-effect of malaria, fear and reaction to the non-virgin needle. My body had had enough and was breaking out in huge blotches. I found sanctuary at a big Catholic mission about ten miles behind the front. One of the nuns had a remedy that stopped the itching and the blotching almost instantly. I slept a long deep sleep on a mission bed.

It was through the mission that I came to see the Biafran horrors that were to leave the most enduring impression on my mind. I was directed to a mission in the Umuiaghu area where I could see a different kind of victim of the war – the orphaned and abandoned children of Biafra. They were also close to starvation. The war of course had disrupted all forms of agricultural production. Relief supplies, mainly from France, rarely got through. What food there was went to feed army bellies.

At the mission, I met Father Kennedy, one of those people who are both strong and good. He took me to what had been a primary school but was now a hospital for some of the many war-orphaned children. There were 800 there. As I entered I saw a young albino boy. To be a starving Biafran orphan was to be in a most pitiable situation, but to be a starving albino Biafran was to be in a position beyond description. Dying of starvation, he was still among his peers an object of ostracism, ridicule and insult. I saw this boy looking at me. He was like a living skeleton. There was a skeletal kind of whiteness about him. He moved nearer and nearer to me. He wore the remnants of an ill-fitting jumper and was clutching a corner of a corned beef tin, an empty corned beef tin.

The boy looked at me with a fixity that evoked the evil eye in a way which harrowed me with guilt and unease. He was moving closer. I was trying not to look at him. I tried to focus my eyes elsewhere. Some French doctors from Médecins sans Frontières were trying to save a small girl who was dying. They are doctors renowned for going into the centre of the darkness to help. They were trying to revive the little girl by thrusting a needle in her throat and banging her chest. The sight was almost unendurable. She died in front of me. The smallest human being I had ever, in all my grim experience, seen die.

Still in the corner of my eye I could see the albino boy. I caught the flash of whiteness. He was haunting me, getting nearer. Someone was giving me the statistics of the suffering, the awful multiples of this tragedy. As I gazed at these grim victims of deprivation and starvation, my mind retreated to my own home in England where my children of much the same age were careless and cavalier with food, as Western children often are. Trying to balance between these two visions produced in me a kind of mental torment.

I felt something touch my hand. The albino boy had crept close and moved his hand into mind. I felt the tears come into my eyes as I stood there holding his hand. I thought, Don't look, think of something else, anything else. Don't cry in front of these kids. I put my hand in my pocket and found one of my barley sugar sweets. Surreptitiously I transferred it to the albino boy's hand and he went away. He stood a short distance off and slowly unwrapped the sweet with fumbling fingers. He licked the sweet and stared at me with huge eyes. I noticed that he was still clutching the empty corned beef tin while he stood delicately licking the sweet as if it might disappear too quickly. He looked hardly human, as if a tiny skeleton had somehow stayed alive.

My mind was assaulted with every kind of affliction that starving children can suffer. There was an English doctor cradling a dying infant who was determined to stand on legs devoid of all strength. In the other arm she sheltered another child with a drip-feed tube through its nose. Half-blind children with bellies like beer barrels (from malnutrition and kwashiorkor) stood on legs like sticks. One boy's arms hung out of their sockets, attached only by thin strips of skin due to the muscular collapse. Others lay dying in their own excrement with flies encrusting their sores.

It was beyond war, it was beyond journalism, it was beyond photography, but not beyond politics. This unspeakable suffering was not the result of one of Africa's natural disasters. Here was not nature's pruning fork at work but the outcome of men's evil desires. If I could, I would take this day out of my life, demolish the memory of it. But like memories of those haunting pictures of the Nazi death camps, we cannot, must not be allowed to forget the appalling things we are all capable of doing to our fellow human beings. The photograph I took of that little albino boy must remain engraved on the minds of all who see it.

Before leaving I found a young girl of about sixteen sitting naked in a hut, looking ill and very frail, but beautiful. Her name, I was told, was Patience. I wanted to photograph her and asked the orderly if she could persuade the girl to cover the private parts of her body with her hands so that I could show her nakedness with as much dignity as possible. But the sight of her stripped me naked of any of the qualities I might have had as a human being. The whiplash of compassion and conscience never ceased to assail me in Biafra.

We all suffer from the naive belief that our integrity is reason enough for being in any situation, but if you stand in front of dying people, something more is required. If you can't help, you shouldn't be there. Was I of any use at all to the Biafran people? Or was I simply aiding a war that was not in their interests, a secession generated by power-hungry zealots with no thought of the anguish and deprivation they left behind when they moved their weapons of destruction on?

I was ravaged and confused by this war as never before, and could see not the smallest justification for it. Or for my presence here – unless it was to remind people, through my pictures, of the futility of all wars.

Even the means of my being there, through the assistance of Markpress, made my position tenuous and dubious. This was a man-made famine – made by the secession and the response to it, made by the greed and foolishness on both sides and, most of all, by the dishonesty of the original conspirators who created the breakaway state.

I never thought I had a great insight into politics. But it doesn't matter when you see what I saw in that mission hospital that day. It does not require much political acumen to see what it so plain that it pushes itself down your throat.

Richard West wrote a strongly pro-Biafran piece which appeared in the magazine with my pictures, though the pictures were not partisan. I would like to think these images brought help to the beleaguered hospitals with their dying children. I knew my pictures had a message, but what it was precisely I couldn't have said – except, perhaps, that I wanted to break the hearts and spirits of secure people. All we knew at the time, though, was that neither words nor pictures could do anything to halt the advance of the Nigerian military machine.

For once I resorted to a little direct political action of my own. One of my most tragic photographs was of a Biafran mother trying to feed her baby with withered breasts. This I converted into a poster after it had appeared in the magazine. Francis Wyndham put a suitable inflammatory caption on it – 'Biafra, the British Government Supports this War. You the Public Could Stop It' – and then we fanned out and fly-posted it around the city. My wife, Christine, and I paid special attention to our own area of Hampstead Garden Suburb where the Prime Minister, Harold Wilson, had his home.

As the months went by and Biafra's position became more

desperate I was eager to get back, but there was a problem. The differences between the pro-Nigerian and pro-Biafran factions on the *Sunday Times* had become so bitter that they could not agree on a suitably neutral candidate to write about the war. Eventually, after much rancorous argument, they agreed to send the veteran Antony Terry. His qualification: he was the Central European correspondent, relatively innocent of African affairs.

He was, however, a very quick judge of a bad situation. When we landed at Uli airstrip the officials there were trying to commandeer all the hard currency they could and issuing huge heaps of Biafran paper in exchange. As Tony came away from exchange control, stuffed with his load of worthless currency, he gave me a look and said, 'They've had it here, haven't they, this lot?'

We went to the front. Terminal demoralisation, it was clear, had set in among the Biafran troops. General Ojukwu had already left, taking with him, among much else, his Mercedes limousine. Mountains of empty wine bottles outside the General staff headquarters testified to the lifestyle the little echelon of top leaders had pursued at the expense of their people's starvation. By now I knew them as opportunist spivs.

I took some food and others things for the children of a man called Chinua Achebe, one of the genuine idealists on the Biafran side. He was a novelist, who wrote a book called *Things Fall Apart*. That was precisely what was happening now. He was a young man, an honourable man, a nice man. I remember the last time I saw him. He took the gifts without any emotion. He had cut off any feeling he may once have had for the one or two Westerners he thought really cared. I felt he was looking through me, as if I didn't really exist. And I could see that the ruin of Ibo culture had made him feel exactly as I had when coming out of Hue – totally shell-shocked.

Biafra finally surrendered on 15 January 1970, two days after my return. Despite all the hysteria, it is only fair to record that the Lagos authorities treated the defeated Ibo with decency. It was the only grace of that war.

19

People Who Eat People

THOUGH I HAVE spent much of my life getting on and off aeroplanes I have never been at ease in them. Once the wheels touched the ground again I would feel in some way redeemed, as if I had been given a new lease of life. Each landing would be a kind of rebirth.

It was this feeling, not the actual air travel, that I was hooked on. By my mid-thirties I had travelled, mainly by air, to over 70 countries; by the end of my career in journalism, to 120. Not all my travels involved wars. I also like exploring other countries for their own sake, though sometimes I got the feeling I might be safer in a war zone. This was especially the case when I teamed up with travel writer Eric Newby and his wife Wanda.

They had met in the war, after Eric had been picked up treading water in the sea of Mussolini's Italy. His Special Boat Section operation had gone awry, he had been taken prisoner and subsequently had escaped from prisoner-of-war camp near the Adriatic. Wanda was one of the Resistance workers who spirited him out. They spent months together in the Apennines before Eric was recaptured by the SS. Since the war their life together had been a more agreeable adventure.

I had run into them first in Sardinia, when they were travelling slowly round the entire Mediterranean. I had gone to get pictures of the bandits who had held hostage and killed a British tourist and his wife. The assignment was not a success. I was chased from the bandit hill town of Orgosola, not by bandits, but by irate old ladies wielding pitchforks.

The occasion however cemented a friendship between myself and the Newbys, which was to confirm my taste for travel.

They took me to India, where they were planning a slow and hilarious 1,200-mile journey by boat down the Ganges. Early in the venture Eric went to interview Prime Minister Nehru, and took me along for the historic man's photograph. In his book *Slowly Down the Ganges*, Eric recalled my bobbing up from a camera position behind the sofa and saying to the Indian premier, 'You must find it difficult to control this rough old lot.' My education still had some way to go.

Later I accompanied the Newbys on a tiger hunt as guests of the Nawab of Paigah, Eric with a Holland rifle, me with my Pentax. Eighteen hours of waiting up a tree failed to flush out a tiger, but eventually brought Eric face to face with an outraged sloth bear. After dispatching one bear, Eric found himself confronted by its angry mate, with no cartridge left. For a moment he thought that he would have to ruin his expensive and beautiful rifle by using it as a club, but then the Nawab, whom everyone called Owly, stepped in and felled the attacking sloth with a shot that narrowly missed Eric's ear.

'Lucky,' said the Nawab, 'I had only that one shot left.'

Afterwards, like someone in a fairy tale, Eric asked the Nawab if there was any favour he might do him, in return for the boon of saving his life.

'What I'd really like,' said Owly, the maharajah-who-already-had-everything, wistfully, 'is the bumper Christmas edition of *Dog World*. You can't get it here because of the currency restrictions.'

I took away an abiding love of India. Kashmir – until the tourists flocked in – remained my favourite place in the world. On its lotus-covered lakes, which reflected the Himalayas, you lived on large fretworked houseboats left behind by the Raj. They were like old Oxford college barges, where bearers still dished up sensational Mrs Beeton-type cheese soufflés.

In the daytime Eric and I would drift round the lakes, among kingfishers and floating islands, some with Moghul gardens on them, in little boats called shikaras. Curtained and cushioned, they were a sort of cross between a gondola and an Edwardian punt. The whole place was a magic amalgam of Mughal and Anglo-Saxon civilisations, and it stayed in my mind through much rougher experiences as an image of how glorious life can be.

I grew less fussy about food after India. I have even eaten rat, when pushed a bit, though I drew the line at dog, which I saw Taiwanese women hanging out to air-cure on washing lines. In Niger and Upper Volta I was able, after a dusty 18-hour drive across the desert, to countenance ostrich, washed down by warm goat's milk. When people who have not enough to eat offer you a delicacy, and would be offended by your rejection, you accept. The Tuareg left an indelible impression on me of human dignity in an ancient way of life. There had been no rain for seven years, and they were forced to beg, surviving in the main on aid hand-outs. Their nomadic way of life will probably die in my lifetime.

Drought and disaster are not the only threats faced by the ancient peoples of the world. The impact of Western civilisation is just as serious a matter. I was shown this graphically in Papua, where I went with Tony Clifton, one of the liveliest of the Aussie *Sunday Times* mafia, to record the gathering of the New Guinea warrior clans at Mount Hagen. It was an astonishing spectacle. To throbbing drum beats, thirty thousand tribesmen were rioting around town in grass skirts in groups of about two hundred. They were decorated in every hue of ochre and Bird of Paradise feather. Where once a bone would do for an ornament, it was now fashionable to wear through the nose the most recherché object that could be found – ball-point pens, plastic cocktail sticks, screwdrivers and bits of copper piping. One man wore across his forehead, to dramatic effect, a trouser zip. Someone had donated, as an added decorative luxury, a five gallon drum of Mobil oil. The tribesmen were gratefully smearing it over themselves, an ochre substitute, as if it was sun cream.

Life in New Guinea today is much more deeply con-taminated by such modern influences as alcohol; then, in the sixties, it was still a place where people ate people. We made a ten-day trek into the rain forest, to the edge of the country of the Porgaiga and the Hewa, both practising cannibal tribes. With us were 60 bearers of the Duma tribe, led by an Australian patrolman. We were taking supplies to the edge of the Porgaiga lands to establish a food dump for a later patrol that would chart the unknown Hewa country and take a census of its inhabitants. Like the warriors, all our bearers wore grass skirts. At night they used them to roof and shelter the temporary huts that they built. They still made fire with two pieces of wood.

Their trekking capacities were daunting. They had wide feet for their size, which took them unerringly over the slippery logs that traversed the ravines. Tony, struggling to keep up, fell between two logs and was saved only by his gut. In revenge for my jokes about his waistline, he pointed to my furry chest when I was washing, saying, 'Jeez man, you look like a busted open settee.'

Despite the jokes, things were decidedly reserved, spooky even, between us and the Duma. Though there was no record of their having eaten anybody recently, darkness brought on a certain nervous tension. One night I introduced a snake, a green rubber job I had bought in Singapore, and conjured it out of my nose. It cleared the camp in second. After the Duma had come trooping sheepishly back, Tony and I found ourselves enjoying a new status, as miracle workers as well as laughter makers.

Most of the laughs, it has to be said, were on us. We met some Porgaiga on the fourth day out, an experience which made Tony feel like a trout in a restaurant tank. They were small and muscular, with droopy Napoleon hat wigs made from human hair clippings and decorated with brilliant yellow button flowers. Dog's teeth necklaces and G-strings threaded with shells and beads covered the rest. Their last known human repast had been two of their own tribe, eaten when they had run out of other food. Hunger was the main motive for cannibalism. It still happened, I was told, in remote villages when someone important died. The mourners would eat him to absorb his strength and intelligence, as Stone Age Britons are said to have done. Head-hunting for cannibal purposes, though rare, was still not unknown. The chief disincentive to the practice was a very nasty brain disease called kuru, in effect something close to dementia.

One evening, at the furthest point of our travels, a member of our party shot a cassowary bird, which is the size of an emu, weighs about forty pounds, and which, for conservation reasons, should not be shot. The Duma tore out the feathers, then gutted it, split open the thighs with sharp bamboo, wrapped it in ferns and banana leaves and cooked it under hot stones. It tasted pleasant, rather like beef. We were told by a smiling Duma that you cooked a human being in the same way. I decided that, even if I had become less finicky about local food, I would always play safe with breakfast. I would go nowhere without my supply of Ready Brek instant porridge.

The distinction between my travel stories and my war assignments was not always precise. I went to Guatemala to do a story about the culture and kept overtaking the civil war. In Eritrea, where I was sent for a story about the revolutionary struggle, I ended up doing nothing but travel, very, very, painfully.

The rebel camps were over 100 miles into the trackless Sahara, and our only method of approach (after effecting illegal entry into the country via Khartoum) was by camel. My desert companions were Colin Smith of the *Observer*, and Charlie Glass, a very pleasant man who later became celebrated both for his coverage of Beirut and for escaping from kidnappers who held him hostage there.

Camels are unattractive beasts, arrogant, disdainful of man, and totally against doing what they're told. They move in a sort of tidal wave, heave and slump motion. If they gallop unexpectedly, you feel they will heave and slump you over their heads.

I was prepared to put up with my camel only because I had become more than a little addicted to deserts. The dry heat evaporates all the stickiness and sweat off your body, so you can travel for weeks without a bath, but, as the Desert Fathers and T.E. Lawrence claimed, the desert also cleans your mind. It triggers the mind, liberating a kind of psychic energy, and making space for you to realise things about yourself. It really does produce a touch of mysticism, a sort of spiritual voice.

That is, if your camel is behaving properly. Colin's was not. Even flogging it (the standard nomad recourse in these circumstances) didn't have the effect of getting it to move. The beast just started frothing at the mouth in a most alarming way, like a washing machine gone crazy. Colin had to get off and walk. We never got to the Eritrean front. After jolting our way deep into the desert, there was nothing for it but to turn round and jolt all the way back.

I found myself in the desert again – this time with writer James Fox – to cover the war in Chad, where my brother Michael had his posting with the Foreign Legion. It was years since I had seen him. The French Foreign Legion does not encourage contact with the outside world. I didn't know if he was being 'Faithful unto Death', as the Legion's motto has it, or if he was simply stuck with it. I had caught one glimpse of him in Paris, on a Bastille Day, where infantryman McCullin, in all the gear – epaulettes, kepi blanc, and white breeches – was marching with the Legion down the Champs-Elysées. They were performing their uncanny slow march with a fixed stare, to a stomach-turning low chant. They looked like dead men on parade.

Michael, at twenty-seven, was now promoted sergeant, and his unit was fighting rebels in the great land-locked country in the heart of Africa, bounded by Libya to the North, Sudan to the East, Niger, Nigeria and the evil empire of Bokassa (the Central Africa Republic) to the South. It was 2,000 miles further into the Sahara than Timbuktu. Chad was so unstable that no fewer than twelve armies could be marching on its capital, N'Djamena, better known as Fort-Lamy. The French had once colonised it. Not they had sent in their Foreign Legion and French troops to back up President Tombalbaye in his struggle against insurgents. He claimed 95 per cent of the popular vote while half the population was in revolt against him. The activities of tax officials had ignited spontaneous uprisings among people who earned, on average, £12 a year. Libya's Colonel Gaddafi, eager to extend his own revolution, backed the rebels, who were mounting a spirited resistance. Short of weapons – sharing one gun between ten – they sported impromptu home-made devices such as barbed spears made from motor car springs, with which they had already killed five Legionnaires.

When James and I arrived in Fort-Lamy, we found events taking us away from Sergeant McCullin. His post, with 2nd para, near Mongo in the south of Chad, had been under heavy pressure. Political exiles from the capital had combined with local chiefs to form a National Liberation Front. The idea was to capture Mongo, the administrative capital of the region, and five other towns. Had it been successful, it would have split Chad in two. My brother's outfit, with the support of the French and Chadian security troops, had fought the rebels off, and the situation had eased.

The immediate attack was now to the North, in the Borkou-Ennedi-Tibesti region, near the borders with Libya, an underpopulated wasteland of desert and mountain ranges where nomads had declared themselves in revolt against the administration. We flew to Faya-Largeau, the largest town in the North, in a French Transal troop-carrier full of young and nervous looking Berets Rouges and a tough Foreign Legion padre with 30 parachute jumps to his credit. He was not a comforting sight.

We landed in the furnace heat of a desert airstrip, where the wind was whipping up the sand. The Berets Rouges, in goggles and peaked caps, looking remarkably like Monty's old Eighth Army, were grouping to move on all-night truck rides into the mountains, to take up positions.

The Legionnaires we had come across were truculent and suspicious, addicted to the consumption of large quantities of alcohol and endless talk about killing. We drove into Faya-Largeau past the wrecks of armoured cars and transport trucks – left there since General Leclerc's march through Libya in 1943. Faya was like some isolated French garrison of the nineteenth century. Guns protruded through battlements and mud walls. The tricolour flew overhead. A tidal wave of the Sahara and its dunes crept up to it as if reclaiming its rights. An old man and his son showed us the magic of the dunes. When you slid down them, they produced an extraordinary singing sound, so loud it seemed to fill the entire desert. My hair stood on end. It was the most remarkable sound I ever heard.

We joined one of the convoys into the mountains, though not without difficulty. I tried to hitch a lift with a Dodge truck which I could see was carrying the Foreign Legion padre we had met on the plane. The padre leaned out and sharply told me it was full. I caught another truck. Three days later, as we were travelling in convoy, the Dodge toppled head first over the sheer end of a sand dune. The padre survived, with three broken ribs.

I went on patrols in which trucks and jeeps would drive into mud-walled 'bleds', or townships, to find horsemen, identified as the rebels, galloping away at top speed. A bloody chase would ensue.

It was after this sortie to the North that I heard some extraordinary news about my brother, in a bar in Fort-Lamy.

'Sergeant McCullin?' the Beret Rouge had said. 'There has been some problem with this man.'

Some months earlier, it appeared, my brother had been involved in a strange incident with his adjutant. The officer had come up to him, apparently in high spirits, and stuck a pistol in Michael's mouth, telling him to stick 'em up. When my brother had warned him, 'Careful, it might be loaded,' the officer told him not to worry and for reassurance turned the pistol towards his own temple. He had then blown part of his own head away.

The French soldier had also heard that there had been some kind of tribunal or hearing. The story sounded so improbable it was thought that Michael must have shot the officer. There were no very close witnesses, it seemed. He thought that my brother had been cleared, but wasn't sure.

It was James who managed to fix the transport to the

McCullin's photographs of the war in Cyprus which gained him the World Press Photo Award in 1964 – a Turkish villager lying dead on the floor of his house is embraced by his bride; a distraught Turkish woman fleeing the village of Gazabaran after her husband has been killed.

(*Above*) An old man gunned down by snipers in Limassol.
(*Below left*) An eighteen-year-old Turkish girl with shotgun seeking revenge hours after the death of her brother.

The war photographer's Press Pass.

Mercenaries in the Belgian Congo under the command of Mad Mike Hoare (right) in 1964.

Alan Murphy, who smuggled McCullin into Stanleyville. Later he died violently in a shooting in the East End of London.

Torment and deprivation of prisoners in Stanleyville.

Don and
Christine with
three-year-old
Paul.

Field Marshal
Montgomery of
Alamein:
an inscribed
portrait for
Don McCullin.

Israeli troops
capturing the
old city of
Jerusalem under
heavy Jordanian
fire.

Israeli soldiers
mock Jordanian
soldiers in mufti,
prisoners in
Jerusalem, 1967.

The athlete, moments before he was shot in the hand in the Tet offensive of 1968 – a turning point of the war in Vietnam.

Civilians being removed from the battle zone in the old Mandarin Imperial City of Hue.

With a fatal wound in the chest, a soldier is transported by tank to a casualty clearing area.

Don carried this victim of a sniper's bullet to a First Aid station.

A Vietnamese civilian tormented by his 'liberators', American marines.

Overleaf) A 'grunt' (infantryman) suffering severe shell shock awaits transportation away from the battle.

outpost. He wangled me on to a 'milk run', one of the French planes that took supplies around the camps. Only one seat was available so James, with some anguish, stayed behind. Arrangements weren't ideal for me either. I would have to return with the same plane – get in and get out in not much over an hour.

As we descended to a dusty runway in the middle of nowhere, and emerged into the hot wind, I saw a lean, dark, shaven-headed figure in dark glasses at the head of a reception committee. Not in the kepi of course, or even the khaki, but in off-duty sports gear, with trainers. He looked very rugged, but was still recognisably my brother.

He spent a long time arm-waving and gesticulating when he learned how little time I had. As he ushered me to the bamboo hutted camp beside the runway he told me he had organised hunting parties and patrols for my benefit. His arms flailed with the unfairness of it all, and I realised that my brother had become more French than the French.

Of his ordeal and the tribunal, he had an extraordinary tale to tell. He had not been punished for the shooting, he said, because the adjutant was still alive. He had lain on the floor, his white neck-towel turning red, moaning, 'What is happening to me?' Michael said, 'You've shot yourself.' Later, the wounded officer was well enough to give evidence on Michael's behalf. It was logged as a self-inflicted wound, and Michael was cleared of all suspicion.

Over lunch Michael told me that Legion training was less harsh than once it had been. He said that if ever he left the Legion he figured on a security job. There were networks that could fix you up, he said, as there were in the SAS and the mercenaries. The main difference between Legionnaires and the mercenaries was financial – the Legion didn't pay much. The Legion was also still toughly disciplined; mercenaries were just a rabble.

He told me that Legionnaires bought women from local tribes. In Algeria four were officially provided once a month, in cubicles, to service some of the company, and Michael recoiled at this. My brother had a contract with a local man for his daughter. It worked out at £5 a month. They preserved the French military priorities: food, then women, and only after that la guerre. But the women you could see walking around in clothes that looked as if they had been shipped in by Oxfam were less than appetising.

The Legionnaire's most common disease, he said, was piles. It came from bouncing around in trucks over endless miles of unmade tracks. Michael's unit would drive across desert scrub to mud-walled oasis casbahs, with their date palms and wells, and flush the rebels out. They would shoot them down as they fled. As in Vietnam, it was a dangerous place to be seen running. If contact was made outside the settlements, there would be battles on the scorched plains between trucks and warriors on horseback.

It seemed bizarre to me, in this era of high-speed jets and rockets, that there should be bush wars going on between tribesmen and Legionnaires. It also seemed an unequal war, between barely-armed primitives and some of the hardest soldiers in the world. Selective pacification, as they called it, seemed more like the sport of hunting men than any kind of political programme.

'I've got a really great present for you,' Michael said as I was about to leave, 'I won it in a poker game.' He then flourished an elaborate hunting rifle, complete with telescopic sights.

'I thought you could go hunting with it today,' he said, 'but now there's no time. Take it home with you.'

I didn't know what to say. It was a made situation, and also a mark of how far we had grown apart. It must have been well over six years since I had used a gun – I had stopped soon after I started taking pictures of war, when I got a better idea of what guns could do.

'What on earth am I to do with it,' I had to say, 'in Hampstead Garden Suburb?'

He was upset by my attitude but I was incapable of accepting his gift. I left thinking Finsbury Park must have done something strange to both of us, to wind up in this godforsaken place. Two McCullins meeting on a battleground in Africa. One offering a bad conscience about not being able to stay, the other offering a rifle.

I felt sad as my plane took off, leaving that lonely figure in the bush. I would soon be home in Hampstead with my wife and children. Then I realised that pity was not the right emotion. My brother was completely at home with what he was doing. I was the one afflicted with doubt and division. For Michael, war was now a disciplined profession. For me, it had become an abhorrence that I could not bring myself to leave alone.

20

WOUNDED IN ACTION

THERE WAS A lethal atmosphere in Cambodia from the start. When I arrived I learned that three American network television men had been ambushed in the jungle and killed by an insurgent force known as the Khmer Rouge. Even more distressing for me personally was the rumour that Gilles Caron, my friend and rival from Biafra days, had fallen into the hands of the Khmers.

I hurried round to the office of Agence France Presse to get the latest word on his disappearance. All I found were a lot of gloomy faces and Gilles's travelling bags, all packed. They had been lodged in the hotel for safe-keeping, but they would never be reclaimed by their owner.

Yet despite the ever-present danger to them, correspondents still thronged to Cambodia and its capital Pnom Penh. Before it was touched by war it was always said to be an exquisite place. Richard West once wrote: 'I have seen the past, and it works.' But even after the country had been sucked into the war it retained its charm. Newspapermen, jaded by the jagged edges of Saigon, came to look upon a Pnom Penh posting almost as R and R. The people were different, softer altogether, with friendlier faces. Compared to Saigon, everything in the Cambodian capital seemed smaller and cosier, and the Americans were much thinner on the ground. Not that their presence wasn't much felt.

When I first went there, in June 1970, Prince Norodom Sihanouk, a ruler of infinite craftiness when it came to playing off East against West and vice-versa, had finally fallen off the tightrope. His replacement by General Lon Nol was said to be more suitable to American interests, and few coups took place in South-East Asia in those days without a suspicion of CIA involvement. In this case the suspicion was almost certainly correct.

The American administration, under President Nixon, was already embarked on a secret bombing campaign in the west of Cambodia to destroy the infiltration routes from the North, down through the Parrot's Beak, into Vietnam. It was no secret of course to the Cambodian peasantry who bore the brunt. The massive scale of this operation, conducted mainly by high-flying B-52 bombers known as 'Whispering Death', was concealed from the American Congress for many years.

The Cambodian army, which enjoyed a less than awesome reputation, had been bolstered with a lot of support from the South Vietnamese army, which operated with the Cambodians in much the same way Americans operated with the Vietnamese in Vietnam. The enemy was invariably described as 'The VC' though in most cases it was the indigenous Khmer Rouge who presented the problem. There were strong links between the North Vietnamese and the local guerrillas, but the Khmers would subsequently assert their independence with ruthless and terrifying effect.

It was a hot sticky day, with a monsoon approaching, as I flew by helicopter towards Prey Veng, 30 miles east of Pnom Penh. It was known to be an area of intense Khmer activity as the guerrillas tried to cut communication between Saigon and Pnom Penh.

By the riverside you could see the Vietnamese of Cambodia as before I had witnessed the Americanisation of Vietnam. Boys were cadging chewing gum and cigarettes. The Vietnamese general I approached for a helicopter ride wore a baseball cap and was smoking a big cigar. To my request, he said, 'Sure, no sweat.'

When we got over the front line, the pilot decided it was too risky to put the machine down. Instead he hovered a few feet above ground while we jumped out. I came down new Marks and Spencer desert boots first and landed up to my crotch in a rice paddy. Any resemblance between the smartly attired photographer who had left Pnom Penh that morning and myself was now purely coincidental.

On an embankment by the rice field I saw a lot of soldiers milling around and two Khmer prisoners, no more than seventeen, bound hand and foot. That evening I made myself unpopular with their captors by giving them some chocolate and some water, which they accepted with a kind of resigned courtesy. They had given up all hope of survival.

Cambodia can be enchanting by day, but it is spooky by night for westerners and orientals alike. The Vietnamese are very superstitious about ghosts. They bedded down two by two for reasons that were not erotic. One soldier said to me, 'Eh you, you want to sleep me?' and I was glad of the offer.

So we paired off in the stubble of the last crop of rice, little twosomes all over the field. My partner took out his 'indigenous rations' – two plastic bags of pre-cooked rice – and spread his groundsheet for us. From the direction of Prey Veng we could hear the sound of tracer bullets, B 40 rockets and 120mm Chinese mortars.

All this was eclipsed by the arrival of what was known as 'Puff the Spooky Dragon', a droning old Dakota with a faint red undercarriage which suddenly burst into an incredible yellow, like a huge sunflower in the sky. The parachute flare glided slowly to earth lighting up the countryside, and then came the pyrotechnics, as the gunship rained down fire on the illuminated targets. For some strange optical reason, however, it actually looked as if the bullets were pouring back into the gunship. In my half-awake condition, it seemed the most phenomenal firework display, a great, if sinister, piece of theatre.

Next morning a platoon of Cambodian soldiers showed up, looking like gypsies. They arrived in basketball boots, baggy trousers and all kinds of exotic headgear. They had AK-47 automatic rifles and a standard-bearer who proudly held the Cambodian flag aloft. The plan was that they should go in first across the rice paddies to see where the fire was coming from and, if possible, link up with some beleaguered troops in a hamlet, less than a mile away. The Vietnamese commander advised me against going with them, but I was too keyed up not to go.

As we set out – a little platoon of no more than a dozen men – the Vietnamese were calling out insults to the Cambodians. 'Number Ten' being the most popular. We crossed three dry rice fields and then some that were full of water. Suddenly a hail of fire rose from a line of trees and the water started splashing up around us like fountains. There seemed to be a great many fountains round me, possibly because I was a head taller than anyone else on the march.

There was a ridge to my right, and I managed to lie in the water with my head almost under while my right hand held the cameras propped on the ridge. I made up my mind to move away from the bank and get behind the radio operator. My one thought was to avoid a head wound, and I thought the big radio should give me some shelter. I was in a panic, and began to feel that someone was drawing a line on my position, and would keep firing at me whatever move I made.

All over the paddy there were figures up to their necks in slime. The absence of any returning fire indicated that most of them had discarded their weapons. I edged away from the radio operator and bumped into three men in black outfits lying face-down in the water. They were Khmer Rouge, killed in the previous day's fighting. I noticed that one of the dead men was wearing 'Ho Chi Minh 1000 milers' – the name for shoes made out of car tyres.

Worry about staying alive mingled with concern to keep my cameras dry. I made it back to the ridge and crawled on my back the 200 yards to the edge of the paddy. When I got up to run the last stretch, it was like a bad dream. My legs were like two heavy weights. I was doing a sort of zigzag run and the mortar fire was hitting the ground all round me, earth exploding in huge cascades. I was labouring under the camera equipment and the sodden clothes and heavy fear.

When we got back, I crashed out in an exhausted state at the feet of the Vietnamese commander, who smiled at me when I looked up. He had told me so. I started to check over the condition of my cameras and found that one of my Nikons had the perfect imprint of an AK-47 round. The discovery was oddly exhilarating. I thought to myself, Boy you've done it again. You've managed to get away with it.

No mood was ever more fleeting. The commander came over again and said, 'We are ready. Are you ready?' Old Skyraider aeroplanes had started to bomb the flanks of Prey Veng to keep the VC's heads down, and the 400 men of the South Vietnamese Crazy Buffalo battalion were moving in.

I crossed one field with them before I heard sniper fire again and lost my bottle. I lay down and became a coward. But I couldn't forgive myself for losing my nerve; shame got me to move again. A Vietnamese corporal came up and shooed me on.

'Go, go, you are with crazy buffaloes. Go, mister, go.'

These buffaloes rarely stood more than five feet in height but their numbers made the advance impressive. We crossed more fields, then dropped down into a little valley and, before we knew it, were trotting along the road into town. It was just gone ten o'clock in the morning but seemed as if a whole day had passed by. The arrival of rescuers was no great occasion for rejoicing. The VC went on stepping up the mortar fire into town.

I found a huge rice store full of women and children crying. I felt wretched in front of them, and they seemed suspicious of me. I pulled out packets of peppermints. At first some of the kids resented the gesture, they thought I was evil, but others began to enjoy the sweets and to smile. Pretty soon you could hear twenty sucking mouths. I found myself getting tearful as I took pictures.

With VC mortars still exploding, reinforcements started to arrive. By nightfall there must have been over a thousand soldiers in the little town.

Around two o'clock in the morning there was a very loud crunch. I woke stiffly and reached for my helmet. Two mortars had landed on the compound where the Cambodian soldiers had been sleeping. Ten or more were injured. I walked away. Enough was enough.

When I woke in sunlight, you could hear the birds. It was a sign, better than any peace treaty. I knew the VC must have moved on. However, there was still work to be done. Near where I had been sleeping I found a low wicker bed with a dead man on it covered by a white sheet. I looked closer and saw two little feet sticking out beside him. They belonged to a pretty little girl with dead staring eyes.

I wandered off and came across two dead Khmers in a pit. They looked like exhausted lovers on a bed. To the official war machine these men were just part of the body-count that was supposed to define military success. It was all highly dubious. Commanders would always overcount and often lump in ordinary civilian deaths just to make up the numbers. The Vietnamese claimed a body-count of 150 VC after the battle but I saw only about thirty of their dead.

I got the first helicopter out of Prey Veng that morning, along with a bunch of wounded Vietnamese soldiers. The pilot, still apprehensive about Khmer ground fire, climbed too quickly for his engine revolutions. As the helicopter plummeted back towards the earth I had plenty of time to review my life, but the only thing I could take in was the extent of the gold fillings in the screaming faces of the soldiers. Somehow the pilot pulled his machine around and we made it back to Pnom Penh without further surprise.

Jon Swain, the *Sunday Times* man in Pnom Penh, had the face of an English schoolboy, which indeed he had been until very recently. He was an alert and resourceful correspondent, always ready to help those who came in with his local knowledge. I asked him to let me know if he should hear of any firefights on the city outskirts. A couple of days later he called in at my hotel to tell me of some Khmer Rouge activity in a place called Setbo, only a short distance from the city. He was due to attend a press conference that afternoon – with Marshal Ky, the South Vietnamese war leader who idolised Hitler – and proposed to run me down there to link up with some Cambodian paratroopers who were probing the area, and to pick me up when the press conference was finished. I felt reassured at the prospect of being with paratroopers, always the elite troops in any army.

We took a route snared with roadblocks but enlivened by friendly Cambodian soldiers. About two miles from Setbo we came across a cluster of highly coloured buses which gave the impression of an English travelling funfair. Soldiers in red and yellow scarves, with personal flower arrangements and wearing flip-flops, turned out to be the Cambodian paratroopers. Their commander said that where we were going there would be 'beaucoup VC'. To me it all seemed too lackadaisical to be real.

The sun was streaking golden light through the leaves of trees beside the Mekong as we stopped on the embankment above it. The trucks behind us were loaded with sacks of rice and pots and pans, but I could also see machine guns and mortars being lifted down. The soldiers grouped and then moved forward. Khmers must have been watching us all the time.

I was walking in front of a jeep, with soldiers probing forward, when the breeze from the river blew off my jungle hat. As I went to retrieve it from the middle of the road, a hail of AK-47 rounds started pouring round me, whipping and lashing. I could see the road spitting dust as the bullets struck, and I dived down the side of the embankment where houses on stilts stood in the water.

I peered back at my hat, still in the road, defying me to pick it up. Bodies, some bearing red wounds, came tumbling down the bank. The commanders then started to mount the semblance of a counter-attack and I went back up to the road with them.

I crouched behind a jeep. As the man with me made to move forward we were rocked by the blast of a tremendous explosion. I could feel ringing in my ears, and stinging in my legs, and the shock waves blasted me backwards. My ears were in terrific pain. I realised I was deaf. I was in a daze and could feel something burning. I looked down and saw blood coming from my legs and crotch.

I tried to get away. Instinctively I wrapped my cameras and

half-crawled, half-scrambled down the embankment. Some men fell on top of me and were treading on my legs. I knew from the pain of their impact that I must have taken some wounds. I dragged myself on hands and knees for a couple of hundred yards, falling into a pit of wounded men – one of them with two holes in his stomach – and then into a pit full of ants. My legs felt as if they were on fire.

With the fate of Gilles Caron so fresh in my mind, I was determined not to be taken prisoner. Like Gilles, we had walked into a classic ambush. I wanted to get at least 300 yards from the point of ambush before I would allow myself to feel at all safe. I thought of hiding the camera bag and swimming for it in the Mekong. It might even ease the pain in my legs.

Then I came across the medics behind a culvert, trying to patch up some raw, red flesh. Two paratroopers saw me and dumped me in a house where there were more wounded. I wasn't taking very much in at that moment. I was only interested in getting my trousers down to see what had happened. My dick was bleeding like a pig but it had only been nicked by a piece of fragmentation. The more serious area was my right leg, which had taken four mortar fragments, one in the knee joint. I had another wound just above the knee of my left leg. I still could not hear properly.

Someone jabbed a morphine needle into my right leg and the next thing I knew I was being dumped unceremoniously with the other wounded on to the back of an open lorry. To my horror, they turned the lorry round and backed 300 yards towards the ambush from which I had just fled. They wanted to pick up more wounded, among them soldiers who had got the worst of the mortar explosion that had hit me.

As they brought the wounded to the lorry and started piling them in, the Khmers suddenly opened up with another round of mortars. The driver ran away. We were left on the back of the lorry taking a lot of incoming flak while the wounded were screaming and trying to hide. I recognised the soldier lying next to me. He was the man who had been just in front of me by the jeep when the first explosion took place. We had shared the fragmentation, but he had taken most of it in the stomach.

With some courage, the Cambodians were still loading the injured on to the lorry under heavy fire. Eventually the driver was located and forced to come back. I cannot say how relieved I was when we drove away from that place.

As we passed the primitive medical station there was new encouragement. Jon Swain, true to his word, had come back in his little black Citroën, and I heard him sing out, 'Okay, matey. You're going straight to the hospital. I'll follow.'

The deafness and the shock were wearing off. I took my mind off the pain by photographing the wounded soldiers. The day had become evening as we wound through the leafy suburbs of Pnom Penh, and caught the sweet smell of cooking. People on verandahs looked down nonchalantly to see the distorted shapes in our lorry. The shock would just begin to register on their faces as we pulled out of view and they realised how close they were to the battle.

The man beside me with the awful stomach wounds sat up and was kicking his legs, pleading for life. Minutes later I noticed he was lying down again, his feet drumming too perfectly with every motion of the lorry. I knew that he had gone. It could so easily have been my dead corpse rattling. I thought, He's gone instead of me.

There were chickens running round the hospital. Jon Swain did not think it was satisfactory. He had me whisked away in an ambulance to a French civilian hospital where I slept for most of the next ten days. The only excitement was a telegram rushed round from the British Embassy. It had been facilitated by the British Foreign Secretary, Michael Stewart, and was a 'get well' message from my fellow *Sunday Times* photographer, Tony Armstrong-Jones.

An ambulance took me to the airport, where I found that the *Sunday Times* had splashed out by buying me a first-class ticket. I couldn't help thinking that you had to go to ludicrous lengths before you merited this privilege.

On the way back I had plenty of time to reflect on my first battle wounds, but there seemed little of a profound nature to be thought on the subject. I must have seen thousands of wounded on battlefields since I first started going to the wars. Why them and not me?

21

BESIEGED

MY LEG WOUNDS did not detain me in England for long. Generous industrial injury terms did not seem to apply to war correspondents, and I had a mortgage to clear and the dream of a new home in the country.

I was back in action again within four months of the Cambodian adventure – under fire with my colleague Murray Sayle in Amman. One of Murray's many nicknames was 'The Camel', which derived from his ability to go for enormous lengths of time without any visible means of sustenance. It was an ability that came in particularly handy when I shared a room with him for ten days at the besieged Intercontinental Hotel. Inside the hotel there were breakdowns of every form of supply – heating, lighting, food and water. Outside there was the near-certainty of death by sniper fire. For the most part, we stayed in.

The siege for us and several score of the world's press was caused by what was known as 'The Battle of the Beds versus the Feds'. The 'Beds' were the fiercely loyal Bedouin troops of the Jordanian King Hussein; their battle-cry was 'Allah, Malik, Watami' (God, King and Country). The 'Feds' were the fedayeen guerrillas fighting on behalf of Jordan's huge Palestinian community.

The conflict centred on who was running Jordan – the King or the Palestinians? A punch-up had been in the offing for some time. All that was required was the spark – provided ultimately by the Palestinians when they hijacked three Western airliners, one of them a British VC-10, and brought them all to land in Jordan at a place called Dawson's Field. It was an amazing feat, which highlighted the government's impotence, and its inability to control what was happening on its own territory.

I went to Dawson's Field to photograph the planes as smouldering ruins. The passengers had already been evacuated, many of them to the Intercontinental. When I got back to the city, the Jordanian army had taken to the streets and were attacking Palestinian strongholds around the city.

In our hotel, a Swedish reporter took a bullet in the leg; just down the road, in a smaller hotel, a Russian correspondent was shot between the eyes. The electricity and the water supply packed up, and we were told the whole city was a no-go area to correspondents. Because the hotel was bursting at the seams everyone had to double up. This was how I came to be living on intimate terms with 'The Camel'.

I did not know Murray Sayle very well, though we had been with the newspaper roughly the same length of time. In his early forties, he was the oldest of the Aussies, and by far the most complicated. He was a large man with a large nose that almost quivered with inquisitiveness. People would say that he could talk the legs off a donkey without ever letting you know what was in his mind. He was considered eccentric though this may have been because he never dressed any part other than his own; he once turned up to a reception at the Athenaeum wearing a crash helmet and a T-shirt with 'Bloomsbury Wheelers' emblazoned across the front.

He had suffered a disappointment in life – the suppression, for alleged libel, of his novel about journalism, *A Crooked Sixpence*, which opened with the rhyme:

> There was a crooked man
> Who walked a crooked mile
> He found a crooked sixpence
> It wasn't enough.

Before Amman my contacts with him had been brief. In the Six Day War I was nervous of him, afraid that he might

145

trample over my inside track on Jerusalem. We should have met up in Prague in the Spring of 1968, when Russian tanks rolled in to crush Alexander Dubcek's hopes for socialism with a human face. I made it to the Czechoslovak border but the word 'photographer' in my passport put paid to any further penetration. An understanding official at the British Embassy in Vienna told me I had 'lost' my passport and issued me with a new one in which I featured as a 'businessman'. While I continued to languish on the wrong side of the border, Murray cruised in with a car brimming with sales leaflets and some cock-and-bull story about a trade fair.

The only time we actually managed to work together was on a story about the American crack troops, the Green Berets, in Vietnam a year earlier. For the most part, he went his way and I went mine but we did meet up at Loc Ninh, an isolated Green Beret fortress near the Cambodian border. Murray aroused hostility in the garrison by going to interview a French rubber planter who was thought to be in the pay of the VC, but this was a mark of Murray's professionalism. If anything, Murray was on the hawkish side in Vietnam – few correspondents wrote as sympathetically about the ordinary American solider – but he was nobody's partisan.

In the Amman siege, Murray was never idle. While at Dawson's Field, he had picked up a charred coffee pot in one of the burned-out airplanes. He used to sit, wholly relaxed in his long john underpants, polishing it back to normal as if he were under contract to the airline to clean it up. Somehow he wangled himself on the organising committee, run on strict prison camp lines, and Murray would receive complainants while polishing his pot. There was no shortage of complaints, especially when the food was reduced to what seemed like pigs' trotters and rice. Resentment also fastened on those people who had presciently filled up their baths before the water was cut off – should they share, or were they entitled to the whole reservoir? The big problem, however, was the odious toilets, eventually solved when Murray's committee organised the digging of latrines in a protected part of the gardens at the back of the hotel.

For much of the time even the briefest glance out of a hotel window was greeted with a barrage of fire from both sides. People kept their heads down, but all ears could pick up the din of battle, and sometimes more than the din. Arnaud de Borchgrave, a snappy dresser who worked for *Newsweek*, went to his bedroom wardrobe to find that a bullet had punctured his suits – all thirteen of them.

It took troops two hours to clear out one half-completed block opposite the Intercontinental. I could see four snipers being led away. Then, during the night, new snipers infiltrated, and it took three hours to clear them. And so it went on.

There was some education to be had from hanging around and listening to the wit and wisdom of Murray Sayle. He believed that journalism only required three things: rat-like cunning, a plausible manner, and a little literary ability. But for me the situation was most unpleasant – cheek-by-jowl with my peers, with no scope for independent action.

After five days I decided to break out on my own, only to be sent back at gunpoint by the Jordanian army patrol just outside. Next day, when the fighting had died down a little, I asked Murray if he would like to exercise a little of his cunning and come with me for another attempt. We both agreed that the objective should be the home of the First Secretary of the British Embassy, who lived only a few streets away and was said to be in daily contact with the King.

This time the patrols were less vigilant and we made it. We returned with the promise that an army jeep would call for us the next day to take us to Hussein at the Palace. We were on to a big 'exclusive'.

The jeep arrived when Murray, taking advantage of renewed water supplies, was in fully soaped condition in the bath. I had to run back downstairs and tell the Jordanian army, and by extension the King, to wait while Murray Sayle finished his ablutions. Fortunately they did.

As we came hurrying through the lobby, you could see the other journalists sniffing that something was afoot. Most of the correspondents had entered into an arrangement to pool their information. The reasoning was that all journalists were operating at a disadvantage, so it was only fair that any available scraps should be shared. I never liked such arrangements, and usually made myself scarce when anything of that nature was being discussed. As we were nearing the door, Arnaud de Borchgrave, the man with the punctured suits, made to cut us off.

'Where are you guys going?'

'None of your business.'

'I want to remind you guys that this is a pool.'

'It's not a pool for me,' I said. 'I don't pool for anybody.'

The exchange concluded with him calling me 'a bastard', and my promise to see him when I got back. Siege conditions rarely improve people's tempers. There was no way Murray and I were going to risk our necks for a pooled dispatch.

We got to the Palace to find King Hussein in high spirits. He reckoned that his gamble had paid off. The fedayeen had been crushed, he said, and the rest was mopping-up. He looked forward to an immediate restoration of law and order, which would include lifting the siege of the Intercontinental.

We got all this, but not quite exclusively. A BBC 'Panorama' crew was there too. And an obscure row broke out between Murray and a BBC man whom I happened to know slightly from Vietnam. Murray seemed to think the BBC crew were trying to pull a fast one by organising a Friday transmission (which would scoop him) rather than the usual 'Panorama' spot on Monday (which would leave Murray in front). The BBC man seemed to think that Murray had poached his questions, though why Murray should ever need anybody else's questions was a mystery to me.

That evening we gathered at the First Secretary's house for a mild celebration. The diplomat's wife was serving the drinks. It was best-behaviour time. I could hear this ludicrous row rumbling up again, and suddenly it took a turn that was to provide me with the most terrifying moment of the whole civil war.

Murray grabbed my arm and piloted me out into the garden, where he proceeded to take a pee over the First

Secretary's rose bushes. Simultaneously the first secretary's wife came out to hang some washing on the line. In an agony of embarrassment, I began thinking that pissing on English roses in a foreign field might even constitute high treason. Fortunately the diplomat's wife did not see us, or pretended not to. I could hear Murray, all oblivious, whittering on about this friend of mine who seemed to have some kind of problem . . .

Later in the week I met Murray glowering over his typewriter in the bar of the Intercontinental. He was saying that nothing now would persuade him to file a story, and I got excited about our missing the biggest story of the week in the world. Murray remained resolute.

It seemed that the Features Editor had got up his nose by telling him to write to the brief 'The City that Committed Suicide'. Murray was saying it was just like those egomaniacal deskmen back home. Their idea was to write the headline first, regardless of what the slobs in the field were saying, and then mangle the words to fit in. He raved on. There was no way this city had committed suicide; most of its citizens were still alive and, being built of stone, it was in no danger of collapse. He was damned if he was going to file to fit the preconceptions of a man whose arse never left the office.

There was much in this tirade with which I could sympathise, but none of it amounted to a reason not to file. We had to do our job, I said, even if we didn't like how others did theirs. I was coming on like a boy scout, but Murray was just winding me up. He had already filed before I entered the bar.

But the last laugh belonged to the Features Editor. My pictures, along with the dispatches of Murray Sayle and Brian Moynahan, all seamlessly welded together, appeared under the headline 'In the City that Committed Suicide'.

22

RAIN FOREST GENOCIDE

I HAVE ARGUED with a lot of journalists in my time, and the fault was often not theirs. I could be bad-tempered and erratic, especially in the approach to a big assignment. Friendships with writers sometimes came under strain, and occasionally broke down. While running repairs could usually be effected at the nearest bar, there would always be some legacy of damage.

There was one writer, however, who always brought out the best in me. His name was Norman Lewis, and in a way I became his disciple. Norman was the kind of man you could pass in the street without realising anybody had gone by. Tall, slightly stooped, with glasses and moustache, it was hard to imagine yourself in the presence of one of the world's greatest adventurers. He was old enough to be my father, and this may have been relevant to our relationship. I had no difficulty in being deferential to him, and he never seemed to find it hard to be kind and considerate to me. Over a period of twelve years we teamed up whenever we could to go to some of the most inaccessible parts of the world, and on only one occasion did we exchange cross words.

It had been a tough assignment among the Panare Indians in the Venezuelan interior and we were weary as we stumbled back across the Orinoco. I had torn the flesh off my ankle while pushing the ferry boat off a sandbar and Norman walked into an iron bar that formed part of the ferry canopy and landed flat on his back with a bloody gash across his forehead.

There were options on the other side. We could charter a small plane that would get us to Caracas in plenty of time for the flight home to England. Or we could make a riskier connection by taxi – a horrendous journey of some seven hours. There was no doubt in my mind, given our condition and the possibility that Norman might be concussed. It had to be the airplane. But Norman didn't trust small planes, which he believed fell out of the air all too frequently. So we took the bruising taxi ride instead. It wiped me out, but it left Norman, in his seventies, as composed as ever.

I served an apprenticeship before working directly with Norman. He had come back from Brazil in 1968 with an amazing story about genocide of the rain forest Indians in the Amazon. Mineral and land speculators, in league with corrupt politicians and officials, had continually usurped the Indian lands, destroying whole tribes in a cruel struggle in which bacteriological warfare had been employed. The food supplies of the Indians had been poisoned and epidemics created by issuing them with clothing impregnated with the smallpox virus.

Norman had covered every aspect of this hideous saga, except the pictures. The *Sunday Times* magazine asked me if I could reach some of the threatened tribes and provide suitable photographs to go with his powerful account. Before I left London, Norman himself gave me a precise briefing on what he wanted, though he warned me that it wouldn't be easy.

I soon began to feel it was impossible. Stuck in Rio, getting the mañana treatment every day from Brazilian officials, I couldn't see any way of getting to the Indians. Eventually a man at the Ministry of the Interior recommended that I go and photograph the Kadiweus, a mounted tribe often referred to as the Indian Cavaliers, who could be reached by a missionary plane.

Though not my objective, I was interested enough to follow this up. I remembered Norman telling me to beware of what he called the ethnocidal tendencies of the North American missionaries in Brazil. He saw them as the instrument by which the Indians lost their land, their self-respect, and finally their identity. I had no structured religious beliefs myself, but this judgment sounded harsh to me. I had seen missionaries in Biafra and other countries, who seemed to me to be working for the general good of the people.

All that I found remaining of the Kadiweus were a few sick and starving women and children who rode even hungrier looking horses down to the mission house to beg for scraps. The American missionary there did not seem greatly interested in them. He was busy on his translation of the Epistle to the Galatians into Kadiweu, and expected to finish the work in another ten years.

'But won't they be dead by then?' I asked.

'Yes, they will,' he said.

'Then what's the point?'

The missionary gave this some thought, and said, 'It's something I can't explain, something I could never make you understand.'

I began to get some inkling of what Norman might be on about.

I really wanted to get to Xingu, in the heart of the Amazon forest, where two dedicated anthropologists, the Vilas Boas brothers, had created a secure place in which a number of endangered tribes had found refuge to live in their own style, without any danger of missionary contact. The Boas brothers shared Norman's view on the subject.

After more days of frustration in Rio, I finally managed to fix it. I flew into Xingu on a Brazilian air force plane as the companion of a visiting doctor of tropical medicine. I presented my letters of accreditation to a short, grizzled, muscular man who said, 'They don't matter to me. We don't want you here, the Indians don't want you.'

I felt like a man who had just climbed Everest only to get turfed off when six inches from the summit. The one thing I had not anticipated was that a photographer would come in the same category of contamination as a missionary. It would be five days before the aircraft returned and, from the hostile reception I was getting, it looked as if I would be spending them with my camera bag unopened.

That evening, as the Boas brothers and their staff were about to sit down to dinner, I said, 'Before I left Rio, I bought a few things – cheese, salami, bits and pieces from the delicatessen – that I would like you to share with me.' To people contemplating another night of rice and beans, this had a wonderfully melting effect. Besides, I had shown respect for the Indians in the short time I had been there. They must have seen that I wouldn't behave like a tourist. Anyway, for whatever reason, there was a complete thaw.

I felt greatly honoured to photograph the tribes, some of which were pitifully small in numbers. Overrun by diamond hunters two years earlier, the Tchikaos had been reduced from 400 to 43. The Kamairos were highly musical, blending their music with religion – 'we speak to the Gods with the sweet music of flutes'.

I was invited to attend a ceremony where the women – naked except for the smallest shreds of rattan – danced frenziedly to the rain god. I spent time with the men – some of whom were 6 feet tall, and all of them muscular – as they anointed their bodies with extraordinary colours and ochres. With the children I chased insects and caught an enormous grasshopper, all of 7 inches long. At the end of it all the Boas brothers set the seal on our friendship by presenting me with a magnificent Indian headdress.

I took the grasshopper back to Rio, smuggled it to England in my camera bag and arrived in Hampstead Garden Suburb in time for Christmas. 'I've got something really interesting to show you,' I told the kids. There were screams of delight when the grasshopper emerged, though ten minutes later it died.

That trip made friends of Norman Lewis and me. We often spoke of making a joint expedition, though it would be another two years before we could get together. By then, early 1971, I was deliberately trying to broaden my range as a photographer. I didn't want to give up war reporting but I also didn't want to get a reputation for repeating the same images.

What impressed me about Norman was about how meticulous his approach was to an expedition. His level of research was quite incredible. I used to think that he had uncanny powers of prediction but in reality he just knew a lot.

'Tomorrow,' said Norman, on the third day of our first expedition together, 'you will see pagan rituals on the steps of a Christian church.' Sure enough, this was one of the strange sights that Chichicastenango, in the heart of Guatemala, had to offer. The church bell had been replaced by an Indian who squatted in the tower thudding an enormous drum.

Chichicastenango was the kind of place that Norman thoroughly approved of, a place where the 'civilising mission' of the white man had been slowly throttled. It was an almost all-Indian town fifty miles from the nearest qualified doctor, and yet it seemed to be in good healthy shape. The combination of Indian life and old Spanish colonial architecture made for a certain style. I can remember writing home from the comfort of my four-poster bed in the Mayan Inn and thinking, This is the life.

Norman loved the small details and turns of phrase in life. I remember inexpertly trying to beat down a man who was selling a silver figure, and I asked Norman to intercede with his gift for languages. After a brief exchange, Norman turned to me laughing and said, 'This is a very smart man. He says he is not dealing in vegetables.' Other sights and sounds were less agreeable.

In Guatemala City, we noticed a large skinhead population but they bore no relation to the British 'skins'. They were the result of police initiative in dealing with the hippie problem. In remote Tekal, the greatest of the ancient Mayan cities, situated in the largest rain forest in the northern hemisphere, the view was suddenly marred by the appearance of fifty combat-ready paramilitaries.

Guatemala was, as usual, in the grip of a civil war, with left-wing guerrillas in the hills and right-wing death squads in the city. The most feared group was called Ojo por Ojo (eye for an eye). After nine o'clock at night (curfew time) the army shot anything that moved. Each morning the *Prensa Libre* would list the corpses found round Guatemala City.

Norman made it his business to find out what progress had been made since 1954, when the left-wing President Arbenz, whose reforms threatened the holdings of the United Fruit Company, was overthrown in a coup organised by the CIA. It transpired that less than 200 families still owned 98 per cent of the land. Norman thought it could be safely said that Guatemala still retained its status as a banana republic, and the most murderous one at that.

Meanwhile, there was still the consolation of small pleasures, and Norman found another one at our last port of call, Puerto Barrios, an almost wholly negro town on the Gulf of Mexico. Upon hearing the most fearful screams outside our hotel, we went to investigate. Round the back of the hotel we found the source of the commotion – dozens of big rats in cages.

'It's highly likely,' said Norman, with his schoolmaster's chuckle, 'that we are looking at tonight's supper.'

23

HIDING BEHIND THE CAMERA

MY FIRST BOOK of photographs, called *The Destruction Business*, was published in 1971. The paper was cheap and the printing diabolical, but I was enormously proud of it. Putting it together gave me the chance to assess where I had been and where I might be going.

I wasn't about to find serious fault with my own work but I could see there was an emphasis on soldiers at war rather than civilians in war, though when the casualty numbers were finally added up it was often the civilians who had suffered the most. In future I wanted to reflect more of what happened to the women and children caught up in war, and the chance to do so came sooner than I expected.

In March 1971, soon after I came back from Guatemala with Norman Lewis, civil war broke out in East Pakistan. The West Pakistan army moved in with the intention of destroying all Bengali ambitions for an independent state. The brutality of their intervention would soon give the green light to involvement by the Indian army.

Like most photographers, I was not eager to go. This was not due to the risks, but mainly because of the lack of them. Both the Pakistanis and the Indians were highly skilled at not letting newspapermen anywhere remotely near the front. I went to the Indo-Pakistan war of 1965 and for me it was a total wash-out. Nothing but a diet of briefings way behind the lines, something for the reporters to nibble on but useless for photographers. If they ever took you to what was called a front, you could bet it was last month's front.

Confident that I wouldn't be called upon, I went ahead with booking our first family holiday abroad. We settled on Cyprus, a place which had a special significance for me. I still read newspapers of the Pakistan conflict, and remember being riveted one morning by a story in *The Times*. It spoke of the possibility of a million people fleeing the war and crossing the border into India. It seemed a staggering number of people to be dispossessed and homeless at one time, and in a country where the monsoon rains were due any day. I spoke to Mike Rand at the *Sunday Times* magazine and he gave me the go-ahead to do what I could on my own. I had less than two weeks, though my deadline this time was imposed not so much by the newspaper as the family holiday.

By the time I flew into Calcutta, a million refugees was looking like a flimsy underestimate. I took a cab and headed north. It was soon apparent that the problem was beyond counting. The road was an endless flow of people: of people carrying the crippled; of the crippled carrying the more crippled; of people on sticks with legs that bent backwards. Every form of human disfigurement, in terms of emotion and physique, was going down that road towards Calcutta.

I stopped at Hasanabad, about fifty miles north, to take some pictures. The little railway station, which would have looked busy with a hundred people on it, was now the only shelter for 8,000 refugees. You could see the families with bundles all down the track.

I arrived near the border where a battalion of the Indian army was camped under canvas. All the soldiers were on full alert. My first thought was that I might stay with them but they said it wasn't possible: they were expecting to be on the move into East Pakistan at any moment. They directed me instead to a church down the road.

The Catholic sisters there said I could have a bed, on one condition. I would have to be ready to vacate it on Saturday night when the travelling Father arrived for a night's sleep before Sunday Mass. It was the beginning of a chain of kindnesses that sustained me through the catastrophe.

Transport was supplied by a bicycle from the

neighbouring farm, and I pedalled off to find the refugee settlements. They were dotted all around, some in old vacant buildings, others in tents supplied by the Indians, still more in primitive grass huts. They all told the same tale of dispossession and misery.

I had a strange anxiety. The rains had not arrived. Each morning as I pedalled out the sky was brilliant blue, almost cloudless. The monsoon of course is a great blessing in a land with the ever-present fear of drought. Now the flooding could only make the plight of the refugees more dire. Either way, the outcome was not in human hands.

I had just five days left, and that morning had travelled less than a mile on my bicycle when I felt the first droplets of rain on my cheek. By the time I got to the little cluster of huts that marked the settlement of thousands of refugees the monsoon was ranging, and its effect was more devastating than anything I could have imagined. Already weakened people were collapsing under the weight of the torrential downpour. Husbands were carrying dead wives, and I could see men and women carrying dead children. There were virtually no medical supplies, and within twenty-four hours of the monsoon starting a cholera epidemic had broken out.

Often I found myself not wanting to look at what I had come to photograph. As I went quietly about my work I was never made to feel intrusive, yet I was horrified and heart-broken. My abiding thought was that those comfortably at home in Britain should see how these people were suffering. I saw one woman cradling her dead child whom she had carried round all day. When finally, towards evening, she squatted down and released the child it seemed even more sad than when she had clung to the corpse.

In a makeshift hospital I saw a man and his four children clustered round the sickbed where their mother lay foaming at the mouth, her eyes spent. The nurse told me that she was dying because she had been given the wrong drugs. When finally she died, the family went into a frenzy.

'What happens now?' I asked the nurse helplessly.

She answered patiently. 'Well, we're going to take the

bodies from here to the dead body tent over there, so the men can take them away.'

The dead woman was carried out of the water-logged hospital and her stretcher put down beside the body tent. The family waded across and lay down beside her while I was taking pictures. They couldn't believe their mother had gone. I felt as if I were using the camera as something to hide behind. I stood there feeling less than human, with no flesh on me, like a ghost that was present but invisible. You have no right to be here at all, I told myself, my throat contracted and I was on the verge of tears.

'Mister, where will you go?' I asked the man in a trembling voice.

'I don't know,' he said. 'To Calcutta maybe.' And what would Calcutta do with him and his family and the two million other refugees? I gave him every rupee I had in my pocket. It was to help me, as well as him.

I photographed the refugees under the monsoon rain for four days before my cameras started to give out. The leather cases disintegrated and the water got in, while my own body became shaky from a diet of tea and bananas. Emotionally I was drained. I thought of my pictures as atrocity pictures. They were not of war but of the dreadful plight of victims of war.

Before flying home from Calcutta I went to visit Mother Teresa's House of the Dying, where I saw marvellous work being done for the destitute. There was a dignity about the place, and I took some pictures of Mother Teresa who, unlike the refugees, seemed very practised before the camera.

As I left I decided to stay with victims and to look more closely at conflict through civilian eyes. There was no need to travel the world to find what I wanted, for the situation was there on my own doorstep, in Northern Ireland.

I can vouch for the effectiveness of the CS gas used by the British army against riotous demonstrators in Northern Ireland. The first time I received a serious dose, in the Bogside area of Derry later in 1971, I went blind.

The demonstration had become ugly, with rubber bullets and great shards of glass from shattered milk bottles flying around. Then, suddenly, a tremendous burning sensation seized my nose and throat, and forced me to close my eyes. I can remember groping my way back from the fray and leaning my face to a wall. I was thinking that if I could zone in on an area of total darkness and flick my eyes open, the trouble would go away. It didn't work. As I stood there in total darkness – eyes, nose, throat, ears, mouth, all burning – I felt a great lump in my back. It was a rubber bullet. Behind me a voice said, 'The bastards. The inhuman bastards.'

I was grabbed unceremoniously by the jacket and hustled away. I thought I must have been arrested by the army. Then close to my arm I heard the voice again, and there was no mistaking the vowel-mangling Ulster accent. I was led a short distance down what seemed like the corridor of a house. The 'inhuman bastards' kept going in a stream at my side as if these were the only words my unseen companion had ever learned. I was made to sit down. When again I tried to open my eyes, it was as if someone had thrown fire into them, and still I couldn't see.

I called into the darkness for a damp cloth, and several voices shouted, 'Get him a damp cloth. A damp cloth here.' In the background I heard the sound of a desperate animal honking. When a stinking floor-cloth was placed in my hand, I managed to clear my eyes enough to make out my immediate surroundings. Through a burning haze I focused on two globes just below me. They were two eyes, so near that they looked like two close-ups of the moon. My host, a midget, was standing just in front of me. For a moment I thought I had woken up in a Fellini film. My host was repeating, 'Are you all right? The focking bastards.'

His eyes were streaming too. Beyond him I could dimly see more people, women, children, dabbing faces. From outside came another burst of loud hee-hawing. Someone said, 'The donkey's been gassed too.' A pall of burning gas lay over everything in that little Catholic community.

For a journalist, one of the prevailing emotions in Ulster

was feeling like a Judas to both sides. It was there again when I left the midget and his little house after thanking his family for their kindness. I had to pass the British soldiers posted at the street corner. I held up my cameras prominently as the badge of my profession, and saw the looks of scorn and heard the swearing under their breath. As far as they were concerned I was consorting with the enemy which they had just tear-gassed.

Civil rights marches, boisterous but not violent, rather like Ban the Bomb demonstrations, were the order of the day when I first visited the province three years earlier. Catholics were protesting about discrimination in jobs, housing and voting rights, though under the surface old sectarian enmities smouldered. The Greens harked back to the Irish nationalist martyrs and those who had died at the hands of the Black and Tans, while the Orangemen owed direct descent from the Scottish mercenaries sent in by Cromwell to pacify and colonise Ireland in the seventeenth century.

On the night of 4 January 1969 the old traditions welled up when the overwhelmingly Protestant Royal Ulster Constabulary led the predominantly Catholic civil rights marchers into a Loyalist ambush at Burntollet Bridge outside Derry. There hordes of men wielding cudgels with nails in, wooden staves and bars of iron swept down on the protest marchers like the wild Picts and Scots of earlier times had charged upon the English from the Border hills. It was the green light for the IRA to gear themselves up for a struggle. They too were hard men, made stubborn because they felt cornered and had nothing to lose.

In the Bogside itself in those days we received great kindness and hospitality from gentle people who felt oppressed by the structure of their lives. I am sure that they did not want to see the blood-letting come to their community, or spread through Ulster, but the stage was now set for just that to take place. When British soldiers arrived to keep the peace they were seen at first by the Catholics as saviours. It didn't take long for attitudes to change when the army took up their stance as protectors of the status quo. Young Catholic girls were tarred and feathered for fraternising with the soldiers and Protestant Loyalists were inflamed by the emergence in the Catholic community of the Provisional IRA, ready to use the gun and the bomb.

I chose the Bogside for the many visits I made to Northern Ireland in 1971 because it was easier to bring out the issues photographically in an area not much bigger than a football pitch than in a large, anonymous city like Belfast. In the Bogside, after the pubs turned out on Saturday afternoons, you could almost guarantee that something would happen. It began with youngsters hurling stones at the troops and escalated to Molotov cocktails and sniping gunfire. Then the army would retaliate. The pictures I took of a charge by the Royal Anglians became famous because it gave such a clear view of the soldiers' difficulty. Kitted out in flak jacket, perspex-visored riot helmet and awkward Samurai-style leg and arm shields, they appeared like Bushido warriors to housewives as they passed their doorsteps. Burdened with all this medieval armour, they were expected to chase kids who could run and turn on a cat's whisker.

One day I was approached by two men in the Bogside who demanded to know what I was doing with my camera. With my usual level of tact I told them to mind their own business.

'If y'know what's good for ye,' I was informed, 'y'll do as ye're told an' clear off.'

I stood my ground and said that I had never cleared off at anyone's behest in all my life, and wasn't thinking of starting now.

Later that night at my hotel, the City, which was eventually flattened by a bomb, a wild Catholic porter called Tommy came up to me after I had been relaying my experience to other journalists in the bar and offered me words of assurance.

'That man who stopped you this aft'noon, I've fixed him. Ye're okay now.'

'What do you mean?' I said.

'Them's the Provos. But ye're all right now. Y'won't have any more trouble. I've told them ye're from the Sunday Times.'

A nine-year-old boy suffering from kwashiorkor.

Fleeing from battle on his first excursion into Biafra with an abortive guerilla mission, Don McCullin is photographed by his French colleague Gilles Caron, who was later killed by the Khmer Rouge in 1970.

Captain Osadebe lectures a dead soldier about hi sacrifice for the cause.

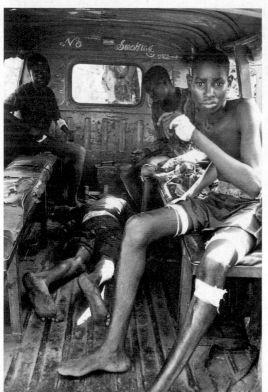

Carrying away a comrade wounded in the face.

An ambulance awaits more wounded before using scarce petrol to drive them to hospit

(*Facing pa* The albino boy clutching empty French corned beef

Michael McCullin, sergeant in the French Foreign Legion.

The camera that recieved an AK-47 bullet.

Cambodian soldiers, looking almost festive in their neckscarves, mourn the death of a child in battle.

Some victims of the ambush, evacuated by lorry, are dead on arrival at a military hospital.

Cambodian paratroopers 14km from Phnom Penh counter-attack after walking into an ambush.

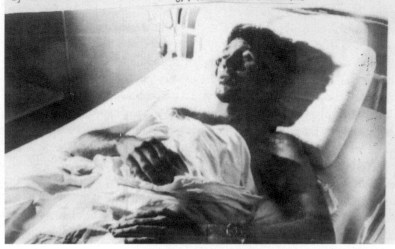

HKP-101-6/5/70:NEAR SETBO,PHNOM PENH: British Sunday Times correspondent
DONALD McCULLIN in hospital bed who was wounded thursday 6/4 when hit
by mortar fragments near Setbo,10 miles south east of Phnom Penh.
UPI RADIOPHOTO SAWADA.kb

The distinguished Japanese photographer Sawada, who took this photograph of
the wounded McCullin, was later murdered by the Khmer Rouge.

Christine, Paul and Jessica in a weekend cottage in Suffolk – the first step
in the McCullin's escape from the city, to be completed when the family moved
into a farmhouse in Hertfordshire.

Bringing out one of the first victims of IRA sniper fire.

A young boy arrested by British soldiers on suspicion of causing riots.

Men from the Royal Anglian Regiment in their samurai protective armour counter-attack in the Bogside.

British soldier takes up covering position on British soil while civilians go home from work.

I didn't have any more trouble of this sort, but it was uncomfortable to know that I had been vetted by the Provisional IRA before I could take pictures freely. It was no more comfortable crossing the lines, passing the army at checkpoints on my way to and from the other side. With tension running high in the Creggan estate, and youngsters setting fire to hijacked lorries, I spotted an older man taking up a position in a front garden near me. I sensed that he was a sniper, although I could not see any weapon as quietly he got himself organised. My companion explained what was going on, and it put me in a dilemma. Here was a man lining up to shoot and possibly kill a British soldier and I could do nothing about it except move away, as I was told, and keep quiet, for I was being closely watched. No British soldiers were killed that day in Derry, but that was just my good fortune. On another occasion I saw a soldier stretchered out of a garage after being shot in the back. I went forward to take a photograph and was confronted by another soldier who tried to beat me back with his baton-gun. I could understand how he felt after seeing me among the Catholic youths who were causing the trouble.

It might not have been a full-scale war but covering events in Northern Ireland was an extremely dangerous business. Apart from being mistaken by one side for a member of the other, at any time I could be struck by a stray missile, a bottle or a brick, and suffer severe brain damage – as could any other innocent passer-by using the streets to go about his or her normal business. The hazards of civilian life in this province are nowhere more vividly illustrated than in an extraordinary press picture of me running from both bricks and an English Saracen armoured car that was trying to run me down in mistake for a demonstrator. The vehicle has its wheels off the ground and looks as if it is trying to seize me in its jaws. Bricks hurled at the Saracen came heading for me.

There was a final irony to my acquaintance at first hand with the Irish troubles. I phoned a contact in the Bogside during one week to ask if anything was likely to happen at the weekend.

'I think ye'd better get y'self over here,' was the cryptic reply.

The *Sunday Times* had other plans for me that weekend, and so I missed what became known as Bloody Sunday, when 13 Catholics were killed in the Bogside in an appalling day of rioting and shooting. I should have been there – or maybe it was Fate that intervened.

PART THREE

Matters of Life and Death

24

PRISONER OF IDI AMIN

WHEN CHRISTINE READ Donald Wise's report in the *Daily Mirror*, that I was among those fellow journalists who had just disappeared in Uganda before he managed to get out of the country, she was sure that I was dead. She knew that Donald and I were close, and that some of the missing Western newspapermen had been taken to Makindye jail, Idi Amin's notorious killing-house.

Tension was already building when I arrived at Uganda's Entebbe Airport in the middle of a power cut. There was talk of a coup, and President Amin had begun a bloody purge of his own police force. I drove the eighteen miles to Kampala on a narrow potholed road with jungle hanging overhead. All the signs of a corrupt regime coming to an end were in the city – no service, defective plumbing, sewage backing up, shops looted or bare of goods. The Asian temple in the centre of the town was besieged by Africans begging with menace. Most Asian shops had been ransacked. Finally, in the Apollo Hotel, there was the vulture-like influx of journalists of whom I was one.

I homed in on the Strangers' Quarter where Somalis, Congolese, Rwandans, Burundians and all manner of Asians – people whom Amin considered trouble-makers – hung out in a crumbling, overpopulated shanty town. I knew from experience that when uprisings or disturbances are in the air, this is the sort of place in which they start. As I moved around, making friends and taking photographs, I was suddenly confronted by a huge soldier with lizard-like eyes. He was dressed in English fatigues, English-style jungle shirt rolled up at the sleeves, combat jungle boots and a soft jungle hat.

'What are you doing?' he demanded in a snakish and hostile fashion. When I told him the obvious – that I was photographing these people – he snarled. 'You are not supposed to be here.'

'Yes, I am. I have a permit,' I said.

His eyes flicked to the permit which he snatched out of my hand. I tried to grab it back.

'No! Get into this car.' The vehicle, driven by another soldier, nosed up to us. This was the sort of car, I thought, that could make you disappear.

'No, I won't.'

A crowd was gathering, for I had become the focus of an unheard-of public scene. A black sergeant was ordering a white man to jump to it and do what he's told. In those days in Africa no black man, whatever his authority, talked to a white man like that. It entailed a calculated abandoning of respect. Repeatedly I refused to get in the car. Even so I found myself eased and nudged towards it quite against my will. Then I was hustled in and driven away, tyres screaming, after the driver had executed a high-speed three-point turn that almost demolished a section of the crowd.

I was taken to a large army complex and left in a room. At least I'm not in some anonymous spot in the forest, I reassured myself. I tried to remain cool and pretended not to care. Two men came in with files – and when I see files I get nervous. The files were placed on the table and there was a babble of conversation in Swahili before the lizard-eyed sergeant left. I smiled and spoke firmly.

'Can I ask you a question? Why am I here?'

'Why were you taking photographs in this district?'

'Because I am working for an English newspaper and have permission to do so.'

'What are these pictures for?'

'To show that life in Kampala is going on as normal,' I said with as much innocence as I could muster.

I was asked to hand over my money and personal

possessions, and I refused. I tried a high and mighty tone. 'No, I'm not giving them to you. You can't have them. I'm here for legitimate reasons, and I want to know why this is happening.'

They left me to cool off for an hour. When they returned it was suddenly all courtesies.

'Well, we're going to let you go. We are sorry we had to bring you here.'

I was so relieved I said, 'Oh listen, absolutely no problem.' Once you've been released you don't fuss about being screwed up for the last three hours.

They drove me back to my hotel. On the way I made a few comments about the lovely Kampala girls, just to keep the mood congenial. I even asked them if they would like a beer, but they declined; they had their duties. It was some days before I discovered exactly where I had been and what these duties were. I had spent my time in the office block of the Makindye prison and my interrogators were members of Amin's secret police. All the same, I don't like being intimidated into not doing my work, so I went back to the Strangers' Quarter, this time taking my tripod for moral support.

I was not far from the spot where I had been arrested when I came upon an excited crowd in the middle of which stood a seedy sweaty-faced man, his suit rumpled, his manner drunken and belligerent. He squinted at me through red eyes.

'Who are you?'

'It's none of your business.' I must be a slow learner.

'Show me your passport.'

I refused. He said he was a soldier.

'Prove to me you are a soldier,' I said with disbelief.

He put his hand into his pocket as if to bring out papers. Instead of papers a clenched fist smashed into my face. I reeled back, clutching for my tripod. As the crowd moved in on me I swung the tripod like some demented Scottish hammer-thrower, trying to get a distance between me and them. Seeing a gap, I took off like a hare up the street. Behind me the mob swarmed and took up the chase, with me as the focus of a great hue and cry. At full spring, I heard a voice call me from an alleyway and I dived into the shadows to draw breath.

'Sir, sir, follow me. I know a way for you.' I had no idea who the African was but there was little choice. Full of qualms, I followed him quickly through a warren of alleys, the mob clearly audible behind me.

With relief I found myself back in the hotel district, and I could see a broad path leading to the Apollo. My guide held me back as a large Mercedes loomed from the end of the street.

'Dada is driving around,' he said.

Sure enough, the gorilla outline of Amin Dada could be seen hunched at the wheel of the car as it drew to a stop before very slowly moving on again.

'Sir, you must leave this country,' my rescuer urged me. 'In two or three days there will be big trouble in Kampala.'

I took a deep breath and bolted as fast as I could for the hotel, arriving breathless, adrenalin pumping. Christ, this job is getting to be a nightmare, I thought.

That night the press met for one of those super-charged drink-ups you tend to have in beleaguered hotels in troubled zones in troubled times. I remember drinking with David Holden, who was in a serious mood. 'I don't like the look of this place,' he said. 'I'm getting out of here quickly.'

I respected David's sense of when to stay and when to go. He was knowledgeable and not easily scared. If anything, he dared too much. A few years later he would be killed in Egypt by an assassin's bullet. Maybe he knew something I didn't know. Anyhow, I listened to David and thought it over. I had some good pictures, though not as many as I would like. I decided to go – but how? Communications were in turmoil. Even British airlines were curtailing their services. It was becoming unsafe for the crews. Alitalia was still flying, but for how long? I wangled a seat with Alitalia on the eight o'clock flight that evening.

Those of us left gathered round the pool for a farewell swim under the eyes of Amin's ever-present security men. I was just thinking about a second dip when a strange murmuring sound drew us to the verandah. Columns of armoured vehicles told us that Amin had mobilised.

Later we discovered that Ugandan guerrilla exiles had grouped in force on the border with Tanzania with the aim of toppling Amin and replacing him with Milton Obote, the man Amin himself had deposed. Obote had the support of Tanzania's respected President Julius Nyerere, but the incursion was botched, driving Amin to paranoid extremes.

The first evidence of this was the armoured cars stationed outside our hotel. Phone and telex lines were cut. Pulling clothes hastily over my swimming trunks, I decamped with Donald Wise to another hotel that might still be in touch with the outside world. When I went back to the Apollo to retrieve my cameras, I found the place surrounded by the Ugandan army. I held back and watched people being brought out and put into army trucks. A European emerged surrounded by soldiers with weapons and was forced to lie face down on the floor of a Volkswagen truck. This is going to be very unpleasant, I thought, if they feel the need to humiliate people in this way.

It crossed my mind to abandon the cameras and make myself scarce as quickly as possible. Almost immediately I saw the risks. I didn't fancy the consequences of being caught running away.

I strolled with a confident air into the lobby, trying to look as if I knew what I was doing while all that was going on had nothing to do with me. A British flight crew was standing stock-still, their faces pale and worried. We exchanged wide-eyed looks but no words. Suddenly I was surrounded by tall burly African soldiers. Amin's Nubians were a daunting sight. They asked me for my room number, and I told them, very politely. Under escort I was led to the reception desk to pay my bill. I took this as a good sign, allowing myself the consoling thought – Alitalia, here I come!

'We will go to your room now and pack your bags.'

Four of them accompanied me to my room and began rifling through my belongings. In a photographic magazine containing some of my Biafra pictures, they came across the pictures of the skeletal albino on the verge of death, which made them giggle and fall about. These people aren't just evil, I thought, they're crazy, mad.

I was marched downstairs again. When I asked where they were taking me, they said to the police station. I clung to the hope that I was just being deported.

The police station was a madhouse. Everyone, black or white, who might conceivably be opposed to Amin had been rounded up and brought in. The crush forced us to sit on each other's knees. I spotted John Fairhall of the *Guardian* in the throng, as well as someone from Reuters whom I knew by sight and the man from the *Telegraph*. Beside me was a young German boy who had lived in Uganda for some time, and who spoke Swahili. Suddenly he started crying. I asked what the trouble was and tried to comfort him.

'I've just heard one of the guards saying we are all being sent to Makindye. It's a terrible place,' he said. 'No one comes out of there alive.'

'No, I'm sure that's not right,' I said.

A man in a short jacket, whom I later discovered was also a member of Amin's secret police, was saying loudly in English – indicating me and Fairhall and the others – 'Who are these people?' The desk sergeant told him that we were journalists and the man registered the word with distaste. 'Journalists,' he repeated. 'They are dirty people.'

We of the press were weeded out and taken to a long Landrover. The man I had seen being pushed to the floor of the truck outside the Apollo was also there. They bellowed at us to get into the vehicle. After a push and a shove, and a few punches thrown, we were heaped in on one another, all tangled up with our baggage on the Landrover floor. It screeched away angrily in a leftward direction. I relinquished the last hope that we were going to the airport.

We disembarked in a yard with verandahs giving on to it. Piled outside the gate was a large stack of empty beer cans – not a reassuring sign. Uniformed men lounged on the verandahs, tossing back cans of beer and chatting up women. As the guards yelled at us to get out of the Landrover, these men put down their cans and came loping over to us with sticks in their hands. Now the bullying tempo started to pep up.

'Get down. Sit down. Take off your shoes and socks.'

One of our group, an ex-colonial policeman, stood straight and said, 'I *beg* your pardon!' *Thump*. The punch landed squarely on his chin and rocked him on his feet. 'What the devil's that for?' *Thump*, came another. I had seen some of this sort of treatment meted out in Biafra and the Congo, though not to whites. My shoes and socks were off in a flash. I was beginning to feel really scared. We sat hunched in a semi-circle, almost in a foetal position, cowering under the baton blows that came raining down. I felt a boot in my back and thought, Christ, we are going to be murdered!

We were shoved into a guardroom. A heavy African body came flying through the air and crashed into our midst. It was a drunken soldier, being punished by his comrades. Later, when it was only half-light, we were taken out to a courtyard and stood against a wall. I was sure we were going to be shot. A guard with the novel experience of holding white men at gunpoint was sniggering in a way I had learned men do when they torment prisoners, before they are dispatched. I'm going to die here, I thought. This is where my life will end, in a dark and dingy African killing-house.

I waited for the rest of the firing squad to arrive, my legs barely able to hold me up. There was a lot of scuffling and running around. Other men came, and Fairhall and the *Telegraph* man were taken away. We were just left there.

Eventually they moved me and the policeman further on. My legs didn't feel as if they were carrying me along. I just seemed to float, as if my crushed spirit were carried on a magic carpet. Dimly in this zombie glide I heard the rattling of keys. A door opened and I saw in front of me another white man. He said genially, 'I'm Bob Astles. Sit down. Have a drink. You look as if you need a drink.'

It was the most needed drink of my life. Later I learned that this man was of the most sinister provenance, but the sound of his voice at that time was like sweet music. Fear had soaked up every droplet of moisture in my body. I felt as if I had spent a month in the Kalahari desert.

'You're in a bloody dangerous place here,' Astles said. 'It's really bad.'

'Don't tell me, don't tell me,' I said.

It transpired we were in the VIP wing of Makindye prison. I had no idea what was to come. I looked round a high-ceilinged room with sub-cells leading off it, fronted with bars like cages in the zoo. All the cells were fully occupied, and there were cots for the overspill. VIP privilege meant that prisoners were not locked into the cells but could move from one to another and into the small communal area.

Among a handful of white prisoners was an English school-teacher who wore glasses and had a very nasty head wound. He had been coshed with a rifle. There were Asians and a brooding Tanzanian among the Africans. One man was locked in his cell with a stack of coffee-table books. He was said to be the richest man in Uganda, and Amin was bleeding his fortune away for privileges and ransom.

Astles was filling me in on these and other more alarming details. Fairhall and the *Telegraph* man had almost certainly been taken to the execution block, where the sledgehammer was the favoured means of cheap and blunt dispatch. Nineteen men in succession had been battered to death, I was told, by a twentieth acting under duress, whose own head was then smashed in by the guard. Astles had grisly atrocity pictures to show around.

All this took place in another block, not far away. They could come for you just as easily here. Astles pointed to the marks of recent terrors in our block – mattresses stained with blood and scratches on the walls. While Astles told his mounting tale of horrors, the Reuters man kept trying to catch my eye.

My mind twitched with the humiliations undergone and fear of what might come. I lay in the dark on my bloodstained mattress in deep shock. Suddenly, in the stillness, I heard the rattle of rifles and then the crashing of doors. A prisoner was thrown into the outer room. There were terrible thudding sounds.

At one o'clock the rattle and crashing of arms approached again. They stopped just short of my cell. I heard howls and beating and whimpering as the Tanzanian man took a terrible pasting before he was dragged away.

'S'all right,' Bob Astles drawled out of the darkness. 'He's for the chop. Poor bastard never stood a chance anyway. They've broken his arms.' He detailed the punishments inflicted on Tanzanians, which were similar to those suffered by policemen of suspect loyalty. Screams penetrated the night from somewhere outside the block.

I dozed fitfully, waiting for the crash of doors again. Humiliation and terror and despair chased each other across my brain. It was wonderful to see the dawn break, but appalling to realise you faced another day of the fear you had just gone through.

My heart thumped at another scuffling approach. The door opened to reveal two Africans holding between them a dustbin, which was steaming. Both had taken fearful beatings. One was covered in welts and bruises, the other had an eye hanging with a sack of fluid. As the jailer loomed up behind them I tried to muster some dry-mouthed spirit.

'What have you got for us there,' I said.

'It's your breakfast,' said the jailer.

The sinister steaming substance in the dustbin turned out to be tea. Rarely has tea tasted so good. And there were hard tack biscuits to go with it. We were fortunate. Prisoners in Amin's jails often starved to death.

As I bit into the hard tack, squatting on the floor, the Reuters man tried to raise morale with a wry smile, 'I heard something funny in Swahili last night. The guard told the jailer that these Wa-zungi cannot run away because they had taken our shoes and socks.' Shoeless or not, I would have run out of there barefoot and broken-legged, over a mile of burning coals and broken glass, if there had been any chance of escape.

While we washed – another VIP privilege – we were out of earshot of Astles. The Reuters man said quietly, 'That Astles – he's not kosher. He's not on the side of the angels.'

Astles was one of the most feared white men in Uganda. He had risen to power as one of Amin's leading advisers, but recently there had been talk of him falling out with Amin, though this wasn't generally believed. If he had not quarrelled with Amin, the Reuters man thought his presence among us more than sinister. When I asked Astles why he was there, his reply was vague. 'I was rounded up with the others,' he said. 'Amin's gone mad. He's just gone *mad*.'

I spent hours staring through the window grille at the egrets and the little weaver birds. From time to time they were scattered by the arrival of a party of vultures.

'They always come,' said Astles. 'They come for the body-truck.'

For four days I looked out through the bars and watched the trucks leaving with the bodies of those executed. They were the four longest days of my life.

A tall officer with a large jungle hat arrived at my cell door carrying a whip. His henchmen were armed with cudgels, knives, daggers and whips. As they all crowded in I thought, in a state of acute alarm, this is it!

'Are you a newspaperman?'

I looked straight at him and said, 'Yes, I am.'

'I am giving you this form. You must fill in this form. I don't want a statement. I want you to fill in this form. If you don't you will be chastised.'

There was nowhere to do it except to kneel down before him and write it on the floor. As I scrawled my name and passport number I thought, At any minute now my skull will explode. The officer's manner suggested barely suppressed rage. At any moment, I thought, I would be whacked in that most vulnerable position. When I clambered back to my feet, the man scanned my writing with displeasure, staring at me after registering each detail.

Astles, who never missed anything, was rocking to and fro and laughing. 'You'll be all right now,' he said. I didn't believe him, but the words raised a little hope in me, soon to be denied.

I was taken to a hut in the yard to collect my shaving things.

Inside I saw a mountain of shoes and pathetic little cases, some held together with string, others no more than bundles. I saw my own suitcase there, shiny new in this derelict heap.

'Leave it there,' the escort said.

I felt dismayed. I've been here before, I thought with dread. And I had been there – in those photographs of Auschwitz and other Nazi death camps. The mountain of shaving brushes and the piles of spectacles, the sort of cases people took from the Warsaw ghetto. I was more stricken by the sight of that room than by people I had seen shot in front of me. I returned to my cell physically drained, smelly, my clothes stained, spent.

In the block were two new prisoners. 'These men,' said Astles, 'were customs officials at Entebbe. They're going to get the chop. They know they're for the chop and would like to have a church service. Would you care to join in?'

A square was formed. I stood on one side, Astles was across from me, the two doomed Africans formed a third side. The spectacled schoolmaster stood in a corner. They started singing, and I tell you there is no more beautiful sound than an African singing hymns in harmony with another African. My mouth opened but no sound emerged as I watched the Englishman gradually slide down the wall in his corner, overcome by the fever in his head wound, the fear in his belly and the sheer sadness of the situation.

I fled into my cell when I heard the keys rattling once again. The Reuters man crouched beside me, tense. But they weren't taking anyone, just pushing someone in.

I went out to find the upright, clean, handsome figure of Sandy Gall, and my heart rocketed with the reassurance that seeing him gave. He told me that Donald Wise had been deported. Then he asked what it was like in here. I said truthfully, 'A bloody nightmare!'

The next day men came and dug half a dozen grave-like pits outside our window. My heart plummeted. We're not going to be released at all, I thought. It's all a con. They're going to kill us. The party of vultures was again in position on the roof.

Then the guards told us, 'You're being released.'

Astles got up and said, 'What about me? Don't I get released.'

'Oh, no,' he was told. 'Not you, Bob.'

He seemed very sanguine about it. 'Maybe tomorrow,' he said. 'Maybe.'

We were taken to the huts and I rescued my suitcase from that piteous mountain. I felt a new spring in my ankles but joy had to be curbed. You can't show joy to those who stay behind.

As we made our way to the main gate indescribable screams pursued us. The Nubian officer with the lizard eyes was on gate duty and took offence at Sandy's look. He was affronted by Sandy's elegance, his cleanness, his composure. He walked across and said, 'Why are you looking at me? There is still time to chastise you, now, before you leave.'

Sandy pushed back his hair. 'I'm not looking at you, old boy,' he said. 'I can assure you.'

As we waited, listening to the terrible thrashing and screaming, there was the sound of a truck starting up. It produced intense joy in me and an undercurrent of fear. What if it wasn't release after all? I had heard that some people went from Makindye to the forests outside Kampala, where bishops and other religious people had been disposed of by Amin. Maybe even now we were being duped.

At Entebbe Airport they gave me the most pleasing document of my life – a certificate of deportation from Uganda. John Fairhall and the *Telegraph* man were reunited with us. They had been in quarters next to the execution block, and we heard with numbness that the sledgehammer tales were true, and more that was unbearable. We trashed our filthy clothes, and on the plane Sandy said, 'Champagne all round, I think.'

Fog diverted the flight from London to Manchester. For four hours after landing we stood back to back with commuting businessmen on a packed train to London. The British Rail restaurant car hadn't been attached. It was, even so, still heaven.

The fields were peaceful around our new farmhouse home

near Bishop's Stortford. Idi Amin's Uganda seemed like another world, though. Makindye had reached into the English countryside. The shock of believing I had been killed brought Christine out in great red blotches. It took two years for them to clear.

25

HANDSHAKE BEFORE HIGHWAY 13

A BRIEF SOCIAL interlude followed quickly on my return from Uganda before I found myself back in the thick of the fighting in south-east Asia. It might seem like a punishing schedule – for both me and my family – but I had accepted the invitation to go to Peking some months before. It was not so much an assignment, more an appointment with history.

With the Cultural Revolution behind them, the Chinese were confident enough to receive honoured British guests while simultaneously responding cordially to President Nixon's overtures, so enabling China to play a pivotal role in bringing to an end America's long and discredited war in Asia. These great political matters concerned me less than the business of photographing a handshake. A pioneer of the British sortie was my own boss, Lord Thomson, the proprietor of both *The Times* and the *Sunday Times*. He had approached me, before Kampala, to be the official photographer of the historic Anglo-Chinese friendship sealing moment when he shook hands with Chou En-lai. Also in the party were Denis Hamilton, the editor-in-chief, Frank Giles, the *Sunday Times* foreign editor, Louis Heren, a seasoned correspondent who later became deputy editor of *The Times*, and Lord Thomson's son Kenneth, heir apparent to the newspaper empire.

On the face of it, our proprietor had few of the conventional attributes of a trans-Atlantic tycoon who was to strike oil in the North Sea. He was below average height and his homely features were dominated by thick pebble-lens glasses which were said to be made especially for enlarging the tiny print of the financial columns. He made it a policy to appoint strong editors and keep his own interference to a minimum. Despite his legendary reputation for meanness, he financed big expansion plans for both papers. As he edged towards his eightieth year, one young journalist had the temerity to ask him if there was anything he thought he had missed in life. Lord Thomson reckoned that he had missed something in not having a proper university education – though perhaps not, he added, for 'then I would have wound up like you, working for a guy like me'.

Most of us endured the nineteen-hour flight, fidgeting and trying in vain to get some sleep, while our proprietor showed no sign of discomfort or irritability. He read a book, located no more than three inches from his nose, throughout the entire flight. Curious to know what he thought it necessary to equip himself with for his conversations with the great Chinese Communist leaders, I kept craning for a glimpse of the book's title but could see no more than it was a thriller by Alistair Maclean.

We were welcomed in Peking by the Red Army ensemble playing the Eton boating songs and tunes from *The King and I*. On the great day, I carefully followed instructions and got into a suit – not my normal attire – well before the appointed hour. I even gilded the lily by shaving, though some misjudgment brought blood out on to my face. I dabbed at it with lavatory paper and all kinds of after-shave without any effect. When the call came to say that a limousine was waiting, I grabbed a handful of the coarse revolutionary paper and raced downstairs. In the chilly air I ripped off the paper that had stuck to my cheek and hung my face out of the car window to dry. As we arrived at the Great Hall a small river of blood was running down my neck.

I was still trying to load my cameras and at the same time staunch the flow when one of the top brass came up to me and said, 'Come along now, Donald, be ready. Be ready on the signal. They'll be here at any minute.'

Concerned Chinese hands were propelling me into position

for the historic encounter between Capitalism and Communism, symbolised by Lord Thomson and the Chinese premier pressing the flesh. It was the ultimate handshake picture.

I missed it.

Later, feeling pretty dejected, I was bullied into taking my place in a group photograph with the whole Thomson party and Chou's men. I stood forlornly at the end in my ill-fitting suit while the blood went on trickling down my face and neck. If Lord Thomson was upset, he didn't make a meal of it. What impressed me about him as I busied myself taking pictures through the three hours of talks – conducted through interpreters – that followed was his spitting precision. As a heavy smoker he had frequent recourse to the spittoon, which he never failed to hit dead centre.

Lord Thomson genially introduced me to Premier Chou as someone who had spent a long time in Vietnam. I was unsure to what extent this endeared me to the Chinese leader. Whatever he thought, I was soon back in Vietnam again to find the old war had taken a new turn.

The superior discipline and vastly improved armour of the Communists had turned the battle of Quang Tri into a rout. For the South Vietnamese this struggle for control in the north of their country represented the beginning of the end, but it was to be a long and bitter finale.

I was with the television reporter Michael Nicholson when we found two badly wounded soldiers at the side of the Quang Tri road and tried to flag down help from the truck-loads of their retreating comrades as they went thundering past. None would stop even for the moment it would take to pick up the injured. I became so angry that I snatched up an M-16 rifle from one of the wounded and tried to stop the next truck at gunpoint. It slowed down but then, as it drew close, speeded up again and roared past. I could hear Mike yelling at me. 'Don! You must be crazy. What would you have done if they'd started firing?'

The answer was not a lot, because my rifle had no

magazine. We managed to manhandle the wounded men on to the bonnet of Mike's car and drove very slowly to the nearest casualty station. Both soldiers died the next day.

At that time, in the early summer of 1972, another two dead in Vietnam meant little to anyone in Britain. Vietnam had become the forgotten war. The rage exhibited in the demos of the Sixties seemed to have been replaced by indifference. Because the Americans under President Nixon had greatly reduced their combat presence in Vietnam, it was assumed that the war had lost its ferocity. Nothing was further from the truth.

I went to Vietnam again with James Fox, the magazine correspondent, and William Shawcross, who was then writing for the news pages. There was a wide choice of battle zones to visit, and everywhere the North Vietnamese seemed to be on the advance. I decided to concentrate first on one of the more southerly theatres, on An Loc and Highway 13, where the close combat seemed to be at its bloodiest.

I had Alan Hart of BBC television to thank for getting me within range. I found him at a staging-area, with a helicopter organised and a full film crew, but minus the eyepiece for the camera. For the want of a little eyepiece they were all grounded, so I had the use of the helicopter.

Approaching An Loc, the fire was so intense that the pilot decided to set me down on a position behind a ridge about three kilometres from the town. As I got out an American adviser told me, 'You've come to the wrong place. This is a very bad place. We're taking a lot of rounds.'

It was already getting dark and I decided to dig in. I offered a sip from my brandy flask to a passing American solider, who declined. Seconds later we found ourselves on the receiving end of the night's first incoming shells and I had this big soldier on top of me in my pathetic little hole, almost crushing the life out of me.

'You know what?' he said when there was a pause in the shelling. 'I could sure use some of that brandy now.'

It was an appalling night under shell fire. Next morning I heard automatic gunfire and got out my field glasses. I could see men all over the landscape, running through paddy fields and down hedgerows. They were coming in our direction, South Vietnamese paratroopers in full flight, many of them carrying heavy red wounds.

A helicopter came down by the ridge and I persuaded the pilot to take me out. Then a party of wounded arrived, and they were all loaded in around me. We flew back to my original staging-area, which looked somehow different. Something was missing. While I was away overnight, VC sappers had crept in and blown 800 tons of ammunition sky high. For concentrated devastation those twenty-four hours were among the nastiest of my life – which said something for the resilience of the Forgotten War. Some South Vietnamese units were suffering as many as 50 per cent casualties.

The suffering caused by the An Loc battle was over-whelming. James Fox interviewed a pregnant woman who was the wife of an An Loc police officer. A bomb from a South Vietnamese plane had hit her house, killing her father, brother and three children. She herself was wounded and some North Vietnamese soldiers put her arm in a splint. Eight days later her husband was killed at a police post by a B-40 rocket. Her only other relative, a younger sister, had been arrested by the North Vietnamese.

After my retreat from An Loc, I took to probing up Highway 13 every day with an American friend in his big old car. We would load up with cold beers, park a mile or so from the action, and walk the rest of the way.

The action on Highway 13 was astonishing to see, especially when the B-52s bombed in such concentration that you could swear nothing would be left alive for miles around. Minutes after the bombers had gone overhead the North Vietnamese would come out of their bunkers and start inflicting more casualties.

One day I was asked if I could deliver some mail to two Americans in a forward position, and so found myself acting as the crawling postman. Ensconced in a culvert by the road, I was assailed by a metallic screaming noise unlike any sound of battle I had heard before. A white flame seemed to be

184

bobbing with the contours of the road ahead, and it was coming my way fast. The missile went past me and headed on for the M-60 tank coming up behind. It made a direct hit.

I went back to the colonel to ask if he'd be kind enough to figure out an alternative postal service and found him pointing to the gruesome sight of a man in an armoured personnel carrier, holding the wheel but without a head on his shoulders. His commander, who had been thrown twenty yards down the road, was being picked up and folded like a child's rag doll.

Besides the B-52s, there were also the Cobra helicopter gunships, crewed by the wildest Americans around. They would drop calling cards on their targets with messages like 'Killing is our business and the business is good', or 'The Lord giveth and the 20mm taketh away'. I wondered too what the conquerors made of graffiti in the lavatories in Quang Tri when it fell: 'Withdrawal is something that Nixon's father should have done 58 years ago.' It certainly expressed a common feeling among South Vietnamese that their country's fate had nothing to do with their President Thieu and everything to do with the Americans.

I came across some South Vietnamese soldiers rejoicing over the kill of a North Vietnamese medic. They were horsing around with an NVA flag and making gestures with their penises as if to pee on the body. In the midst of their celebration I saw a little red book and asked the lieutenant if I could have it. He had to play with me for a while, pretending to rip it up, but eventually he gave it to me. It was a diary, meticulously kept, and I wanted it to have a further journey, a further life. Eventually extracts from it appeared in translation in the *Sunday Times* under the banner 'Diary of a North Vietnamese Soldier'.

Cambodia was regarded as no more than a sideshow to Vietnam, and, in consequence, it received little attention. As Vietnam faded from the news, Cambodia disappeared almost without trace. Yet when I next visited Cambodia, in the spring of 1973, the country was literally being torn apart.

Caught between the ravages of American bombing and the cruelties of the Khmer Rouge, it was now a land of refugees. Almost a third of the seven million population had been forced to flee their homes.

I arrived in Pnom Penh to find that the main topic of conversation among the press corps was a German photographer who had persuaded a Cambodian soldier to cut off the heads of dead Khmer soldiers and hold them up for his camera. It was enough to tell me that war-freaks were in the ascendant.

I couldn't get out of Pnom Penh fast enough. I went down to the airfield and hitched a ride on the first old Dakota going south. The friendly Taiwanese pilot eventually brought us down expertly on a road that had been converted into a runway. There was a little township nearby, but I forget its name. People were waiting to get on for the flight back, among them a lady who took an interest in what I was doing. She said her chauffeur would be pleased to drive me into town.

No sooner did we reach this little town than I heard news that came as a sickening shock. It hit me like a heavy blow to the solar plexus. The old Dakota that had deposited me here less than an hour earlier had been blasted to smithereens by the Khmer Rouge at the end of the runway as it was taking off again. Everyone on board had been killed, including the friendly lady whose driver had just dropped me off and the Taiwanese pilot with whom I had been on such good terms on the flight in.

I felt a rush of panic. If the Khmers were that close to the airstrip they were much too close to me. My nerve started giving out as it had never done before under fire in the thick of battle. Ghastly images of savage Khmers bludgeoning me to death invaded my mind and wouldn't let go. Soldiers fighting, however fiercely, was one thing but to end up one of a million corpses in the Khmers' killing fields was something else, and I just wanted to be out of it. I junked my US army fatigues, bought some cheap regular clothes and made my way back to the airstrip to spend most of the day using too much imagination.

Nothing was taking off. My stomach churned in a knot of fearful tension. Towards five o'clock in the afternoon I heard the distant sound of an aero engine and prayed that it would make a stopover. Pandemonium broke out as the aircraft circled a few times before landing. A fat Chinese man, who seemed to be in charge, waved me away when I asked him if I could be taken to Pnom Penh. Once the cargo was unloaded the aircraft would return almost empty, but he kept shouting that I couldn't go because I was not on the manifest. When his attention was diverted I threw my gear into the DC3 and climbed aboard.

'Come down, mister,' the irate man called as he spotted me. When I refused he surrendered with a shrug and the plane took off almost vertically, like a rocket. I gazed down at the ashes of the morning's tragedy, still smouldering, as we banked steeply away.

Nightmares dogged my sleep long after I returned home from Pnom Penh, and to this day I carry a scarred memory of the time when I experienced fear running riot.

26

DEATH ON THE GOLAN HEIGHTS

WITH THE AMERICAN retreat from war in south-east Asia went a parallel decline in American enthusiasm for Israel in the Middle East. The Arab oil cartel changed perspectives there, and in October 1973 an emboldened Egypt and Syria mounted a lightning assault on their old enemy during the Yom Kippur holiday.

It was like an echo of Ho Chi Minh's successful Tet Offensive, and I was sent in with a full *Sunday Times* team to cover the war from the Israeli side. On 17 October, in the second week of conflict, my colleague Nick Tomalin was killed on the Golan Heights front. The car he was driving, some distance ahead of mine, was blown to pieces by a Syrian wire-guided missile.

Nick was forty-two and, many of us thought, the best English journalist of his generation. He was one of those writers who could do everything well, from turning a funny gossip paragraph to producing long and moving dispatches from the front line. His feature, 'The General Goes Zapping Charlie Cong', opened more eyes to the war in Vietnam than a thousand photographs could ever have done. There were many on the *Sunday Times* who thought that Nick should become the editor in the unlikely event of Harry Evans tiring of the job, and I was one of them. He was no popularity-seeker; indeed he could be prickly and sharp with those who displeased him, but I cannot think of a single journalist who did not admire him.

We had never previously gone to war together, though we

often operated in the same theatres. This was not entirely a matter of coincidence; like me, Nick had a preference for working alone. Unlike the Six Day War, when some correspondents failed to turn up until after the last shot had been fired, the entire *Sunday Times* photographic first team – Steve Brodie, Frank Hermann, Sally Soames, Romano Cagnoni and my old friend Bryan Wharton – were soon in action. With the benefit of surprise, and greatly improved military discipline, the Egyptians chose the Day of Atonement to attack from the south while almost simultaneously the Syrians piled in from the north. We all knew this would be longer and bloodier than the 1967 engagement.

I made for the Golan Heights where the Syrians had taken out a good deal of Israeli armour in fierce fighting. As the light began to fade on my first recce I made my way to a kibbutz where a number of photographers had agreed to meet for a meal. We pushed a few tables together and made a party of it. Apart from his commitment, there was no need for Nick Tomalin, as a writer, to be so close to the front. I can remember him turning round imperiously and saying, 'You know, something has struck me as very strange about you photographers. Not one of you has asked for the bloody wine list.'

He had arrived in Israel before me and was enjoying himself, shooting out that slightly cockeyed look from behind his glasses to see if everybody was with him. Already he had sent home a detailed brief on the war's progress by smuggling it past the censor in the shoe of a friend returning to London. It provided the core for the Insight team's story, and it was typical of Nick to contribute in this way to team efforts on the *Sunday Times*. Now the essential individualist would, I knew, be out to get a big story of his own.

Nick drew me aside before going to bed. 'I heard you have a spare combat jacket,' he said. 'Would you loan it to me? Can I come and get it in the morning?' I assumed he was teaming up with Frank Hermann to go to the front.

I was lacing my army boots at around 6 am when the tap on the door came and Nick was standing there with an air of impatience.

189

'Can I have that jacket you said you'd lend me? I want to get away now . . .'

'Shouldn't you wait for Frank?' I said.

'No, I can't,' Nick said. 'I've got an arrangement with this man from *Stern* magazine. He's got a Peugeot, and I told him I drive a Peugeot. So I'm going to act as chauffeur while he takes his pictures.'

I asked about Frank again, but Nick snatched up the combat jacket and raced off. 'See you later,' he called over his shoulder. That was the last time I saw him alive.

An hour or so later, when the rest of us had sorted ourselves into two cars and had been gathered up by the inescapable Israeli escort, we began to move slowly up towards the Golan Heights. Tanks hidden in groups of cypress trees caught my eye. A black pall of smoke rose from a valley some way ahead. Soon an Israeli officer in the road was flagging us down.

'Will you stop here please,' he said. 'You cannot get any further. There's been one journalist killed already. A man from the Sunday Times.'

I got out and went straight up to him. 'Listen, I'm from the Sunday Times. What's happening?'

'I don't know, and you cannot go to see. The car was hit by the Syrians. They're just over there and, as you can see, we're here. Your friend was in the line of Syrian fire.'

There could be no certainty that Nick was dead. Perhaps he was critically wounded and waiting for help. I thought of his wife Claire, and of my own family and of what they would have a right to expect if I were lying badly wounded. I became like a man possessed, taken over by madness, no longer in control. I put down my cameras and pulled on a helmet. I ran in a stooped position to make my head less vulnerable. It was extraordinarily quiet. 'Why are you doing this? Why are you doing this?' a voice in my head kept saying. I passed dead Syrian soldiers lying near some knocked-out Russian tanks.

There was no chance of going unobserved by either side and I expected to stop an AK-47 round at any moment. If I could see the shape of a body, I told myself, I'll turn back. No one could survive in that blaze. I was angry, willing Nick to be alive so that I could take him back. When I got nearer, I could see no shape in the car. Perhaps he had been thrown out. I made my way round to the other side of it and found him lying there. I tried to talk to him, so far gone was I with terror and grief, though there could be no doubt that he was dead. Picking up his glasses from the road, I ran back in the same eerie stillness.

I was speechless when I returned. Terror had drained the moisture from my body, from my lips and my mouth. I gulped down mouthfuls of brandy. I clambered into the back of a car where I could shed the tears for Claire and his kids in private.

On the way back to Tel Aviv we talked, and it didn't take long to piece together what had happened. Nick's German companion had been Fred Ihrt, one of *Stern*'s senior staff photographers and a very experienced operator. They had seen the dead Syrians by the burnt-out tanks and Nick had turned the car down the narrow side road. When Fred leapt out and started taking pictures, Nick had driven on a little way to where the road widened out and he could do a three-point turn. The missile hit the car as it was returning to collect the photographer. With a spare five-gallon drum of petrol behind the driver's seat, the explosion had been devastating.

Philip Jacobson met me in the hotel lobby. 'You're to go back to London, did you know?' he said. 'Message from Harry says he doesn't want you taking any more chances. Frank, too.'

At the airport I was singled out for a disagreeable strip-search. I was never given a reason for the humiliation. Maybe they had me logged from the time of the Six Day War, when I had managed to evade the censors. If they were trying to lay hands on my Yom Kippur pictures they were wasting their time, for they didn't exist.

27

THE TRIBE WHO KILLED CHRIST

THE QUESTION I'M most often asked about going to war is – how much danger money did you get? And I can always detect a certain incredulity when I give the only possible answer: 'None.'

I have a letter of contract, dated 13 February 1974 – almost exactly ten years after I started going to the wars – in which the *Sunday Times* agrees to pay me £5,392.80 a year, in return for which I am pledged to make myself available 47 weeks of the year, and not to work for any other British national newspaper. Work for any other publication of any kind had to be cleared with the editor of the magazine, and while I retained the copyright of my pictures, Times Newspapers could use them at any time without a fee.

While £5,000 was certainly a reasonable wage in those days, it was no more than was paid to senior sub-editors who never emerged from behind the security of their desks in Gray's Inn Road. Compared with earnings in the field of advertising and fashion photography, it was of course not even modest.

There is no reason to believe war correspondents are less grasping than other human beings, but I have never come across one who went to war to get rich. There were some journalists, good ones too, who would not go to war if you gave them the Mint. Others would show up at the front without permission and no more than a faint hope of recouping their expenses. Like every other journalist, war correspondents might expect a bit extra, usually in terms of time off, after a good or a particularly harrowing job, but danger money never came into it. And really, when you think about it, the idea is laughable. The amount of money that would compensate you adequately for getting your head blown off doesn't exist.

My life, though, was about to enter one of its less dangerous phases. The death of Nick Tomalin had been a brutal shock. Nick had been good friends with most of the top executives on the newspaper, with Harry Evans in particular, and while unquestionably he had acted on his own initiative, the question arose as to whether he would have used his initiative in this way if so much had not been expected of him, or if there had not been so much enthusiasm for going to the limit for the paper.

Inevitably Nick's death cast a shadow over the paper's swashbuckling style. I cannot remember a memo on the subject going round, but there was a definite sense of reining in, of a new caution, particularly in the foreign field. It was a change of mood rather than a decision, and for that reason its effects went deeper.

The main consequence for me was that I found myself doing more but safer assignments. This trend was accelerated by a change of magazine editorship. Under Godfrey Smith, and his young successor Magnus Linklater, I had enjoyed the easiest of rides. Both were genuinely curious about foreign parts and would, after little persuasion, allow me to go almost where I pleased. This situation changed when Linklater gave place to Hunter Davies who, though a very considerable journalist, made no secret of the fact that he was less than infatuated with happenings beyond Dover.

For eighteen months I didn't cover a war of any sort, though I was rarely idle. Coming from Carlisle, Hunter Davies was keen on the North and I was up there several times, photographing Hadrian's Wall at its best and the dust-ridden steel town of Consett at its consistent worse. After Consett we got a lot of flak. A local schoolmaster wrote in: 'Now that your reporter and photographer have crawled back to their holes in London, we're rather proud of our . . .' I'm always amazed by how lovable awfulness can become.

I took a spin around Japan with Alex Mitchell who was charmed by the opportunity to dismember the corporate state, and I did a long story about racist hoodlums in Marseille with Bruce Chatwin. We tried to trace hoods who machine-gunned Algerian settlements by night, but there was also a High Society element to the investigation.

One evening Bruce and I were invited to dinner by the estranged wife of the Mayor of Marseille who seemed to occupy the official residence with a woman friend while the mayor and his new lady were away. As the wine flowed the two women started competing for Bruce's favours. The mayor's wife brought out all her jewellery, which she had had crushed into a huge dice. She threw it on the table, saying, 'I've had my jewellery refashioned.' Not to be outdone, her companion then brought out her own dice and threw it down. Bruce sat there egging them on with that angelic, mischievous face thrown back in laughter, and that is the image of him that came back to me when I heard of his tragic death in 1989.

The most interesting enterprise of this peace period was the investigation I made with Norman Lewis of the disappearances of Aché Indians in Paraguay. When a new road to Argentina was driven through the rain forest habitat of the 'white Indians' – as the Achés are called because of their light skin colour – land prices shot up and Indian hunts began. Many of those captured were taken to a camp at Cecilio Baez and about half that number never seen again. In response to an international outcry, the Paraguayan government dismissed the camp's administration and invited the American missionary group, the New Tribes Mission, to take over. Norman Lewis was not reassured.

The New Tribes Mission drew support from the born-again Christians in the Bible belt of the American South. It was aggressive in its pursuit of Indian souls and not too fastidious in its methods.

To Norman's mind, the way the missionaries attracted Indians with gifts of knives, axes and mirrors as bait, and then would 'integrate' them into their settlements, was scarcely better than methods adopted by the more rough-hewn Indian-hunters. Those Indians who didn't die of white man's diseases (like the common cold) were rapidly demoralised and, in white man's hand-me-downs, fitted only for poverty-stricken lives in the teeming city slums. The Indian clearing services provided by the missionaries were appreciated by many Latin American dictatorships who would show their appreciation by handing over chunks of land. A Paraguayan army officer once told Norman that missionaries were more efficient at clearing Indian areas than the army. 'When we go in we shoot some, and some get away. They get the lot. When the missionaries clear an area they leave it clean.'

Norman and I flew to the Paraguayan capital of Asunción with the idea of seeing conditions in Cecilio Baez for ourselves. The Paraguay of General Stroessner, Latin America's most enduring dictator, was not a place that disgorged its secrets easily. It was probably this discretion that made it attractive to the many Nazi war criminals who lived there. When Norman spoke about our mission to a distinguished local anthropologist in Asunción, he was advised against seeking a permit from the Ministry of Defence. The best method was to go in by village bus with two hired trusties, otherwise we might be the ones to disappear.

We decided to enlist the help of the British Embassy and found a willing accomplice there in Julio, a Paraguayan schoolteacher who worked part-time on the Embassy staff. It was Julio who smoothed our way to the Ministry of Defence, where we met polite, but vigorous, attempts to dissuade us. The official explained his reluctance to give us a permit by reference to his last bad experience. He said that a French couple, ostensibly on a scientific mission, had filmed the Aché in Cecilio Baez indulging in sexual intercourse and that this film had surfaced in the blue movie parlours of Panama. Then, after a few days, the barriers seemed to come down and conveniently Julio found the time to drive us halfway across Paraguay to Cecilio Baez in his 2 CV.

It was a long drive and heavy rains made the dirt road impassable. We diverted for the night to Julio's home in Caazapá. Julio was a most entertaining companion, chatty and well-read, but I remember Norman saying to me that he had never before come across a schoolmaster who held himself in quite the way he did. That evening Norman came up to me and said with a quiet chuckle, 'I accidentally opened the door to Julio's room and saw our schoolmaster buckling on an automatic pistol. He also had a dagger strapped just above his right ankle.'

Next day Julio showed us how to have a good time in Caazapá in the rain. He explained that vendetta duels used to be conducted conveniently close to the cemetery. Since the showing of the film *High Noon*, they tended to be held in the main street. A sudden buzz of excitement led me to believe a duel was being laid on for our benefit, but it was only a local bullfight.

I became excited photographing the storm clouds and the effects on the light, and this obviously moved Julio, who told me I was opening his eyes to the beauties of Paraguay. And while I didn't feel nervous of Julio, whose presence was presumably designed to protect us, I thought it reassuring that the man with a gun should admire what I did.

It became clear that this particular mission to Cecilio Baez would have to be aborted, but there was one more diversion on the way back to Asunción. In the little town of Coronel Oviedo there lived the Great Witch of Paraguay. Her name was Maria Calavera (Mary Skull) and General Perón of Argentina was said to have been one of her regular clients. Her speciality was helping people to put their affairs in order by predicting for them the exact date of their death.

This was not the kind of information that I was keen to acquire, but Norman couldn't resist. I'm not sure what he got out of Mary Skull but he had a quiet smile on his face when he returned to the car.

We made another run to Cecilio Baez a couple of days later, this time in a Landrover with a driver (again referred to us through the British Embassy) who was an English veterinary surgeon with no discernible armament about his person.

Clearly we were unwelcome at the camp. The head missionary, who looked like a crop-haired marine, grumbled about our turning up three days after we were expected. With a slight edge of surprise on our side, we tried to allay his concern by saying we had no intention of making blue movies as the French couple had. The missionary looked blank. There had never been a 'French couple'. He surprised us by saying he had 300 Indians in the camp, for this was considerably more than we had been led to believe and suggested that mission care was indeed keeping more Indians alive. He explained that the overriding purpose was to bring salvation to those in a state of sin. All the missionaries in Cecilio Baez 'worked with the unreached'.

While Norman was still talking, I slipped away and started taking photographs. The stench of neglected sanitation in the hutted camp area was overpowering. One thing soon became obvious: there were nothing like 300 Aché in this camp – at most there were 50 Indians, all of them in pitiful condition. The young children all had distended stomachs and decayed teeth that told of malnutrition. The adults all seemed unfocused and listless. Some of the young missionaries hovered uncertainly around me while I took pictures, though I achieved some immunity when a little flaxen-haired boy, the son of one of the missionaries, decided to take a liking to me. I accepted his offer to carry my tripod.

As I went over to a little hut, a missionary started gesturing no admittance. I went in and found two old Aché women, emaciated and very close to death. In the next hut lay a young woman with untreated wounds, a small tearful boy beside her. I asked my missionary boy what had happened and he, unaware of the grown-ups' party line that everybody in Cecilio Baez had come there voluntarily, told me the truth. All three women and the boy, he said, had been taken in a recent forest round-up; the youngest woman had been shot in the side while trying to escape.

This confirmed Norman's evidence, from other sources, that some of the missionaries went on Indian-catching raids. Indeed, it was wholly impossible to credit the notion that the Aché could be 'attracted' to this place without coercion. It could be that the missionaries were saving Indian souls but the evidence of neglect of their bodies was there to be seen.

While we were going about our business the younger missionaries formed up a rank and sang hymns. Norman described it as the most sinister experience of his life, and it wasn't a moment I wanted to prolong.

We tangled again with the New Tribes Mission some years later when Norman heard a curious story about the Panare Indians who lived in the Venezuelan interior. The Panare were known for their immunity to any white man's attempt to civilise them, and resistance to evangelism was enchanted by the lack in Panare language of words for sin, punishment and guilt.

A census-taker had come across a Panare community in the Colorado Valley and had tape-recorded them singing their ancestral songs. She returned a year later with the intention of playing back the songs to entertain the Indians. Once the tape-recorder was switched on, the Indians leapt up in panic and denounced the voice of the devil. For Norman, this was a sure sign of New Tribes Mission activity.

We made the expedition to the Panare in the company of Paul Henley, an anthropologist who spoke their language and who was an adopted member of the tribe. The first Panare we saw told the whole story. He was a young man in the traditional red woven loincloth astride a bicycle bearing the message 'Christ Saves Us'. The Panare, it seemed, had been half-saved, incorporating bits and pieces of Christian culture but essentially going their own way.

We were allocated one of the thatched longhouses and made welcome – up to a point. The Colorado Valley Panare did not want me to photograph them. At first I thought this might be a prohibition imposed by the NTM missionaries, but then the missionaries all took off in their charter plane soon after our arrival, leaving behind them a piggy bank for every Panare child and a reworked version of the Crucifixion story in which the Panare killed Christ. It was still 'no photographs', even after the missionaries had gone.

The Panare are a highly photogenic people, lithe and graceful in movement, and I could just imagine the art editor's response if I got back saying, 'Listen, they were really amazing-looking Indians but I don't have any pictures.' I started trying to win hearts and minds with my small repertoire of conjuring tricks and succeeded in elevating my status with the Panare children. The adults were harder to crack. Paul Henley told me that my best chance of beating the ban would be to photograph them in some kind of action. The opportunity came with a most unusual fishing expedition.

The operation began with a trip into the mountains to cut down quantities of a liana called enerima before the Panare gathered in force on a quiet reach of the Tortuga river, a tributary of the Orinoco. Some fifty Indians lined the bank while the lianas were crushed and put into baskets which were then rinsed in the flowing water. In a couple of minutes the water began to turn milky. Soon you could see fish leaping out of the river and going doolally. This was the signal for the Panare to move in with their spears. Norman estimated the full catch at around a ton.

The enerima must have contained some kind of nerve poison. It did not kill fish but just paralysed or stunned them temporarily. While this astonishing spectacle was in progress I was able to take photographs almost at will, though photographing the Panare remained a delicate and difficult matter.

From Colorado Valley we would make excursions to other smaller Panare communities. Some of these required Norman and me to undertake intrepid treks across country, even wading rivers waist deep. In one such crossing Norman, who was ahead of me, stopped to draw my attention to a host of humming birds skittering along the bank. Suddenly he began hopping up and down alarmingly in the water.

'What is it?' I said. 'What's wrong?'

'I'm not sure, dear boy,' his benign voice floated back to me as he tried to regain his composure. 'Feels as if something is biting at my crotch.'

The cause of this discomfort was not easy to discover but

eventually we spotted the tiny fish, only a few millimetres long, that were trying to make a meal of poor Norman's genitals.

The most bizarre location we visited was close to a diamond mining township called Tiro Loco (Crazy Shot). There the Indians traded fresh vegetables for the miners' pots and pans.

Norman bore with me while I enjoyed some freedom among the diamond miners. They were some of the most evil-looking characters I had ever come across, but that didn't seem to inhibit them from asking me to take their pictures. Here you could actually see drunks being pitched head first out of saloons into the street, though we were assured by one citizen that you had to work hard to get yourself shot. The only hotel in town turned out to be a whorehouse. While neither Norman nor I was accustomed to frequenting such places, it excited me to be taking my first whorehouse pictures. For me the whole place was rather like grabbing at a live wire.

As the light faded I took to gulping down quantities of local beer, known as Pola, while a raucous crowd was assembling for the cock fight. Through the haze I became aware of Norman saying, 'Have you finished your work?' Yes, I suppose I had, I admitted in a slurred voice. 'Well then, shall we go?' he said. As ever Norman's delicate invitation had the force of a command.

28

WAITING FOR POL POT

THE KHMER ROUGE were busy in the spring of 1975 dropping Russian rockets on the Cambodian capital, Pnom Penh, and killing people left, right and centre. Thousands of mines laid around the city were claiming a dozen amputees daily. The airport was under constant fire from Khmers who had overrun all the country save this last small enclave around the capital. Even twelve-year-olds were being kitted out by a beleaguered government, handed an Armalite each and pushed into the front-line defences.

The situation was so desperate when I arrived it was hard to know where to begin. Combat photography seemed almost inconsequential beside the real story taking place in the hospitals, where conditions could only be described as Crimean. Patients with ghastly wounds littered the floors while the few remaining doctors tried to keep pace with demands for emergency surgery. There was no time for bedside manner or finesse of any sort. I watched a twelve-month-old baby having the wound left by its amputated arm stitched hurriedly as if it were an old football. The speed-sewer was not a doctor but the only man available who could work with a needle. While the blood-letting went on all around Pnom Penh operations were being cancelled for a lack of blood transfusions. Along with the carnage went the starvation. More than 50 babies a week were said to be dying from malnutrition.

When the Red Cross started to withdraw their medical teams, I knew that the writing was on the wall. Pnom Penh and every person in it would soon be at the untender mercy of

Pol Pot, the fanatical leader of the Khmer Rouge. For correspondents it was big decision time – whether to stay or go. The Khmers had already bumped off more than twenty correspondents; disposing of a few more would give them little trouble. Yet to people like Jon Swain the idea of leaving the city seemed like a betrayal, like walking out of a theatre before the last act.

I was very much of the cut and run party. Not through cowardice but as a matter of common sense, though eventually the moral authority for the decision was taken out of my hands. Harry Evans sent me a cable requesting me to move on to Saigon. I remember Martin Woollacott drawing me to one side and saying, 'I'd be careful in Saigon if I were you, as I do believe your name is on a blacklist.' To be honest, I didn't think much of the warning because I didn't see how a government on the verge of collapse could be much concerned about who was taking the photographs. I also thought it would be a lot healthier in Saigon than in Pnom Penh when the Communists came marching in.

Indeed, everyone thought that the Khmers would prove to be much crueller than the North Vietnamese in victory, though nobody anticipated the genocidal nightmare that was to come under Pol Pot's regime in Cambodia.

I flew into Bangkok on the day after receiving Harry's message and shipped my Cambodia film back to London. For security reasons, I usually carry my film back, but I had no idea how long I would be in Vietnam or what communications would survive the crunch. As I boarded the aeroplane for Saigon, I received a curious amplification of Woollacott's warning from John Pilger of the *Daily Mirror*.

'I don't want you to think I'm being funny,' he said, 'but would you do me a favour. When we arrive in Saigon, would you totally detach yourself and not have anything to do with me. Because if you are on the blacklist, I don't want to draw attention to myself by being with you. So if you don't mind – nothing against you meant by it, of course.'

I didn't hold anything against John either, because I knew he was only protecting his ability to operate and do his work.

All the same I couldn't help feeling a bit leprous as we touched down and I watched John disappear through passport control. No hold-up on his part. Then I presented my own passport. The official disappeared with it for five minutes and then came back with a squad of 'white mice', as the Saigon police were called, determination written on their faces.

'You very bad man,' they told me, 'you no stay in Vietnam. You go, you go, you go now, back to Bangkok.'

There was a rush as they tried to overpower me, a lot of pushing and shoving and a bit of a scuffle. I crashed back on a desk, breaking an airport telephone. An officer told me I was on a special list of people who were not friends of Vietnam, and there was no way I could enter the country. I was locked in a little room to cool off. At no stage was I told why I was on this special blacklist, though I could only imagine it was because of my coverage in 1972 when I had photographed a demoralised South Vietnamese army in flight from Quang Tri.

From a window in the room I could see a number of English journalists drifting about, among whom I spotted my friend Mike Nicholson from ITN and quite a few others. I shouted through the grille to attract attention, and to find out what was going on. It turned out that David English of the *Daily Mail* had chartered a whole aeroplane to take Vietnamese war orphans back to England. I knew there was little chance now of my entering Vietnam, but I might at least avoid being sent back to Bangkok.

I managed to get out a request for a seat on the refugee plane. And the message from David English came back, 'You're welcome absolutely to join us, but would you do one thing? Would you mind caring for one of the children on the flight?' I got word back that I'd be delighted, and I was on.

Once the Vietnamese realised that I was prepared to go quietly, any further objections dissolved. I got back my passport and joined David on the runway. My long experience of Vietnam ended with a flight home cradling a nine-year-old spastic boy and a pretty three-year-old girl with a gigantic abscess on the side of her face.

29

A CHRISTIAN MASSACRE

I FIRST VISITED Beirut in 1965 when its decadence had style. While staying at the Palm Beach Hotel, I decided to cross the road one day for lunch in the St George, the last known watering hole of superspy Kim Philby before he surfaced in Moscow. Philby was evidently more of an English gentleman than me – I was turned away for not wearing a tie.

Below that surface correctness, Beirut was a raffish place. The city excelled in the provision of drugs, brothels and financial services. It was like one great big racket that worked for everybody – or everybody with money. It was also known as the safest place in the Middle East. The greatest danger in Beirut when I first went there was of being knocked down by a whole Lebanese family parading on Hamra Street in high Gucci fashion.

Journalists were drawn to the place, partly for its quality as a listening-post in the Arab world, but chiefly because its communications were so good. I must have passed through Beirut half a dozen times without actually working in the Lebanon. The last such stopover was in 1974, when James Fox and I had completed our portrait of the new king of Saudi Arabia in an opulent apartment owned by the arms dealer Adnan Khashoggi. I was offered a lift back to Beirut in Mrs Khashoggi's private aircraft, which was equipped with a cinema and a good supply of expensive chocolates that Soraya Khashoggi's entourage consumed in great quantity when they weren't playfully throwing them around. Finsbury Park never seemed so far away.

When we landed in Beirut, Soraya said, 'I expect you to take me to dinner tonight,' and that sent a shiver of fear down my spine. We ate Lebanese in a small restaurant near the harbour, and then she expected me to go dancing, which produced another stab of fear for I was well out of practice. I was relieved finally to make my escape from the high life of the rich in Beirut. That style had only a few more months to run, and even as I played the tongue-tied escort I detected that something strange was in the air.

For years the whole structure of Lebanese society had been biased to protect the economic and political privileges of the elite, which was mainly Christian. The Christians had the politics tied up with their hold on the Presidency and a system of representation that ensured the Muslims, no matter how numerous, could never achieve power. It was a Levantine version of Northern Ireland, yet with guns even more freely available. The social divide was also important. As the rich Lebanese got richer, so the poor became destitute. To this explosive mixture were added the Palestinians, who had descended on Lebanon in huge numbers after the sacking of their bases in Jordan in 1970.

As the slum areas and Muslim ghettos of Beirut expanded they overlapped the Palestinian refugee camps. Pressure on the city increased further with the arrival of more refugees from the Israeli bombing in the South. Alliances between the Left and the Palestinians began to form and the predominantly right-wing Christians became more and more paranoid about keeping a grip on what they had come to regard as *their* country. Their most concentrated venom was reserved for the Palestinians.

One morning a bus full of Palestinian schoolchildren was riddled with fire and all the enmities erupted at once. The serious fighting began in April 1975 and the business and banking district in central Beirut was soon a battlefield. The kidnappings were worse than the shelling, for these were the expression of long pent-up hatreds. The bodies of the unfortunate victims – some with their private parts cut off – would usually be found in the rubbish dump a day or two later. There's nothing worse than vengeance in the Middle East.

When I climbed aboard my flight from Heathrow to Beirut in November 1975 I could tell that the rich had already made good their escape. There was not a soul in the first-class compartment. Desperate for company and conversation, the pilot summoned me up to the flight-deck and plied me with rather more drink than I could normally handle. I sobered at the sight of the Beirut skyline. I could clearly see the Hotel St George and nearby the Holiday Inn and the Phoenicia lit up by gunfire.

The airport buildings were lit by candles, which gave a sinister slant to formalities like passport control and getting a taxi, and when a policeman took my taxi driver to one side for a quiet talk I became unreasonably nervous. I knew that I would have to keep my imagination in order.

We drove through the darkened city, eerie without lights. There had been many cases of people being killed in their baths by snipers at night, or while just watching television. The snipers were still there on the Moor Tower, a large unfurnished building, and in the abandoned hotels which looked down on West Beirut. But the population had learned how to make their ugly job more difficult after dark.

I checked in at the Commodore Hotel within earshot of sporadic firing. Several thousand rounds would go out before the night was through. The Commodore itself enjoyed some limited immunity from the conflict due to its reputation as the overseas journalists' main hangout. Two local newspapermen had been tortured and killed, and had their tongues cut out and their eyes gouged, but the Western press escaped the worst. Even the most murderous factions were keen to impress the justness of their cause upon the world.

My problem was deciding which faction to follow. Colleagues I spoke to in the hotel thought I would have a hard time with the Left or the Palestinians. They would not let you see any action first-hand and their propaganda machine was too sophisticated – you were taken to see only what they wanted you to see.

I went off to get myself attached to the Christian Falange. I crossed the Green Line, an imaginary dividing line between the factions in the Muslim area, and made my way to Ashrafiyah district, a Christian stronghold. I found the Falange headquarters there and experienced no difficulty over accreditation.

They gave me a pass stamped with some indecipherable script and I moved straight in with a group of fighters holed-up behind the Holiday Inn. I found myself in a warren. People had made tunnels between the houses so that they could run from one to another without being seen. It was like a tube network. One night I slept under a magnificent chandelier, but the normal conditions were squalid and rat-infested. The Falange fighters existed in a litter of half-eaten kebab sandwiches and soft-core pornography in which the faces and pubes of the contorted women would be blacked out. The stench of the unburied dead was something to be endured.

I gained the fighters' trust by staying with them under fire, and after a few days I was taken to the Holiday Inn, which was occupied round-the-clock by the Falange to pour fire into West Beirut. Bizarrely, the lifts were still working and I was taken to one of the upper floors to meet the resting troops who were lying around cleaning their Kalashnikov AK-47 rifles. Other fighters were on the top floor getting theirs dirty again.

They weren't very excited to see me, but neither were they totally hostile. One of them, who I thought had an extra-ordinary amount of hair for a fighter, turned out to be a strikingly beautiful woman. She reminded me of the character played by Maria Schneider in Last Tango in Paris, and I could feel my depression, induced by the days and nights in the warren, beginning to lift. She was the first woman I had ever seen in war combat. Two days later she was hurling hand grenades and tied-up dynamite into the nearby Phoenicia Hotel.

The Holiday Inn billet had its disadvantages. The cellar had survived almost intact. Beer, brandy and champagne were among the easiest commodities to come by. I stayed there for three days, but always went back to the rat-holes at night, where I slept with one eye open and one ear cocked for the tread of the man coming to mutilate me. At dusk, the Holiday Inn made me nervous, because the military advantages of the day became vulnerabilities by night. There was no seeing the enemy from afar, and the danger of being trapped was considerable. Some time after I left, the Holiday Inn was overrun by leftist factions, including one popularly known as 'The Looney Tunes'. They cornered some members of the Christian Falange on the top floor and cut off their penises before throwing them alive off the roof.

One morning I was told by a fighter, 'You are going to see something good today, my friend.' He smiled and told me to get into a jeep. We took off, with a man standing, legs astride, in the back with a 30-calibre machine gun. We screeched to a halt at a gathering of some 200 or 300 fighters.

A woman came over to me with some blue ribbon and safety pins. As she put the blue ribbon round my neck, I asked her, 'What's this for?' She couldn't understand English, but the man beside her told me, 'It's for identification. Look, all the fighters have one. In case we shoot each other.'

Staccato orders were shouted and there seemed a lot of confusion. In times of confusion I've often found it a good idea to play the dumb fool. There's time enough to be smart when you're actually doing the job, but a little false naiveté in the lead-up can be very beneficial in terms of information.

I heard the name 'Quarantina' mentioned several times, which didn't mean much to me other than the fact that it was one of the many districts in the city. But gradually I learned that it was a Muslim ghetto that had somehow planted itself in Christian East Beirut, in a poor area near the docks. It also contained many Palestinians, and these Falange fighters were going in there.

'We're going to clear out this place, get all the rats,' a fighter told me.

More fighters arrived, and the day was wearing on. Suddenly one of the fighters approached me with a big grin and said, 'Look, photograph that.' He pointed to something I hadn't noticed on a telegraph post. Someone had arranged in the form of a collage the dismembered pieces of a cat. It was a sight which clarified my view of the people I was with and made me nervous for Quarantina.

I went running in with the first wave. It was evening and raining hard. They all wore hoods. We stopped behind a low wall and watched people being shepherded out of a hospital for the insane. People came to the windows of one wing. One of the Falange fighters shouted and when he didn't get a proper answer he shot a burst of automatic fire into the window.

A Falangist followed me into the main building and looked out of the same window as I had. There wasn't much to be seen but he took a sniper's bullet across the bridge of his nose. The first drop of Christian blood incensed the Falange.

When darkness fell, the shooting quietened down and the hospital became a Falange dormitory for the night. I bivouacked in a windowless corridor with an Arabic obstetric diagram at one end and a morgue at the other. Next along was a Falange who spoke good English, as a result of working for a British airline. He was a great Anglophile, and we talked ourselves to sleep, though it was hardly sleep – more an unconscious wrestling with bad thoughts.

There was the same snip-snap of sniper bullets in the morning. Everyone seemed to have shrunk into the centre of Quarantina. An old American truck, like a Dodge pick-up, was brought up with a huge 50mm machine gun mounted on it. The Falangist on top was pouring out fire indiscriminately.

I spotted an old man lying dead in the street, a pitiful sight, and went over to take a picture. The Falange fighter accompanying me said, 'Take no photos, my friend. Otherwise I kill you.'

For the moment, I did as he said. The Falange had taken casualties from snipers that morning and were in no mood for an argument with me. Although my papers allowed for photographs, when the killing started they amounted to nothing. I was trying to take pictures of things they did not want to be seen, and that made life difficult.

I heard screaming and shouting and saw women and children being herded from a stairwell. Two men were standing with their hands up, looking very disturbed. The women were giving them furtive glances. They were obviously husbands or brothers and they were being followed by a gang of Falange. I photographed them. A Falange fighter came over to me and cocked his rifle. It was the same man who had threatened me before.

'I told you no photographs; I'm going to kill you,' he said.

'No, no, I didn't photograph you, I photographed only the women,' I said. Of course it was not true. I had got him as well. He tried to wrench the camera out of my hand. I ducked away and said, 'Look, I've got a pass. Look.'

He calmed down and I backed towards the stairwell where the two men were still being held. The Falange had an old M-1 carbine trained on these two men and they shot them down at point-blank range. As he was falling, one of the men used what air was left in his lungs to say 'Allah'.

I held one of the banisters, tight. Hang on to yourself, I thought. You're going to see a lot of this today, so hang on. Don't give the game away now.

A lot of people were surrendering, crying, begging and pleading, and some were being put aside, segregated. Women and children went one way, men and older boys were led off another. The very old seemed harder to categorise. I saw one captured old man being forced at knifepoint to take down his trousers in the middle of the road. They wanted to find his sons, but when he said he had no sons, they turned the whole episode into a taunt against his manhood. Another old man I saw did not live long enough to be humiliated. He shouted defiantly at a Falange fighter and was instantly shot in the belly.

I saw three young men being pushed into a factory yard. Then I spotted the English-speaking fighter I had slept beside the previous night.

'What are they going to do with these young men?' I asked.

'I don't know, my friend,' he said.

'You do know what they're going to do. They're going to kill them.'

Don McCullin took this portrait of President Idi Amin before he declared a state of emergency.

Don McCullin's portrait of his friend Norman Lewis.

Premier Chou En-lai recieves press baron Lord Thomson, his son Kenneth and a *Sunday Times* retinue, including Don McCullin on the fringe, nursing a cut chin.

The road to An Loc being bombed by a B52.

The beginning of the Christian Falangist pogrom against the Palestinians. Families a driven from their hom that are then put to th torch. Women and chi dren are taken out of sight of the execution their menfolk, as the guard warns the photo rapher that he will b killed if he goes on taking pictures.

The mandolin player, photographed despite a death threat to the photographer.

Macho Christian Falange fighters posing in the shattered ruins.

David Cornwell, alias John Le Carré,
by Don McCullin.

A religious leader undergoing rifle practice
on the outskirts of Tehran.

Roger Cooper's photograph of Don McCullin in the company of the mujaheddin
in Afghanistan in 1979.

The dawn of a new Zimbabwe as victorious guerillas hand in their weapons in 1981.

ɔvernment troops flush ɪt left-wing guerrillas in the ɪttle for Usulután.

(Facing page)
An hysterical Lebanese woman
attacks the photographer after
discovering her entire family
entombed in their destroyed
apartment building

Palestinian youths, born in
Lebanese camps, undergoing
intensive training for the day
when they will liberate their
Palestinian homeland.

Sabra mental hospital, where
the staff fled, leaving two
women to care for fifty
children who are tied to their
beds for safety.

Lord Olivier interviewed by Melvyn Bragg for television, photographed by Don McCullin.

Claude, Jessica and Alexander.

We could both see a group of Falange putting fresh ammunition into their magazines in preparation. I said to the man, 'Last night you and I spoke as human beings, and you spoke of your love for English people. Try and stop what is happening now. Try and stop it because the world's press is here and it will look bad for you.'

He tried to say it was not his responsibility but we were attracting attention. Another fighter came over to me and said, 'It is not your business. Leave this yard.'

I think they knew that I had photographed the situation, for a few minutes later the three captives were being booted out of the place. They had a temporary reprieve but their chances of surviving through the rest of that day were very slim.

Great hordes of people were surrendering now. As an area was cleared the torches went in. You could hear eucalyptus trees exploding as they also burst into flames. Everything that was burnable was burnt. The whole scene was something out of the Dark Ages, like our image of what happened when the Goths and the Huns swarmed across Europe and Asia, pillaging and burning. It was more than frightening, it was catastrophically fearful, like the dawn of a new dark age. I photographed, and went on photographing.

Again I heard the distinction: 'No photographs, leave the district.' And this time I did as I was told.

That evening I met up with Martin Meredith in the Commodore and we agreed to go back into Quarantina the next day. As we came up to the Green Line we were stopped at a checkpoint, and I could hear a lot of screaming outside. Our driver said, 'They want your pass. PASS.'

Thoughtlessly I produced the pass from my pocket and put Martin, myself and the Canadian journalist who was travelling with us, in mortal danger. All hell broke loose. They came running around the car, and said, 'Get out. We're going to kill you.'

They hauled us out of the car and started bundling us towards a house. We had to pass through scores of weeping and wailing women, women who had just been widowed in

Quarantina. We were pushed into a room, and a man came up to me and said, 'We are going to cut your throat.'

I asked him what for, and he said, 'You are a spy. You are an enemy. You are Fascist Falange.'

I knew then all too well what I had done wrong. I had tried to get through a left-wing Muslim checkpoint by flourishing a Christian Falange permit. With emotions running so high against the Falangists, this was a perilous mistake. Unfortunately, the throat-cutter did not seem to want to understand the mistake.

'You are a Fascist Falange,' he kept repeating, 'you are a spy.' He then lapsed into an ominous silence.

As we waited to see what our fate would be, people kept cracking open the door to cast an evil eye over the fascist spies. I was in bad shape not only with my own fear but with guilt at having put my colleagues at risk. Eventually higher authority arrived in the form of a young man in a leather jacket with a fur collar. He was mercifully brisk.

'Mr McCullin, you have made a big mistake,' he said. 'These people want to kill you. You have given these people a Christian Falange pass. I know you have to have this pass, but they don't understand it. They are dealing with the survivors from Quarantina whose loved ones have been murdered, and they want to be revenged. I know you are only doing your job, and that you have to go from side to side, but my friend, be very careful, because you are very close to death.'

He asked if we would like some coffee. So shocked were we that we could hardly muster enough saliva between us to say we would. I had to resist an impulse to stoop down and kiss the man's feet.

I took some photographs of the refugees outside, then Martin and I headed off into Quarantina. There was no mystery about what had happened to the men who had been led off on the previous day. As we made for the north of the district, where fighting was said still to be going on, we started passing heaps of charred dead bodies. The streets were strewn with scores of dead Palestinians.

I remember seeing an overweight man, wearing a cardigan,

a cable-knit cardigan such as you can buy in Marks and Spencer, lying on his back with his eyes open. Next to him lay a woman, I think his wife, who was still holding a bunch of plastic flowers. A plea for mercy. One of the Falange came forward and set fire to their clothes.

I photographed very carefully and only when I thought I wouldn't be seen. I was still shaky from the checkpoint incident and I didn't want to push my luck so early in the day. We came upon Christian Falange looting homes that had escaped torching. They came up the road carrying their booty of television sets and cassette players. I marvelled at the capacity of people to covet the possessions of those they despised. The looters had very little time. We saw a fire truck go by and then stop to spray petrol over some abandoned shacks which were then set alight.

In an area of small factories I saw a fighter from the Holiday Inn with a shaking old man backed up against the wall, threatening to cut off his privates. On the other side of the road a captive group was being kicked systematically in the face and stabbed. Then I saw the girl fighter from the Holiday Inn looking shame-faced and alone. There was argument going on between a Palestinian and his captor and I asked her to interpret.

'One of these prisoners is claiming that he and his son are members of the Arafat family. So, you know, they will survive for the time being.' She looked at me with embarrassment and walked away. Surreptitiously I started taking pictures.

One brutalised man summoned up the courage to run. As he ran the fighters started firing at him. Bullets struck the wall by Martin and me and fizzled like worn-out fireworks. The fighters ran after the man and we ran after the fighters, willing the man's escape, but he ran into another bunch of Falange who kicked him to the ground. One of the fighters stepped up and emptied a whole magazine into the man's head.

Again we got the message: 'You two, leave this place now. And do not take any photographs, or you will be killed.'

As we moved on I saw a pile of dead bodies which had not yet been burnt. I was shaking as I took a picture quickly.

Further down the same road we heard strumming. A young boy was playing a mandolin ransacked from a half-burnt house. The boy was strumming it among his mates, as if they were at a picnic among almond groves in the sun. In front of them lay the body of a dead girl in puddles of winter rain.

My mind was seized by this picture of carnival rejoicing in the midst of carnage. It seemed to say so much about what Beirut had become. Yet to raise the camera could be one risk too many.

Then the boy called over to me. 'Hey, Mistah! Mistah! Come take photo.'

I was still frightened but I shot off two frames quickly. This, when it's published, will crucify this lot, I thought.

As we picked our way over the rubble on the way out I could hold it down no longer. 'The bastards. The BASTARDS,' I yelled out loud. 'I'm going to get you bastards!'

Martin looked startled, but I didn't care. I had pictures that would tell the world something of the enormity of the crime that had taken place in Quarantina. The Christian Falange knew it too, for soon afterwards I heard that they had put out death warrants for two photographers. One was for the person who had taken the picture of a Christian soldier toasting victory in Quarantina with champagne, the other was for the photographer who had taken the picture of the boys with the mandolin.

It was my duty now to get myself and my pictures back to London as fast as possible. Martin advised against the airport. Conflict between the pilots, who were mainly Christian, and those who controlled the surrounding area, mainly Palestinian, had totally disrupted all flights. Lingering at the airport was never advisable. It was a prime site for kidnapping.

I left the Lebanon by a less predictable route. There were still a few drivers who would risk the Beka'a valley, though it had been heavily infested with sectarian guns. Two innocuous Japanese typewriter salesmen who had found themselves marooned in the Commodore Hotel recruited one and I hitched a lift with them. It was a bone-shaking eight-hour drive through the valley and on into Syria. With my last reserves of energy I managed to organise a Pakistan Airways flight from Damascus to London. The film survived intact, but I was emotionally burnt out.

30

PICNIC WITH ABU AMMAR

HUNTING FOR, WAITING for, watching, reacting to the disasters of the world had taken a grievous toll on my spirit. You cannot walk on the water of hunger, misery and death. You have to wade through to record them. I was chilled, numb and lonely. My head ached with the intensity of my experience, the intensity of my thinking. It had taken all the energy, all the self-discipline I had to keep myself working to survive, to not go home to a scalding bath, a warm fire, clean clothes. I felt I had seen so much horror that it was likely to destroy me.

I needed to be at home. I needed the peace of my own country, England. Yet when I go home and sleep in my own bed, I soon become restless. I am not shaped for a house. I grew up in harsh surroundings. I have slept under tables in battles for days on end. There is something about this that unfits you for sleeping in beds for the rest of your life. My wars, the way I've lived, is like an incurable disease. It is like the promise of a tremendous high and the certainty of a bad dream. It is something I both fear and love, but it's something I can't do without. I cannot do without the head-on collision with life I have when I am working.

My violent experience in Quarantina led to further work in the Middle East. Naim Attallah, the publisher of Quartet, proposed that I should produce a book with Jonathan Dimbleby, whose journalism I much admired, exploring the identity of the Palestinians. This assignment, along with others for my paper, would see me returning regularly to the

Middle East trouble spots through the late seventies, when the war in Lebanon raged on bloodily and unabated, with only short pauses for exhaustion.

I was drawn to the place less by the conflict than by my sympathy for the Palestinian people, whom I had first encountered in refugee shacks and shanties in Gaza before the Six Day War. Dispersed in the Arab world, they seemed to me surprisingly similar to the Jews – hard-working, highly motivated, an intellectual elite providing a professional class for many another country.

There was also a rougher edge to the Palestinian movement. In Jordan they had not confined themselves to regaining their own land but had created a revolutionary state within a state, and had become a threat to King Hussein. Fatah supporters had screamed round the city of Amman in Landrovers bristling with sub-machine guns, a personal vigilante security force for Palestinian establishments, and not always above extorting contributions to the cause at gunpoint.

Ousted from Amman, they had regrouped in Lebanon and emerged behaving in a similar fashion in Beirut. By then the Black September extremists had taken measures like the Munich massacre, with which I could in no way go along. Like some of the Christian warlords of the Falange, some of the Palestinians reminded me of Chicago gangsters of the Thirties.

We would see the spokesman of the different factions by turns in the Commodore Hotel – where they would come to give informal press conferences. They would like to mingle with journalists, but even more they liked the indulgence of the playboy life. It was like a curious and unnerving variety show.

Getting to see the Palestinian leader, Yasser Arafat, was far more complicated. As the Public Enemy Number One of both the Christians and the Israelis his movements were highly unpredictable, perhaps even to himself. He had a number of dens around Beirut, but there was never any advance warning where he might be at a given time. After long negotiation Jonathan and I were told we would be allowed to see him. It was only after a hair-raising drive in a Mercedes, squashed between two garlic-breathing, heavily armed guards, that we realised exactly where – at a picnic for the Beirut University brigade of Fatah, held in the dappled shade of olive and cedar trees near a decaying yellow stucco villa in the hills above Tyre. The roads round about were blocked by Japanese jeeps and British Landrovers filled with Fatah commandos pointing their 106mm recoilless rifles at the sky. Fear of the arrival of Israeli intelligence was as intense as ever.

Lebanese and Palestinian Fatah supporters brewed lamb and chicken in large cauldrons and drank tea and coffee, until at noon Arafat's convoy swept up in a cloud of dust and a confusion of military all shouting orders. The small, paunchy and unprepossessing figure of Arafat, in a well-pressed but not well-fitting uniform, was soon lost in a sea of followers trying to embrace him and kiss his hand.

It as not until he launched into a passionate oration on the evils of imperialism, the glory of the Palestine martyrs, the need to sacrifice one Palestinian for every mile of lost Palestine, that you could sense the demotic power of the man, the voice pitched on a rising tone, the gestures perfectly timed.

The gathered students, refugees, young fighters, were rapt. By this time my own brief encounter with Arafat had come and gone, and I had concluded that he was both charming and enormously wily.

Before the speeches we had eaten at trestle tables. My main concern was to photograph him. I noticed he had that knack common to world leaders of pausing just the right time for the motorwind of the camera. Though Arafat himself was relaxed, his bodyguards, like leopards about to spring, fixed their eyes on my lens in moment by moment alert, as if the camera might hold an assassin's bullet.

He extricated himself from my focus with great skill. 'Here,' he said, hospitably, offering me a large piece of lamb from his plate. 'Eat. Eat. Enjoy.' By the time I had choked it back, and got the grease off my fingers enough to work the camera again, he had swept benignly away.

Now we were to meet even more alarming members of El

Fatah's revolutionary council, in the course of hearing the Palestinians' story from their own lips.

We spent a week with the man under whose force's fire Murray Sayle and I had been when we were holed up in the Intercontinental Hotel in Amman. He was a legendary figure among the Palestinians and later figured as a leading character in John le Carré's book *The Little Drummer Girl*. His name was Salah Tamari.

Jonathan's contact with him was through his wife, Dina Abdul Hamid. The story of Salah and Dina was an astonishing one. She was a Hashemite princess and the first wife of King Hussein of Jordan, whom she'd divorced because of his lady-killing propensities.

Salah and Dina had married in remarkable circumstances – during the actual siege of Amman, where Salah was commander of the Fatah forces, and therefore the leading foe of his love's ex-husband, the King. During that time, we heard, Salah had kept constantly on the move – making only one pause. This was to hijack a priest and get him, at gunpoint, to perform a marriage ceremony between himself and Dina.

Now they lived in a fine but ancient villa, in an old garden, outside Sidon. He was a handsome, dominating man, made of equal parts of unpretentious warmth and, I would also think, anger. He was a man who had seen much action at close quarters. He had held the line against the Israelis at the battle of Karameh. We had much to talk about. Through him we also met other Fatah leaders, Abu Douad and Abu Moussa, and another legendary figure, who with Arafat had founded El Fatah on the West Bank of Jordan, Abu Jihad. His name meant Holy War. I remember seeing him with his daughter and, after he was killed years later by Mossad, I thought sadly of that little girl. But I couldn't altogether yield to the charm and humanity of the Palestinian leaders.

Salah himself was a Bedouin born in Bethlehem. His uncle, a tribal judge, had ridden a horse carrying a sword by his side. That was in the days when the lands which later became Israel were 95 per cent owned by the Bedouin, and 70 per cent occupied by them. When the British needed American and Jewish financial support in World War One, they duplicitously ceded a Jewish homeland after it had been promised independently to the Arabs. But in Salah's uncle's time this homeland had been a small unthreatening settlement. Abu Douad had grown up happily side by side with Jewish Palestinians. He still did not hate Jews at all. Only the militant Zionists.

Hitler changed everything. The flight from genocide made ordinary Jews, not just Zionists, heedless pressers of a path into lands that for 2,000 years had not been their own. Extremist Zionist organisations, the Stern gang and Irgun, had used all known violent means to destroy the British administration which had tried to stem the flow of new migrants. Aeroplanes were dynamited, banks were robbed, British officers were kidnapped, British sergeants were lynched and hung from trees. Virtually all the tactics later deployed by the extreme Palestinians had been used by Irgun first.

This terror was used with popular support in the West. The American scriptwriter Ben Hecht had written, in the *New York Herald Tribune*, to the Irgun: 'Every time you blow up a British arsenal, wreck a British jail, send a British railroad sky high, let go with your gun and bombs at the betrayers and invaders of your homeland, the Jews of America make a little holiday in their hearts.'

As the British moved out, the wilder extremes of the Jewish movement began 'cleansing operations' in the Arab villages. Jacques le Reynier of the International Red Cross found bloodcurdling evidence of a My Lai style massacre at Deir Yassin. Abu Douad, as a twelve-year-old, was present at another grim massacre of Arabs by Israelis at Ramlan. It had been called by the Palestinians ever since, The Catastrophe. Douad says that it is right the West should never forget The Holocaust, but they should also remember The Catastrophe.

The Palestinians fled throughout the Middle East. From being judges in Palestine, Salah's family became labourers in Kuwait. But exile, over two generations, changed the nature of the people again. Like the Jews in exile, they became intellectuals, lawyers, powerful businessmen and, as in the case of Arafat's twin brother, respected physicians – and also militant revolutionaries.

The dreadful cycle of violence, born of Palestine, continued. Soon after I arrived back in the Lebanon, I heard that, in revenge for Quarantina, the Christians of Damour in southern Lebanon had been driven out, and Damour sacked. In return 30,000 Palestinians had been besieged in the fortress of Tal Al Zaater.

I was in the country again soon after the Syrians marched in to exercise what was called a peace-keeping role. The Syrians, always regarded by the Israelis as their most formidable foe, had arrived initially by invitation of the Saudis, though the Syrians had their own interest in that they saw Lebanon as a part of Greater Syria. Like the other militias on the streets of Beirut, they did not much care for journalists. I was arrested for photographing a Syrian soldier who had perched himself on the bonnet of a car and was waving his pistol joyously in the air.

Even with the 'peace-keepers' in town, hysterical militia-men of all varieties continued to fire wildly at the smallest excuse. You would still get the occasional incoming shell. And if it was sometimes quiet at weekends it would be because all the fighters were off in the mountains where they did their training and inhaled their deadly doctrines. The dictum of the Christian Guardians was: 'It is the duty of every Lebanese to kill one Palestinian.'

One day the sight of my camera got me arrested by a Palestinian militiaman. He seemed to be under the influence of drugs, and I had to think fast. I said I was a friend of Abu Ammar, which is Arafat's nom de guerre.

'You are really a friend of Abu Ammar?' he asked.

I replied that I was, and that I had been playing chess with him that very morning, and asked if he had seen the photograph in the newspaper. In fact, there was a picture that day of Arafat playing chess with a BBC friend of mine. I was asked, 'How did our chairman play? Did he beat you?' I replied that of course he did. He looked at me, smiled and put his arms around me and gave me a huge squeeze which the 9mm Russian pistol in his waistband made rather painful. He then held me back from him and looked me in the eyes and said, 'I am very pleased. You can go.'

There was a chilling aftermath to my Palestinian wanderings with Jonathan. I got involved with some of the Nazis who had done so much to create the Palestinian problem in the first place. It happened through my friend Tony Terry, with whom I had last worked in Biafra, where he arrived sweltering and resplendent in black suit and red sock suspenders post-haste from some north European conference. On that occasion he'd had to use his considerable astuteness to plumb the African politics he was encountering for the first time. On this occasion, in the autumn of 1977, I was being sent to meet him in West Germany, very much his home ground.

We were going to see a group of extraordinary old Nazis, with whom Tony had ingratiated himself. They were the survivors of Hitler's own personal SS guards, the *Leibstandarte* Adolf Hitler. They included an enormous blond man, at least 6' 6" tall, who was treated with much deference. He turned out to have been Hitler's personal bodyguard.

They were, unbelievably, trying to scrub up their image. They had produced a sentimentalised publication about their war efforts. From its glossy pages you would believe that the SS were into no more than genial comradeship and healthy living. As it happened Tony had been a commando in the raid on the German U-boat base at St Nazaire and held a prisoner of war for three years. He had thereafter worked in British Intelligence investigating atrocities committed by this very same unit. He was not at all impressed by their attempt to burnish a latter-day reputation as social workers, but he was a master at not showing his distaste. He'd talk politely to these appalling people, purse his lips when Adolf's name was admiringly evoked, give a little smile and move on. He only let the emotion out when he sat at the typewriter.

We wound up being invited to their reunion dinner held in

Nassau, which had been their garrison town during the war. What went on inside the hall was in some ways more interesting than what when on with the old Nazis at their revels. There were a few anti-Nazi demonstrators about but the solid citizens seemed very solidly on the side of the SS.

Among them was a reserve officer in the present West German army who told us, 'If I had been asked to become a concentration camp guard I would have done so as a matter of course. But things are different nowadays.' I hoped they were. I left with the queasy impression that it was not just in the Middle East that the old wheels were turning full circle.

31

SHADOW OF DOUBT

I HAD BEGUN to wonder where home was for an old war-horse like me. While I was away in some dreadful hell-hole I yearned to be back with my family; when I was at home, tinkering around with the outhouses attached to my farm-house in Hertfordshire, I itched to be away again in foreign parts. One thing had to be recognised – things were changing at the *Sunday Times*. Lifestyles rather than life were coming into fashion on the magazine.

So much of my war reporting had involved watching national identities take shape that I began to ask myself who I was. What were the English and what did they represent? What for that matter did I represent? I decided to take to the road in my own country to find out. For the better part of two years I travelled round England, discovering it, taking pictures, sometimes for the paper but often at my own expense. I was searching not only for the English identity but for a key to something in myself that would enable me to turn a corner into a new world. What I found was that my eyes had grown accustomed to dark. All I saw seemed to echo my childhood and the scenes of deprivation, dereliction, death and disaster, smashed minds and broken bodies, that I had witnessed in other countries.

I immersed myself in the industrial communities of the North and soaked up the desolate beauty of cities like Bradford. Though not myself down-and-out, I could not help identifying with the derelicts and outcasts of society. I went into the slums it was hard to believe still existed in England, where people brewed their children's tea in old beer cans, where wallpaper hung in great furls from damp walls, where fungus grew around greasy stoves that occupied (as in my childhood) the centre of impoverished homes that boasted few other amenities or possessions.

I ate and slept in a Salvation Army hostel, to breathe in its life. I spent weeks photographing in mental hospitals. One of my own fears has always been that I would lose my sanity, and that I too would be institutionalised. But the scenes I witnessed in the hostels and hospitals and on the road fed a social anger in me.

There was a darkness in my own country that I reacted against, but there was also a darkness in me. When I photographed people at English seasides they looked unhappy. It crossed my mind that the unhappiness was not in them but in me. I was still seeing the dead bodies I had crawled past and touched in other people's countries. Burning stubble at evening time in English fields reminded me of scorched-earth strategies, and that is how they came out in my photographs. Mallards rising in the mist from marshes looked like formations of B-52 bombers. In English woods rain drumming on the leaves transplanted me back to tense jungle patrols. I was happiest wandering like a lost soul on open moorlands with heavy rain clouds overhead. I longed for winter, for the abrasive struggle with the weather and the nakedness of the landscape. People told me it was a form of masochism.

When I published my book on England, called *Homecoming*, it was described as over-sombre, a collection of war pictures taken in times of peace. At about that time Associated Television made a documentary about my war photographs in which I was asked about my attitude to war in the future. I had a ready answer. I wanted to photograph just one more war, do it well and say, finish. In reality life is rarely so tidy. War itself is never tidy.

While on a dangerous job I would overcome the fear of leaving England by telling myself I worked for a great newspaper. The paper was as large a part of the identity of all its journalists and photographers as we were of it. Few of us realised how large until the *Sunday Times* closed in November 1978, and stayed closed for a whole year. It is always sad when a newspaper dies for lack of money. When it closes for lack of common sense it makes you angry.

The reason for the closure was a decision to move away from traditional hot metal printing methods and go for the new computer-based typesetting technology. The great Lord Thomson, whom I had accompanied to China, had died. His son Kenneth, whom I had also befriended, was eager to press ahead with modernising his inheritance. So was the *Sunday Times* management team. The print unions were all for standing still. No compromise meant no solution. *The Times* and the *Sunday Times*, which both sides were intent to preserve, disappeared from the streets.

Journalists and photographers, who were not part of the dispute, were left stranded. Most of us continued to be paid, but newspapermen without a newspaper are pathetic creatures. Few are prepared for the demand of anonymity. I would go into the Gray's Inn Road building and feel like a morgue attendant. People would drift about in ones and twos, like the inmates of a mental institution, giving one another suspicious looks of the kind you expect from the paranoid schizophrenic. Nobody really knew if we should or shouldn't be there. Without the newspaper you could feel the erosion of loyalties and trust. For me, it was unbearable to think of the risks I had taken to produce this or that story for a newspaper that now had absolutely no value. It all seemed farcical.

No one thought the closure would last for more than a few days. As it stretched into weeks, then months, until finally it seemed it would have no end, I found it hard to work up enthusiasm for anything. Like everyone else, I watched the Iranian Embassy siege on television. I wasn't looking for danger for a newspaper that didn't exist. If the management and the printers were not prepared to take any risks in negotiation, why should any journalist do so? Only when the Victoria and Albert Museum approached me to mount a retrospective exhibition of my work was I dragged out of the doldrums.

Apart from Henri Cartier-Bresson, I could not remember another contemporary photographer being accorded the honour of a major exhibition at the V and A. I confess I felt uncertain as I printed up the pictures to be exhibited in the pigsty I had converted into a dark room. It is one thing to show pictures of horror and suffering in a newspaper whose function is to reflect what is going on in the world and quite another to put them up on gallery walls to be admired. In the event some 40,000 turned out to see them, most of them young.

The exhibition led directly to a most agreeable meeting. My agent, Abner Stein, wanted me to produce a book of the V and A photographs under the Conradian title *Hearts of Darkness* and asked David Cornwell, better known as John le Carré, to write an introduction to it. He agreed, so long as he could meet me. I felt a little overawed, and attempted to read one of his books by way of preparation. *The Honourable Schoolboy* was said to be based on some of the people I knew at the *Sunday Times*, but even the portrayal of our Far Eastern correspondent, Dick Hughes, thinly disguised as 'Old Crow', couldn't keep me going. Dyslexia had impaired my concentration too much for the complexity of his plot and his prose. I put the book aside and made a mental note to avoid literary discussion.

When David Cornwell arrived at my home, Christine fed him watercress soup, for which he thanked her very nicely. I showed him the chickens and he became the first person ever to be invited to cross the threshold of my dark room. In the cowshed we came upon my discarded copy of *The Honourable Schoolboy* trodden into the mud. He pretended not to notice. We got on well and talked on into the evening. As he was leaving I remember saying to him gravely and rather gauchely, 'Maybe you can tell me where I'm going, whether life is just beginning or just over.' What a question to be asked of anyone after only a few hours' acquaintance!

Of course he was unable to tell me, but he produced the sort of surgical operation on my psyche for the book that I am sure I did not deserve. Yet he helped me to put a painful, self-searching period behind me. He thought my work was 'the product of a restless, slightly puritanical mind, deeply ill at ease with the world's condition and his own.' He could say that again! Another passage made me feel more uncomfortable:

> He has known all forms of fear, he's an expert in it. He has come back from God knows how many brinks, all different. His experiences in a Ugandan prison alone would be enough to unhinge another man – like myself, as a matter of fact – for good. He has been forfeit more times than he can remember, he says. But he is not bragging. Talking this way about death and risk, he seems to be implying quite consciously that by testing his luck each time, he's testing his Maker's indulgence. To survive is to be condoned and blessed again.

Could it be true? I can't altogether deny it.

We became friendly, and later I went with him to Beirut in search of locations for the film of his book *The Little Drummer Girl*. Sensibly the filming was moved to Jordan. We went looking for Salah Tamari and Dina while we were in the Lebanon and found their handsome villa locked up. We clambered over the wall but came away none the wiser as to where they had gone. Later I discovered that Salah was in an Israeli jail.

32

EARTHQUAKE IN IRAN

I WENT TO Iran just before and just after the revolution and I can't honestly say that I took to that country on either occasion, though I did very much take to a man I met there who the Ayatollah Khomeini later had imprisoned.

Since he was jailed in 1986, Roger Cooper had been described in the British press variously as 'an academic' and 'a businessman', and by the Iranians as a spy. I knew him as a newspaperman and a very good one at that. He travelled round with me on both my tours in Iran.

Roger is the nephew of the poet Robert Graves, which may partly explain the endearing eccentricity of his nature. He wore sandals and rode a bicycle, and carried all his gear – notes, knife, pepper-grinder and other vital equipment – around in an outsize woman's hessian bag. He had lived in Tehrān for many years and spoke Farsi (and indeed many other languages) like a native. I liked this man at first count. There was a bit of sparkle about him.

He was brilliant in traffic jams. A torrent of Farsi would emerge from Roger and the offenders would back off. He would tell them, 'As Allah is my witness, you will be punished.' Like Norman Lewis, he got enormous enjoyment out of the small things in life.

I once stood in line to use a rudimentary but popular urinal in a railway station when the man in front of me turned round and started talking to me. I smiled weakly, not understanding a word he said. The man then had an exchange with Roger behind me, at which Roger broke into a bellowing laugh.

'You're not going to like this, Don,' he said, rubbing his eyes. 'He wants to know why my friend is so rude that he doesn't bother to answer when spoken to. When I told him you didn't understand the language, he said, "Well, I spoke to him in Turkish, isn't that good enough for him?" The funny thing is the Iranians consider the Turks to be thick.'

When I first went to Tehrān, in the autumn of 1978, radical students were out on the streets shouting 'Death to the Shah' and were gunned down by the army. The official death toll was 100, but Roger wasn't satisfied until he had counted the fresh graves in Tehrān's main cemetery. He put the figure nearer 500, and he felt sure there would be more in other places. Only a short time before my arrival 70 theological students had been shot in a disturbance in Qom, one of Iran's holiest cities.

It was clear that we were witnessing the death throes of a regime. The Shah's autocracy, underpinned by Savak, all-pervasive and much-feared secret police, was finally losing its grip. We were watching the beginning of a major revolution, with major international implications. Iran's oil, and its proximity to Russia, made its political destiny of special interest to the major powers. Britain had substantial interests there, particularly in construction; Israel and South Africa depended on Iranian oil, but the interests of the United States, which had paved the way for the Shah by a CIA-engineered coup against his left-wing predecessor, Mossadeq, exceeded all others. Now, after years of sustaining the reliably anti-Communist Shah, and unloading huge defence contracts, the Americans were faced with a situation in which the only predictable thing was an end to the Shah.

In those early days, I don't think anyone could tell which of the Shah's many enemies would emerge triumphant. Most of the noise was being made by radical students bent on social revolution but a more solid opposition was emerging from conservative Muslims led by the mullahs, worried at the pace of Westernisation. Suddenly the political disaster that Iran had become gave place to a natural one.

An earthquake in the desert flattened the oasis town of

Ṭabas in thirty seconds. It was said that 20,000 people had died. Roger and I managed to fly in on a military aeroplane. While we were there, sleeping under canvas, there was a second tremor which I count as one of the most unnerving experiences I've ever had.

I thought I could handle most disaster situations but nothing quite prepared me for the scale of the dying that comes with an earthquake, or the sight of bulldozers burying hundreds of bodies. The bodies had to be buried fast to prevent an outbreak of disease, but when you see men laying their shrouded dead babies in the path of the bulldozer, it becomes hard to hold a camera. While I was in Ṭabas, the Shah flew in and I took a photograph of the King of Kings coming down the steps of the aeroplane. The whole story of all the political and natural disasters was written on his ravaged face.

It was impossible to keep politics out of anything, even disaster relief. The mullahs were there with their field kitchens and many people remarked to Roger on how much they were achieving compared to the government's feeble effort. There was also a group of young medical students from Mashhad University who were inoculating against typhus. They dismissed the clergy's efforts as 'propaganda'.

We went on to Mashhad, where a most exquisite mosque with a turquoise dome was surrounded by tanks. Roger had an appointment with a mullah who told us – 'for our own safety' – to turn round and go back to Tehrān before the airport was closed by the army. Seeing our reluctance, he went off briefly and came back with two little boxes, planting one in Roger's palm, the other in mine. They contained two of the most beautiful turquoise stones.

'There's no way I can accept this,' I said to Roger.

'Will you do *me* a favour, and keep it,' Roger hissed. 'He will go mad if you try and give it back. It's his way of trying to show us hospitality even while he's telling us to shove off.' So we flew out with our precious stones, and I later had mine made into a brooch for Christine.

It wasn't exactly a window-shopping sort of situation but I

was entranced by the carpet soukhs near the British Embassy. There was obviously great depth to Iranian culture, though not much to its cuisine, which mainly consisted of boiled rice with a knuckle on top. It was incredible to me that a country which could come up with Persian carpets and turquoise domes should content itself with such lousy food.

Roger and I travelled to many little villages and other towns like Tabrīz, where religious fundamentalists had burnt down cinemas and banks, apparently as symbols of Western decadence. It was always tough going. The men seemed surly, and it was hard to know what to think of the women with so many of them shrouded in the chador.

It was a relief for us to go up into the Kurdish Hills, where the landscape seems to have an almost Biblical quality, and people were genuinely pleased to see us. I know that a lot of journalists fall in love with the Kurds, but there's good reason for it. The men are always ready to smile and the women go in for gloriously cheerful colours, golds, reds and blues. I was fascinated by the way they lived on top of their houses as well as in them, though really it was a practical way of being ready for any dangerous approaches.

My particular Kurdish friend was a young man of twenty-four who showed me round his village and told me of his nation's history. Said to be descended from the Medes who were conquered by the Persians over 2,000 years ago, the Kurds preserve a distinct national identity. I asked my friend how he managed to acquire such good English in the mountains. He said it was the result of a brief descent to Hatfield College in England.

A year later I went back to the Iran of Ayatollah Khomeini. Savak had been swept away along with the Shah, but the torture ethic survived under the mullahs. Public hangings also made a big comeback, and when the gallows broke there was usually a machine gun handy to finish the job. The United States, the Shah's great ally, had become the house of Khomeini's 'Great Satan'.

It was a pleasure to see Roger Cooper again, though he was

now in constant demand. Tehrān was thronged with newsmen from all over the world, trying to figure out what the Iranian revolution was all about, and Roger seemed to be the only one who could actually read a Tehrān newspaper.

Most journalists were concentrating their efforts on the American Embassy and the hostages story. President Carter had already made his big mistake, trying to free the Embassy staff with a military operation. There was a belligerent, gloating atmosphere in the capital. I did a couple of shifts facing the dragooned, drummed-up chorus outside the American Embassy denouncing anything and anybody from the West, including me. I was relieved when Roger managed to break loose from his commitments so that we could leave Tehrān.

Iran is a country of many ethnic groups. Almost half the population is composed of minorities like the Kurds, the Turks, the Arabs and the Baluchis, and most of them live outside the capital. Our idea was to get to these minority peoples and see how the revolution was affecting them.

We decided to take the train to Tabrīz, where there was a large disaffected Turkish community. Despite the mullahs' prohibition on booze, Roger would not be parted from his home-made elderberry wine, and brought along a bottle with him. We both refreshed ourselves at the station before he plunged the bottle down to the bottom of his hessian shopping basket for maximum security.

The train moved off. Not long into the journey we were visited by the ticket collector who was accompanied by a grim-looking, unshaven revolutionary guard. At that stage of the revolution the guards were more feared than the army or the police. They had powers to dispatch people after only the most tenuous legal proceedings. When the ticket collector departed, the revolutionary guard poked his head back in the door.

'I smell alcohol on your breath,' he said to Roger. 'I would like a cup.' He then left, saying he would return shortly.

We had three tense minutes in which to decide whether this was a puritanical guard trying to get us to incriminate ourselves before hauling us off, or whether he was another secret sufferer from the dry revolution. I let Roger make the decision. He reckoned the guard probably needed a drink. When the guard returned and pulled down the blind I realised, with relief, that Roger was right.

In Tabrīz the revolutionary guards were out in oppressive strength. I tried to photograph some local Turks being roughed up by the guards and immediately found myself rammed up against a wall. Again it was Roger who extricated us from a nasty situation, but it took a lot of talk to some pretty thuggish characters. I'm no expert on revolutionary theory but in revolutionary practice you always see very unpleasant people on the rise. When bad things have to be done they are usually better done by bad people. The demand for them in Iran and the Lebanon was plain to see.

We got up to the Kurdish Hills again to find that revolutionary guards had rampaged there before us. The Kurds had fought them off but they had left many dead – among them my young friend from Hatfield College. He had been dragged out of his car and executed on the spot.

On the way back to Tehrān I witnessed another kind of carnage. With flights disrupted, Roger and I took a taxi 400 miles along the country's most famous road, once used by rally drivers going from Tehrān to Tabrīz, then through Afghanistan and into India. I was hoping to sleep but was kept wide awake by the spectacle of one appalling motor wreckage after another. Some were rusting and had obviously been there for years, perhaps to discourage reckless driving, though there was no sign of this happening. In any event, this seemed to be the area with the clearest continuity of policy from the tyranny of the Shah to that of Khomeini.

One day Roger said he'd heard of something incredible happening just outside Tehrān on the edge of the mountains. According to his information there was a secret firing range out there specifically for churchmen. It was true.

As we approached the range we were met by a mullah with a 9mm pistol where you would normally expect a prayer-book to be. Naturally it was the old story – no pictures. Then Roger really started to lay it on, telling the mullah how glorious the revolution was, how keen we were to further its aims. He cited my revolutionary credentials, and how I was 'close to Arafat'. The mullah was still having none of it, but I could see that he was intrigued by the Arafat reference, probably because the Palestinians were identified as fellow revolutionaries.

I drew Roger to one side to tell him that I just happened to have in my hotel room a copy of *The Palestinians*, the book I had done with Jonathan Dimbleby, and as a matter of policy I always carried my room keys around with me. Next minute we had the cab driver roaring back to Tehrān to get the book while Roger continued to work on the mullah. Two hours later we saw the dust of the cab charging back. Roger advised me on a suitable inscription – some perjury about wishing the revolution well and this group especially well. Roger handed the book over to the mullah, then turned to me and said, 'You can do it. Take the photos.'

Photographically it was amazing. Khomeini had spoken of a 'twenty million person army', which sounded ludicrous in a country of 35 million people, but now I saw how he could do it. There were mullahs everywhere lying down with splayed legs, trying to get their Kalashnikovs up straight. Some were having trouble with their skirts, and those who weren't tended to have turban troubles while in the prone position. They were banging away, with every appearance of enjoyment, and a few were already quite good shots.

There were squads of girls and young women too, many wearing the chador but some in informal gear, also learning to be marksmen. I noticed that the women tended to get a poorer choice of weapons. Some had G3 rifles which have a very nasty kick. Only the lucky ones had AK-47s. The general effect was of seeing a synod of Anglican bishops and several troops of Girl Guides getting down to some serious gunplay together.

At that time, before the outbreak of the terrible war between Iraq and Iran, I was most struck by the elements of farce in the situation, though it did occur to me that a country which set out to militarise its clergy and its women, two of the greatest restraining influences against war in any society, could probably do a lot of harm.

33

A SHORT WALK WITH THE
MUJAHEDDIN

BY THE SPRING of 1980 the *Sunday Times* was anxious to reclaim circulation lost during its closure, and spending money as never before. The lid on the foreign budget flew off. Everyone seemed to be on the road. I pursued my projects in Iran and the Lebanon, and also took a short walk in the Hindu Kush.

The summer saw me in Sinbad the Sailor outfit, with a brand new pair of Doctor Marten's boots, trekking beside Roger Cooper and some vicious-looking members of the mujaheddin up the Khyber Pass. Well, not directly up the Khyber, but close. We were entering Afghanistan illegally while the Russians were in occupation. Our forty mujaheddin, we had been told, were bent on giving the Red Army a bloody nose, and we had to blend in with them. We had been secretly vetted, turbaned and supplied with very wide, very baggy trousers. After travelling to Peshawar, where we collected food, we were to join a band of guerrillas who were heading north into the mountains.

We stood on a parched area of hillside with two large and heavy sugar sacks containing our supplies – predominantly pilchards. All we had been able to buy on the North-West Frontier were tins, which the mujaheddin escort would have preferred us not to bring, but I had learned my lesson about going on long marches without sustenance. Besides, guerrillas in mountain country usually have mules to carry such things.

When our hosts arrived, bristling with arms and moustaches, they brought no mules and immediately set off in an upward direction into trackless country, leaving Roger and me standing with the sacks. When Roger translated from the Farsi the news that they didn't want to carry the sacks, I complained that I couldn't carry the cameras *and* the pilchards for a hundred miles over the Hindu Kush. Two aggrieved Pathans were then deputed to heave up these daunting mountains of food.

Before long we stopped for target practice. A small hand mirror was produced and placed a hundred yards away for the guerrillas to fire at with their AK-47s. Nine out of ten of them missed by a wide margin. It was going to be quite a show, I thought, when they engaged the Russians. Roger and I felt it prudent to decline their invitation to have a go.

For four days we kept up the hard walking through immensely rugged terrain, along crystal streams packed, I noted wistfully, with darting trout. We stopped at mud-walled villages and I slept in Afghan fortified houses, eating with our hands from the communal pot. I was dubious about this, but it was obligatory for the sake of good relations.

It was for the sake of relations as well as my fastidiousness that eventually I broke into the sardines. That was when I discovered why the streams were still well populated with trout. The Afghans don't like fish.

We made more of a hit with Roger's field glasses. They passed from hand to hand, and that was the last we saw of them. The one boy in the band was blamed for their disappearance, though he was clearly not responsible. Other journalists told us later that this was par for the course. Indeed we may have got off lightly. Making people carry heavy sacks was reason enough to bump off a Westerner or two on the North-West Frontier.

Two Russian MiGs came rushing through our high valley and we were forced to take cover under mulberry trees. I knew now that we were close to a Russian outpost, our presumed objective, and I made efforts to pin down our commander on when we would be arriving at the front. Always his reply was, 'Soon. Very soon.'

The MiGs came over again, and once more I pressed the

commander. This time he surprised me. 'Three o'clock. We move at three o'clock.'

With a few spare hours in which to prepare ourselves, Roger and I went to bathe in one of the crystal streams. Be clean, I thought, if you're going to the front, in case you have to meet your Maker. I lay back luxuriantly in the clear water, then leapt out swiftly. I was covered in leeches. We got them off and returned to find the mujaheddin snoring in a cave. I said to Roger, 'I don't believe this lot intend going anywhere near the front.' Roger tried out his Farsi again, and so it proved.

'We are not taking you to the front in case it brings the Russian air power down on us.'

Instead they took us to an old Russian helicopter that had been shot down long ago and looked remarkably like one that had appeared in every TV news report I had seen. They posed on it for the camera in a practised sort of way before Roger announced that they were taking us next to see a newly captured gun which they planned to turn on the fort. It turned out to be a Russian Howitzer with flat tyres. There was no way it could be moved, and no way either that the Afghans were ever going to become close-combat fighters. The terrain has never made it necessary. They are nevertheless very effective at long range, as the Russians found to their cost. You can starve people by surrounding their positions, even cut off whole areas. Because of the frequent ambushes, no one could get to them. You can achieve a total amputation, but it is a long and slow business that doesn't lend itself to the camera.

For the whole eight years of the Afghan war no journalist who went in ever came out again with any credibility. They all got the same old run-around, the same Russian helicopter shot. So after 70 miles of hard hill-walking I was feeling pretty fed up and said to Roger, 'We've done all this sweating for nothing. I won't walk another mile with these people.'

We started back in the care – if you can call it that – of two unfriendly brigands from the guerrilla gang. So protective were they of their charges that after prayers one day they left their rifles behind. 'Oh dear,' one of them gestured, hitting the side of his head comically, as if to jog his memory before going back for them.

Roger became highly suspicious of their conduct. 'You know the old Afghan tradition,' he said. 'If they want to bump you off, which they often do just to be rid of you, they wait until you're asleep and then drop a great rock on your head.'

'In that case,' I suggested, 'you sleep while I watch. Then you can do the same for me.'

We slept at night in caravanserais when we could find them, so as to be with groups of people. In the morning our guards said their prayers and then we would be off. One day, as we were climbing a steep escarpment, the MiGs came sweeping in again. They bombed the caravanserais below and we heard frightened whinnying as half the camels ran away.

Further on, I washed my feet in a stream in what appeared to be an abandoned village. I had an enormous blister and my boots were filled with blood. An old man appeared with a filthy bandage on his finger, the top of which had been chopped off. While I was treating it with antiseptic, two surly Afghans with rifles came up. A shouting match ensued. They thought we were Russian spies, and the old man, deeply insulted at the slur on his new friend, went for them with a knife.

I launched myself after him like a rugby forward, and just held on to his wavering old hand as it brandished the knife. I brought him away with my arm around his shoulder until we reached the outskirts of the village, where we shook hands and said goodbye. In all this our two protectors were nowhere to be seen.

That night we kept guard in turn in the open, scanning the astrological positions of the great galaxy of stars.

Fifteen miles from the Pakistan border, Roger started to look very strange. He was forty-eight years old and the strain was beginning to tell. He had a hiatus hernia and was building up a fever. Somehow he staggered through on aspirin and at the border fell into the nearest transport, which happened to be a pick-up truck full of refugees. Physical tiredness swept over us like a tidal wave, but there was still the Pakistani post to pass. We were entering illegally of course, just as we had left illegally. Black with the sun, with light Caucasian eyes, we were dead-ringers for Russian spies for those with suspicious minds.

As I lay drowsing at the border post I felt a digging in my back. 'Come down, mister, come down.' Roger, on his last legs, collapsed into manic laughter. Two English Sinbads climbing down from a Japanese truck. Two escapees from Sadler's Wells and Gilbert and Sullivan, were being taken under armed guard to a police station in Peshawar. I wondered if illegal entry came under the Islamic laws on flogging.

After much explaining we ended up before the turbaned District Commissioner at a very grand residence. 'Well, gentlemen, I suppose you'd like a cup of tea,' he said. I felt we were all right as we sat there on the lawn in our filthy garb, gazing into the fading sun. I knew when I saw the arrival of the cucumber sandwiches.

Afghanistan was a lesson to me. I had always thought that shared hardship brought you closer to people. The Afghans were a special case. I approved of their aims, but despite sharing a hard time there was no way I could feel affection for them.

I am not so sure about Roger. I saw him in London a few months later, after he'd created quite a stir coming through Heathrow in full Afghan rig. I brooded on about the wretchedness of our adventure with the mujaheddin, but he said it hadn't been so bad. While convalescing from his fever, he told me, he had learned Arabic.

34

THE UNEASE OF CHANGE

I WAS NOT surprised when the *Sunday Times* did not use my Afghanistan pictures. There wasn't much mileage in the same old boring helicopter, the posing mujaheddin, and the static gun. When my Beirut pictures also flopped, few being used, I was uneasy. They were of a different order altogether – outstanding anywhere in the world. Finding a home for them was not difficult. Publishers were pressing; I planned a new 'Beirut in Crisis' book, but I was worried about what was happening at the newspaper.

Although the *Sunday Times* had regained its readers, the Thomson family had lost its appetite for the fray. In the autumn of 1980 Ken Thomson put *The Times* and the *Sunday Times* on the market. He was exasperated by the long struggle with the printers.

The best buyer in his view – though not in that of the journalists – was the Australian proprietor Rupert Murdoch. He was already well-represented on Fleet Street through his ownership of the *Sun* and the *News of the World*.

There were printers who thought that they had done everybody proud by seeing off the Thomson family, though this proved, to say the least, short-sighted. In industrial terms, Murdoch would soon butcher and knee-cap all his printers with his move to Wapping.

Murdoch was deeply unpopular with *Sunday Times* journalists, who had tried to get his deal blocked by the Monopolies Commission, but his first moves as the new proprietor were cunning rather than inflammatory, beginning with a change of editor.

Harry Evans (ill-advisedly as it turned out) left his firm power-base in the *Sunday Times* to become editor of *The Times*. On the *Sunday Times* he was succeeded by his deputy, Frank Giles, a well-respected journalist but without Harry's fire.

Through 1981 it appeared that Rupert Murdoch might content himself with just picking on the printers, but the journalists' time would come. We were in a phoney war period, watching, waiting, as some of our structure began slowly to crumble beneath us. Some of the best journalists, feeling the first tremors, made a decision and left. We had yet to experience the full force of the landslide.

In this time of unease I had much uneasiness of my own. Too many of my assignments were half-baked, or going off half-cocked. Either my timing, or the newspaper's, or possibly both, was falling off.

I got to Rhodesia when it was becoming Zimbabwe, but only after the guerrillas had already won and were handing in their weapons. I had to content myself with taking pictures of them with these arsenals, which were like a dream memory sequence of all the weapons in all the wars I'd ever known – from the old British Lee-Enfields and Stens of Cyprus through the guns of Vietnam to the present.

I headed for the Tamil troubles in Sri Lanka with Ian Jack, but I failed to get around the army's block on photographers going to the front. I felt really low about that. Though one can't expect to win them all.

I had more success in India, where I went with Simon Winchester. We did a story about police torture of suspected criminals in Bihar – the notorious Bhagalpur Blindings – but even there I was conscious of missing *the* picture. The most wanted criminal in Bihar at that time was a woman bandit leader called Phulan Devi, who was said to shoot her lovers when she tired of them. I never did get to photograph Phulan.

Back in England there was frustration of a very different kind. I was subjected to a lengthy Press Council case.

THE UNEASE OF CHANGE

It had seemed a mundane magazine assignment: to photograph the Liverpool Police in action. Police treatment of suspects had become a hot topic. Controversial too were stop-and-search campaigns. I photographed, among much else in this connection, the routine searching in a police station of a poorly dressed old man who seemed much the worse for drink.

Flak, the first of this sort in my long career, came from an unexpected quarter – not from the police, but from the old man's solicitor. He took a complaint to the Press Council, asserting that I had invaded his client's privacy. He was said to be particularly incensed because the searching officers were wearing gloves, giving the impression that his client was unclean. My fault was said to have been failing to ask the man's permission before taking the photograph. These were moot points of course. I had been invited by the police to photograph events freely, both on the streets and in the station, so I assumed that there was a general clearance. In addition, the old man did not seem to have any objection at the time.

I lost the case and was given a Press Council reprimand. I didn't feel guilty, but it left a nasty taste in my mouth. If consistently pursued, the Press Council's line would make photo-journalism and news television almost impossible. No film of any arrest, demonstration, disaster, riot or disorder, war or crime, would be possible if all those depicted had first to give permission.

While this was rumbling on interminably in the office, other uneasiness was troubling the tranquillity of life at home. A coolness was imperceptibly pushing Christine and me apart. It was always her way to walk through troubles with her head held high, but our difficulties now were of a different kind. I think she sensed there was another woman though I had never hinted at it, and hadn't really thought of it that way, for I still loved my wife.

I had met Laraine Ashton at a high-life cocktail party at the Ritz – not part of my customary stamping ground. After my lonely prowl through the under-class of English society and the publication of *Homecoming*, the *Sunday Times* magazine had sent me on a lightweight jaunt in the opposite direction, to the Paris fashion shows. It was a stunt typical of those ambivalent days just before the closure – man of action in haunts of beauty sort of stuff. I enjoyed myself, believing I had earned a respite from stinking foxholes under constant bombardment, but at the same time I felt faintly corrupted by the exercise. Somehow I knew that photographing beautiful women was not part of my calling, much as I admired the skill of my old friend David Bailey in this field. It was in Paris that I met Bailey again after a long absence since our capers in the Sixties. With the paper's closure, and my future livelihood shaky, I began to see much more of him and to find my way around that glittering world in which he always seemed to shine. So it was that I found myself at the Ritz, with Bailey's wife Marie Helvin introducing me to Laraine.

We dined that evening at Langan's Brasserie, where somehow Marie had arranged a separate table for Laraine and me away from the rest of the party. I felt relaxed and talkative as I gazed into those huge eyes under that great shock of blonde hair.

A week later Laraine appeared at the Olympus Gallery with a copy of *Homecoming* and asked the receptionist if I would sign for her. I signed it and a connection was made. By then I knew that Laraine was not only very beautiful but also a high-powered businesswoman who ran her own model agency. She invited me to her flat in Notting Hill, which seemed to me the most stylish apartment I had ever seen. We sat on the floor in front of the open fire and drank wine and talked in the flickering firelight. I stayed late, but not very late because I had to pick up my gear and be off before first light on an unromantic story about oil rigs in the North Sea.

That was how the affair began. It had its fire and its fights, and a romance I yearned for. I was no longer the lonely outcast of the *Homecoming* book. I didn't expect it to last, but it did. We were too strongly attached emotionally to bring the affair to an end.

While Christine grew silent a change was taking place in me. I lost the avid energy that had propelled my career. I was less drawn to the thick of the action. I no longer wanted, if I ever had, to commit a long-drawn out suicide in the pursuit of heroism. I wanted to live without testing my courage all the time. Yet war was still a part of me. It was important to me to know that I could still face it out there, still keep my head under fire, if I had to, and yet I also knew that this part of me was doomed. I couldn't go on doing these things for much longer. I was looking for that one last war to express all I knew before walking away.

35

WHITE TOWEL FROM THE CAMINO

REAL

WHEN THE CHANCE came I had a premonition that all might not be well. It was a feeling that did not go away as I flew off once again a few thousand miles across the world with a few rolls of film, a bag, and a knowledge of the violent course of revolution. In this case the revolution was another in the chain that started in the Caribbean with Castro, and it set off the usual avalanche of American arms and aid for the government side. El Salvador, declared President Reagan, would never become another Cuba.

When I arrived in the small but strategically significant Central American state in the spring of 1982 I was not to know that this was where I would really come unstuck, nor that in a few days I would be sitting in a guerrilla camp eating red kidney beans and hearing over a crackling radio that four journalists had just been killed for attempting what I had succeeded in doing. All the same, I found a certain tension mounting in me.

Part of me relished being in Latin America again, amid that decaying Spanish architecture and the tropical vegetation. Another part of me felt a certain unease in relating to the situation that I had read up. There were the nightly murders, adding up to 200 deaths a week. Most victims were kidnapped and shot in the back of the head. The bodies were deposited on rubbish dumps on the outskirts of the capital, San Salvador. A massacre had taken place on the steps of the cathedral just before my arrival. Extreme right-wing death squads dominated the towns while left-wing guerrillas operated from the hills.

Elections were pending, to determine which political direction the small state took – a matter of great concern to the United States. The American networks were there in force to cover events, one news team having as many as thirty-five reporters. So frenzied was the buzz in the Hotel Camino Real that I even heard one TV man in the next cubicle in the lavatory communicating with his colleague in the dining room by walkie-talkie radio. In this mêlée I made contact with Philip Jacobson to plan an escape from the vociferous mob. He suggested teaming up quietly with a *Newsweek* photographer by the name of John Hoagland, who not only spoke Spanish but had a truck at his disposal and knew the lie of the land.

Polling day dawned to a bloody sight before Hoagland arrived. The Left had spirited their people into the capital during the night, taking up positions near the polling booths to oversee what they called 'corrupt elections', and the army had been set against them. I ventured out early in the morning to track down the source of gunfire that had disturbed my sleep. In the hour at which most capitals have their water-carts out dowsing the streets, I found soldiers dragging corpses by the heels through the accumulated rubbish and swinging them up on to open lorries. The guerrillas had been cut to pieces. It was not a good omen for an open ballot.

Election over, I was free to penetrate the guerrilla strong-holds, despite the government decree that anyone doing so would be counted an enemy and shot. I took this as merely intimidating propaganda. In Hoagland's absence I teamed up with a French cameraman I knew who had made contact with the guerrillas and was trying to get his crew to one of their encampments.

In true Hitchcock style, we met his mysterious contact in a downtown hamburger parlour. We had equipped ourselves with a Volkswagen camper from which all gear had been removed save the cameras and mikes. It didn't do to look as if we were heading far up-country. After a long drive on rough dirt roads we arrived in the large square courtyard of an old hacienda in the hills. The camper was concealed in a barn and we slept until cock-crow. While we were still drinking coffee brewed by one of the women at the farmhouse, couriers arrived from the main guerrilla unit to conduct us to our destination. My spirits were rising. This could be the big scoop.

There followed several hours of hard hill-walking, burdened down with video cameras and sound equipment. Great caution was needed to avoid an army ambush. We kept to hidden tracks and stole like ghosts across the main highway near the town of Berlin, so called by the ex-Nazis who settled there after the Second World War. In the villages we were greeted warmly by the peasants and felt among friends.

Sore of foot, tired and hungry, we came at last upon the guerrillas' outlying guard post. A loudhailer was broadcasting to the camp when we arrived. Women, children, whole families were running around like chickens. Armed men with Kalashnikovs and rocket launchers lounged in hammocks. Many of the guerrillas seemed to be no more than sixteen or eighteen years of age. Joining a food line got us the camp issue – a bowl of red kidney beans – after which we slept on the ground in the open.

The following morning camp routine was interrupted by a sudden tension as people clustered round the radio. Someone told us in a halting Spanish accent that four Dutch journalists had pleaded for their lives after being caught trying to make contact with guerrilla fighting units. They had been shot in the back while running away.

In a state of some alarm, as soon as our work was done we set off on the long and wearying journey back to the vicinity of the Pan-American Highway – a dirt-road where a journalist had been killed in a car the previous week. We were striding out along a path when just ahead we saw a movement. It was an army patrol. Doubling back to avoid detection, we returned to the farmhouse by a circuitous route. By this time we were looking very rough – haggard, unshaven, and covered with dust.

All was unnaturally quiet at the ranch, and the peasants appeared to have fled. When at last they emerged from their hiding places they were agitated and told us the army had been in the vicinity, searching for Western journalists. The man who had taken us there in the camper-van had since driven it away. We spent an uneasy night awaiting his return.

The van and its driver were still absent the next morning, so we rolled out of the ranch at early light, with all of our equipment piled on a farmer's creaking bullock cart. The peasants had offered to get us as far as the Highway, and that took courage on their part. There we waited by the roadside for one of those Third World mountain buses, packed with people going to market in the capital, their produce netted on the roof.

There was no room inside and so we were loaded on to the roof. We swayed and lurched our way downwards until we reached a small town where a bridge had been blown by the guerrillas. Telegraph poles and telegraph wires were also down. By the bridge we ran into an army checkpoint. My heart started racing as they took all the males from inside the bus and made them turn round and put their hands behind their heads.

Then they called up to us, 'Come down, señor. Come down.'

Our Spanish guide started talking to them, and there was much brandishing of our Salvadorean passes and our passports. Pandemonium broke out. A small boy of about eleven had been seized and was being picked up and pulled around. They had found wrapped round his waist like a cummerbund the revolutionary banner he was smuggling into town. They took him to an opening two hundred yards or so down the road, a barracks or police-post of some sort. I could hear his cries and wailing, and our guide said, 'That little boy will probably die when it is dark. They run as couriers for the guerrillas, and the army knows that.'

I thought wildly and briefly of making a fight for it. The French cameraman had a long scar down the side of his face and the look of a hard man. His sound engineer was built like a rugby forward. But then the small boy was returned with tears in his eyes, and they calmed me down.

Now it was our turn. My instinct to fight immediately turned to one of flight as I sensed the soldiers' level of aggression pumping up in that manner I had seen in Biafra and in Uganda. While our guide negotiated eloquently on our behalf, I was making plans to run. My heart pounded when the cameraman turned to me and said, 'They want us to go with them in their truck.'

As the truck lurched sharply away we were sitting knee to knee with escort guards festooned with ammunition. I envisaged at the very least a most disagreeable search and interrogation, and probably something much worse. I reached in my bag, as if rummaging normally, and dealt with what could immediately incriminate me. With my hands unseen, I exposed the easily developed black and white film. The colour film could not be developed before Philip Jacobson had time to raise an outcry about my disappearance. Barely had I done this before the truck came to an abrupt stop.

The lieutenant in front leapt out and took off his shirt. With care he draped round his muscular torso several bandoliers of ammunition, Rambo-style. He picked his way to a spot some fifteen yards down the road where another man stood with a gun. This is it, then, I thought.

Still ideas of running raced through my head, though I knew it to be futile. Even if my legs would carry me, there was nowhere to run to.

I could hardly believe it when the lieutenant came back and got back in the front of the truck. So we weren't to be left as bodies in the ditch. It was not reassuring, however, to be taken on to an army barracks.

In the event, we were simply held at this army complex for a few hours. We were not even interrogated hard. They chose to believe our story of being stranded without transport after filming in the villages near the highway. All the same I was shaking internally. From the township – called Usulután – we chartered a light plane back to San Salvador.

*

A day or so later I was in shape to start my promised journeys with John Hoagland. We conceived the harebrained scheme of hunting for gunfights and guerrilla hideouts, and hanging out a white flag from his Dodge truck. We had an object for the purpose – a white towel from the Camino Real hotel.

We found ourselves in trouble sooner than we thought. Entering a small country town held by Government forces, Hoagland prowled round the edge of it while I focused on the square and market place. Then, without warning, a staccato of gunfire erupted. I dived on to the floor in the covered market, feeling brave enough in time to photograph the peasants who were also cowering there. The sound of bullets hitting the corrugated iron roof was astonishing.

I started shouting – 'John, where are you?'

'Hello, I'm here, man,' he called as bang, bing, ping, pong, pang, the bullets ricocheted and detonated off the roof. It was like a thunderstorm, this sudden outburst of fire. It came and quickly went. Our main concern then was getting ourselves safely out of that town.

A day came when we got word of a big battle near the country's second major army garrison, the garrison near Usulután where we had been taken for interrogation. The army had a spotter plane up when we got to the area and we could hear heavy firing. Without noticing we ran into a position where the guerrillas had taken control of the road. There was a fallen tree ahead, blocking our path. Behind the tree was a rocket launcher and behind that a young boy. He was aged no more than fourteen. John was able to start an amiable conversation with the guerrillas in Spanish.

'They've captured a small hamlet outside town,' he said.

'Any chance we could get in there?' I asked.

Overhead a spotter plane, like those I had seen in Vietnam, was circling. We sank into the dappled shade of some banyan-like trees with the guerrillas, who were in radio communication with their newly won position. John translated: 'OK, man. We can go in.'

They took us slowly through ravines and dried-out river-beds and dried-up roads. It was very hot. There were men, armed guerrillas, on all the hills, watching us go in. At length we reached the mangroves and the newly won conquest.

The guerrillas – about 150 of them – seemed to outnumber the villagers. They proudly showed us a couple of dead soldiers, a rather unpleasant sight.

I wasn't keen to stay too long. I knew that the army was bound to retaliate – and soon. They would not be able to accept the loss of face involved in losing a position so close to their stronghold, and when armies reclaim lost ground, they do it with as much firepower as they can muster, and that meant a lot more than anything at the disposal of our guerrilla hosts. We took our pictures very quickly.

I said to John, 'Can we take any wounded with us? Take them to hospital?'

'Hang on, this might be tricky. Let's take it slowly.'

John began to reason with the guerrilla commander, sorting the thing out. Ten minutes later he said, 'OK, man, we can take them.'

People started appearing with their wounded. One man was brought out in a garden chair with a bullet hole in the side of his stomach. Another had received a bullet through his arm and a wound in the chest cavity.

'There's one more,' John said. 'And it's going to be nasty.'

We were then taken into a house where a man was lying on a handwoven rattan carpet into which a pool of blood was soaking. At first I could see only his shoulder blades and the twisted torso. He had been hit in the face. The whole area from nostrils to throat had been blown away.

We brought him along a beautiful gladed track to the road. He was making a horrible noise and flies were trying to settle on the congealed blood around this orifice. A dog, scenting the blood, came after us. I asked one of the women accompanying us for her white shawl to cover the man's terrible injury.

On the way back from this foray we ran into an army encircling movement, but as some of the wounded in our truck were soldiers from their unit, we were helped on our way.

There was no one around at the hospital when we arrived. When I found some of the staff lounging around in the dark at the back, I started shouting in English, which is not widely understood in the country. When they saw our travelling wagon and its burden of wounded, they just stood and stared. I clapped my hands and slowly they lifted down the wounded, except the man whose jaw had been shot away. I became angry and opened the truck door wide, lifting him down myself. As I carried him in I hoped to God he wouldn't fall or faint on me. They laid him on a trolley and took him away.

I kept returning to Usulután like a bad dream. A guerrilla onslaught on the town itself took John and me and an American girl photographer back there one afternoon when the town was under heavy gunfire. We saw a group of soldiers, almost as young as the guerrillas, firing without helmets on down a road. They were ill-equipped and undisciplined, and went into some houses and started clambering across the roofs. I followed them but Hoagland wasn't keen and the girl dropped behind as I climbed on to a roof for pictures of the soldiers. A rattle of gunfire rang out. As the soldiers took cover I found myself falling backwards, trying to hang on to Spanish roof tiles. They were giving way under the weight. Just before I hit the ground I got my elbow in position to break the fall and protect my spine. I was in a frenzy.

I jackknifed off the ground and rolled over in the dirt. The pain was indescribable. I seemed to be paralysed all down one side. The inhabitants of the houses were taking cover from the gunfire and the soldiers had cleared off as I writhed in agony on the ground. An old lady came out and threw up her hands in horror at the sight of me. I did not want to be caught and taken by the guerrillas for a mercenary, so I dragged myself back over the roof in the reverse direction from the way I had come, back in the direction of Hoagland. I dropped into a courtyard where the pain started hitting me terribly.

Crawling on my hands and knees into a doorway, I heard the crackling of a military radio. It was some kind of communication post, with a solider in residence. I dragged myself into the room and tried to speak to him in English, but he didn't understand. I lay on that floor for twelve hours through the sleepless night. I thought I had broken my hip, but my abiding worry was that the guerrillas would kick in the door and throw in a grenade.

In the morning the gunfire had stopped, and a woman and a small boy appeared at the door. She screamed with surprise but quickly recovered and made a splint for my left arm from a cardboard box. A truck eventually arrived and took me to the same hospital I had visited with a cargo of wounded only days earlier. They put me in plaster and released me on to the streets once the battle was finally over. Victorious soldiers were parading, and among the crowd I found John Hoagland and the American girl.

'Jesus Christ, man. I was worried,' Hoagland said. 'I thought you were killed. God, am I glad to see you.'

As the effects of the morphine shot they had given me in the hospital wore off so the pain once again became severe. John and a very kind journalist from *Time* magazine organised my return to San Salvador where Philip Jacobson took over and had me X-rayed. (There had been no X-ray unit in Usulután.) My arm was broken in five places. I was put on to the first flight out with – for the second time in my life – a first-class ticket paid for by the *Sunday Times*.

I seriously wondered whether it was my luck or my skill that was running out.

PART FOUR

The End of the Affair

36

THE TASK FORCE GETS AWAY

EL SALVADOR WAS the beginning of my undoing – of my health, of my marriage, of my career. I was going home to a family which had always had to live with the fear of my coming back a broken man. My wife had seen me injured before, and I had suffered the pain of seeing her pain, and her dread of what might become of me. Now it was not just in my own home that I would be inflicting pain, for there was also Laraine.

On the flight back to London my mind drifted over the emotional tangle in which I was now caught. Laraine knew about my wife but not how close I still was to Christine. Christine did not know about Laraine, though I guessed she suspected something. I swallowed more painkillers, poured some more beer, turned up the Panasonic.

My spirits were lifted at the airport by Mike Rand, the *Sunday Times* art editor and friend of many years, who brought with him a newer friend, the writer David Blundy. They took my films and whisked me straight to the Middlesex Hospital where I lay for the best part of a morning, naked under a sort of shroud. Staff kept coming up with a cheery 'Hello' and lifting the sheet inquisitively before I could stop them.

'Could I have my clothes back?' I said finally. 'I'm tired of being a peepshow.'

Then someone, a visitor, walked up as I lay waiting, and I saw it was Laraine. It was like going public on our secret.

My hip wasn't broken, but my ribs had been snapped like

dry twigs, sending paralysis down one side of my body. It was to take almost two years to restore reasonable mobility to my arm.

I went home to an unhappy household. My wife had discovered my affair with Laraine. I should have made a complete break but could not bring myself to abandon her or the children. We lived in a home we'd built together, and my ties to both family and place were still very strong. I had made the mistake a lot of men make; I had allowed myself to fall in love with someone else. It was a savage time emotionally.

It was not long before I began to fret about work also. A crisis in the Falklands was blowing up. With my arm in plaster, like a broken jackdaw wing, I got on the phone to the office, disturbed that they hadn't already been in touch with me about it.

'Listen, I want to be in on this,' I said.

'Yes, okay. We want you to be in on it,' I heard down the line with the merest touch of hesitance. 'Do you think you can make it?'

'Yes, I can make it,' I said with concocted bravado. 'I can get my hand up to my face now. I've already taken some pictures with one hand. Of course I can do it. So will you get me on to this task force?'

'Okay, Don. Everyone here'll be working on your behalf. We'll get you on if we possibly can.'

We were in the fourth year of Thatcherism, and the magazine was now in the hands of a new Murdoch-appointed editor, Peter Jackson. Already policy had started going against too much hard photo-journalism and further into softer areas, like consumer goods and fashion. Mike Rand and the rest of the old crowd on the magazine were hanging in, but it wasn't always an easy matter.

One day Mike had come on the phone and said, 'We have a problem.'

'What?' I said.

'I don't know how to tell you this, but there's a real battle in the office. Jackson's spiked your Salvador story.'

I said, 'He can't have. He can't have thrown out those

258

Salvador pictures. If he's done that, I'm going to resign.'

'Jackson says it's because the Falklands task force is assembling. He doesn't want pictures of dying Salvadoreans when there might be dying *British* soldiers at any minute.'

'That can only be an excuse,' I said.

It would be weeks before the task force made any contact, assuming they ever did, and British soldiers dying then could hardly exclude Salvadoreans who had died already. Those pictures of El Salvador had been taken at some cost. I went to the office and spoke to two friends there, Phillip Knightley and Stephen Fay. I was pacing up and down like an angry lion. There was more than my pictures at stake, there was a principle. No front-line photographer could be expected to go out and take risks if they were to have their work junked for non-photographic reasons when they got back.

In a fuming condition, I typed out my resignation. Knightley called out, 'What are you doing? No, don't resign. You *mustn't*. It would be very foolish. See Frank Giles. Try to negotiate this one with the editor.'

Despite his good offices, I went over the top. The editor was out, so I slid my resignation under his locked door.

Giles called me in to see him soon afterwards. He was adjusting his clothes, shooting his cuffs to expose his gold Rolex, grooming himself as if he had difficult things to say. But in this case he was generous. He was searching for a solution, trying to prevent me from falling into my own emotional trap.

'I'm not going to accept your resignation,' he said. 'What we need is some kind of compromise. Don't panic. This can be sorted out.' Agreement was reached. They would reinstate my story. I would withdraw my emotionally charged resignation.

But Jackson still wanted to impose his will. Mike Rand had made a brilliant cover from my Salvador pictures. It was all laid out and in proof. Jackson chucked out the cover. I was very fed up at this: I had an arm which the doctor said would never be 100 per cent again, which might mean fewer prospects, and now the hard-won cover was thrown away.

For all the danger and damage, I felt I had received a wretched award.

I threw myself into the Falklands prospect. The selection system for the task force was that each newspaper put forward the names of journalists they wanted to go, and the Ministry of Defence decided which of them actually went. The reason for this was said to be the need to limit the number of correspondents. There were other reasons too, it emerged.

I phoned the MoD. 'My name's Don McCullin and I would like to check my name is down for the Falklands on behalf of the *Sunday Times*.'

'Yes, we know who you are, old boy. We'll put your name down on the priority list.' It should, I thought, have been there already. 'There's no problem. Don't worry about it. We'll come back to you.'

They didn't. I could see the task force getting away without McCullin being part of it. I started drinking. It was painful to me not to have been one of the first people they had approached. I even wondered, in the light of the Salvador episode, if my own newspaper had blocked me. Whatever it was, there were no signs I was going to be aboard one of the ships that were leaving almost daily. The *Uganda* set sail, the *Canberra* got away. I plotted their course. They were going to Ascension Island, before they made the long run to the South Atlantic. I was heart-broken.

I convinced myself that the *Sunday Times* had deliberately avoided establishing my credentials. It was utterly plain I wasn't going. I was frantic, and more depressed than anyone can imagine. I wanted to be with the British Task Force. I had been with every other serious army in the world in the last twenty years and had more experience of battlefields than any senior officer or soldier going down to that South Atlantic war.

I made one last desperate effort. I went to the Imperial War Museum and discussed the situation with their photographic department. I knew they had sent a woman artist to paint and draw pictures of the action, and asked if I could also go to the Falklands as their official photographer. They said they were amazed I wasn't already on the high seas, steaming south. I was promised a speedy answer to my suggestion. It came soon enough. They would very much like me to go for the Museum but they could not afford the fee.

'I'll go for one pound,' I said in a rush before they could change their mind.

They promised to make arrangements immediately.

Weeks went by. The last ship to leave headed south. I sent telexes to government ministers and was on the phone constantly. I knew that Commander Jeremy Moore had not yet departed and that he would be flying to Ascension and joining the convoy there for the last stretch of the voyage. I also knew that one of the trustees of the Imperial War Museum was an Air Vice-Marshal, and that if they really wanted me to go then he would be able to fix it for me to fly with Moore. I waited on tenterhooks.

There was no explanation. It just didn't happen. I became overbearingly demonstrative. I felt a terrible humiliation from my arm and everything else.

Yet it was not my arm that had led to this situation. Nor had the *Sunday Times* dragged their feet on my behalf. It wasn't until I read an article by Fred Emery, an old Vietnam hand, in *The Times* that I discovered the real reason. Those chosen to accompany the Task Force were, for the most part, inexperienced people, and this was a calculated policy designed to keep the flow of information under tight control.

I later learned that my name had been on the original list at the Ministry of Defence to go to the Falkland Islands but it had been struck off by higher authority. By whom exactly? Mike Nicholson of Independent Television News and Max Hastings of the *Evening Standard* were the only really experienced, senior war correspondents who got there. They worked impeccably. Max knew how to get himself in, and his stuff out. Few others did. It became a very British wall of censorship. The Falklands war was – and is now – pretty poorly documented, even at the Imperial War Museum, not to say the *Sunday Times*, which didn't have a photographer there at all. Only one reporter, John Shirley, went for them.

Only two photographers were there for the entire campaign, and of those one was an agency man.

I wrote a letter to *The Times*. This was most unlike me, but I was angry. I dictated it and Christine typed it out. I felt I had earned the right to be at the Falklands War with my own blood. I'd spilt blood in Salvador, I'd spilt blood in Cambodia, but when it came to my own country, my blood wasn't good enough for them. I would rather have bled for England, bled in the Falklands, along with my own army. But that army was denied me.

It was a point of honour. I felt dishonoured by my own country. I sat awake at nights, a man of forty-six, in tears. I was boozed up and tearful when the bulletins and dispatches started coming back from the Falklands.

37

BREAKING POINT

I WAS SAVED from too much vodka and introspection by another war. While the Task Force was mustering in the South Atlantic, a new conflict broke out in the country I had been drawn back to again and again over many years – the Lebanon.

This time the Israelis, incredibly, were to press their war against the Palestinians into the city of Beirut itself.

There were risks in my getting there. A death warrant was still out for me in East Beirut, and there was no quick way into West Beirut. The airport, of necessity, had been closed. I could only get there in good time by boat from Larnaca in Cyprus, and that boat docked in Jounieh, above East Beirut.

It was an edgy crossing. The boat, which was run by a forceful blonde woman and her chap, was called the *Ark*. I felt I needed an ark. I was still in a pretty raw state. Indeed, I had a row with some Lebanese who pushed in front of me in the queue, which was not wise. While I slept on the overnight crossing, the offended Lebanese inquired of the blonde lady who I was and where I was going. His story was that he wanted to make amends, to invite me to his house. I didn't believe a word of it.

'It sounds to me,' I told the lady when she reported it to me, 'more likely he wants me killed.'

Landing, showing my passport and crossing through East Beirut to the West, was a tense business. But the Christian Falange had, it seemed, forgotten or lost track of my offence in Quarantina. They let me through. I went to the

Commodore, where I found my old friend from New Guinea days, Tony Clifton, covering the Israeli advance for *Newsweek*. I was there when the Israelis arrived.

What they did to that sad city was really quite unbelievable. They bombed it and shelled it with phosphorous shells. Children were burnt, people were maimed. The civilian population of West Beirut came under a rain of fire. It was very hard to stomach.

Darting round, trying to work under this assault, was a daily gamble. One day Clifton and I set off for his office as a great cluster of shells and rockets started exploding in front of us. We ditched the car and ran for the shelter of a nearby building. We took cover under the alcove of the stairs. Emerging during a pause in the shelling, we saw women and children running among a host of burned-out and broken cars. We ran back to the Commodore hugging whatever cover was available.

'It's a miracle you turned back before you reached the *Newsweek* building,' a journalist told us. 'It's taken two direct shells. One of them hasn't exploded. It's still lying there in Tony's office.'

The Israelis' main objective was presumed to be the Palestinian camps of Sabra and Shattila. The aim was to destroy at least Arafat's power-base, and if possible the man himself, but from the widespread nature of the shelling it seemed as if they were intent on reducing the whole of West Beirut, if not to complete ruins, then at least to the maximum of tears. There were strange rumours of new types of bomb being used, bombs that could suck up air and collapse concrete buildings at one blast. There was no mystery about what the phosphorous shells could do. They could reduce people to shrivelled burnt husks.

A small but pressing concern for newspapermen as they covered such wretched sights was that they worked under threat of kidnapping. Kidnappings which were not all political. Beirut was more than ever a lawless city, a lair for bandits, spivs and thugs. The Commodore was full of such types, profiteering from the media, running film to Damascus at a cost of hundreds of thousands of dollars. When the local driver of a British TV team was killed in the shelling, his brother came to the hotel and took the TV reporter and his cameraman away at the point of a Kalashnikov, to hold them hostage for ransom, by way of compensation. Their station came through eventually with £22,000. The brother bought, it was said, a Mercedes with the money.

Yet these risks paled to insignificance beside the suffering of the population. The consequences of bombing a mental hospital are something it is hard to wrap the mind round, but this is what I saw one day.

I was taken to a half-ruined building in the Sabra area at least half a mile from any PLO post. It had been attacked with artillery, rockets, and naval gunfire, despite the flags on the roof – one white, the other bearing the Red Cross. Shells had rained down on that hospital, decapitating people who were sitting in their beds, killing them with blast debris, slicing into them with glass shards. Most of the staff had fled the bombing, except two of the most courageous. Now the wounded insane were tending the insane. They were to do so without relief for five days, cut off by the battle. An insane woman kept coming up to me, thinking I was a French doctor from the old days. She was carrying a spastic child. She kept saying, 'Where shall I go Sir? Sir, what shall I do?'

In the wards children had been tethered to their beds, pushed into the middle of the room for protection from blast and debris. Now they lay in pools of their own urine and excreta, which were covered in flies, while the sisters desperately tried to get round. There were hundreds of patients, and only two staff.

One of the sisters took me to the most helpless and uncomprehending of their children. They had put them in the safest place in the hospital, a windowless small internal room. The sight was appalling, as of two or three litters of new-born rats on the floor. They were children with severe congenital defects. They were blind, incontinent, deformed, sometimes mongoloid, writhing in their own secretions.

'When the bombing came,' said the sister, 'to put them in here was all we could do.'

I took more pictures in the geriatric wards. One elderly and dignified patient came up to me and said, 'How did this happen? Have the sane no conscience?'

Twenty-six patients and staff had been killed and seriously wounded in the shelling. The sight of that hospital will never leave me.

Not long after the mental hospital bombing, I was present when a huge modern apartment block took a direct hit. It was an expensive block for the very rich. It was one event in a sequence of endless horrors in Beirut but, like the mental hospital, it scarred my brain.

All the press corps had turned out after the huge explosion. It was close to the Commodore hotel. The Israelis were bombing here, it was assumed, because of Arafat. He had a number of 'safe' houses in the city and it was suspected this could be one of them. He would travel unpredictably between the locations, often with heavy security guard. The Israelis tried to follow him around with their firepower.

They had many spies in West Beirut, posing as vendors and janitors. A seemingly simple-minded old man who had sold hard-boiled eggs on street corners turned out to have been their forward control officer. These people, it later emerged, helped co-ordinate the Israeli assaults.

When we reached the site of the explosion, there was total devastation. The whole building had collapsed. People were tearing at the concrete. There was a man half-hanging out of what was left of this building, still alive. He was dragged out. Then we stood, not knowing what to do.

Suddenly there was a scuffling and a spine-chilling screaming and wailing. A large buxom woman came round the corner in an uninhibited paroxysm of grief. Men were trying to comfort her, to restrain her without touching her. You cannot touch another man's wife in the Middle East. My mind was slow and stupefied with horror. I did what I rarely do – clumsily I snatched a shot of her. The woman charged at me in hysterical outraged anger as a Palestinian with a 9mm pistol tried to wrench the camera from my wounded arm. Then the woman piled into me. She hurled herself at me and battered and pounded me about. For a moment I became and felt like all the evils that had ever beset this city. I felt for every reason or unreason in the world that somehow I deserved this punishment.

A few hours later a journalist approached me at the Commodore. He said, 'That woman . . .'

'Don't talk about it,' I said, 'Don't tell me.'

He told me first of her circumstances, the reasons for her anguish. Other journalists had asked her about her fight with me. She had told them of her grief – how her whole family had been exterminated in that bombed building.

Then he told me the rest. 'As she was telling her story, a car-bomb went off just where they were standing. They were unscathed. She was killed outright.'

It was to be my last serious war assignment. The final image of war for me would be that grief-stricken woman and the wretchedness of those children in the Sabra mental hospital. Yet I did not know this at that time, for I became absorbed in a wretchedness of my own making. I did the most painful thing of all in a painful life. I think now it was also one of the wickedest things I ever did, and it hurt me almost as much as seeing my father die. I left home and began to live with Laraine.

It was a situation in which no one could be happy. I had to choose to give up Laraine or give up my family. But I felt there was no choice, even with my wife and children crying at the door of our house. I drove to London in the darkness, down the M11, trying not to look back.

In time I bought a house in Somerset, and Laraine and I threw ourselves into doing it up and working the garden. We travelled all over the world together, and when we were in London the phone never stopped ringing with invitations to exciting events. We talked of having a child. It seemed like a perfect time, but I was dogged by a shadow of conscience, even though my wife and children became forgiving.

I took some time off work, not with the thought of giving up but to let the upheaval in my life settle down. When I returned it was to another assignment with Norman Lewis, and just the prospect of it was enough to restore the light to my professional world. I had such fond memories of our times together in Latin America when, the day's work done, Norman would lie in his hammock, looking out over the Venezuelan savannah, and I would add some lime (which I had scrounged from the Indians) to his glass of vodka. I would watch him quietly and contentedly sipping his drink in this beautiful and lonely place, and was as happy then as I have ever been.

The sequel was to be bitterly disappointing. The Vietnamese were gearing up for their tenth anniversary celebrations as a united country but there was little prospect of Western journalists being allowed in. Norman felt sure, however, that they would make a few exceptions. His credential was a long record of support for a united Vietnam, whatever the political colour; mine was the distinction of having been thrown out by the expiring South Vietnam regime.

The Vietnamese refused to issue us with visas. It was not a rejection on the Falklands scale but it was a rejection none the less, and it hurt. As in earlier times of stress I went back to the Lebanon, where war was still raging. That turned into a farce.

The Druze was being hammered by 17-inch shells from an American battleship that had recently been taken out of mothballs, while the Christian Lebanese army was also engaging them in a spirited battle in the Chouf mountains. From the roof of the Alexandria Hotel David Blundy and I watched this million-dollar firework display, ducking behind the concrete lift-shafts whenever we saw tracer bullets coming in our direction.

Before going into the Chouf we received a private briefing by the Lebanese General Aoun, during which David's eye settled on a clockwork toy on the general's desk. It was irresistible. David's obsession for wind-up toys knew no bounds. His long arm snaked out and, without taking his eyes off the general, he began absently winding it up. It then shot out of his grasp and started leaping furiously all over the briefing table. Like some huge cat, David was trying frenziedly to pounce on it and stop it. The general droned on as if nothing were happening.

In the mountains our escorting officer steered us clear of the front, though David never did lose his obsession with clockwork toys or dangerous places. One of them was El Salvador, where he was killed some years later.

38

THE NASTIEST PLACE ON EARTH

THE RUMBLINGS SINCE Rupert Murdoch's arrival at the *Sunday Times* became much more ominous towards the end of 1983 when there was a change of editor. Frank Giles, a survivor of the old regime, was edged into early retirement to make way for a man little more than half his age.

Andrew Neil, then thirty-four, although he looked much older, was said to be Murdoch's first choice as editor. He was appointed, it was said, to shake up the newspaper, to get those staff who would serve the new Murdoch purpose hopping in fear of their lives, and those who would not on the road. The idea was, in business parlance, to emerge with a leaner, fitter and more profitable enterprise, stripped of all unserviceable assets. It was a sign of the Thatcher times.

I didn't have much chance to appreciate Neil's early impact because the magazine had mercifully sent me off to 'the nastiest place on earth'.

The plan was for Simon Winchester and I to identify and then go and explore the place that best fitted that description. It obviously had to be one of those African republics where the leader always had a fresh supply of blood in the fridge, but the problem was deciding which one. In the end we homed in on the island of Fernando Po in the Republic of Equatorial Guinea where, as Simon later put it, independence had 'transformed purgatory into utter hell'.

The country had not long since got rid of its Amin-figure. Macias Nguena Bioko, the deranged leader of a tribe known as the Fang, had led the revolt against Spanish rule. As

270

president of Equatorial Guinea, he ruled by terror, super-stition and arbitrary edict, killing off countless subjects and twelve of his own ministers. The church was banned. When his wife Monica ran off, he issued a decree forbidding any child to be named Monica. Life after Macias had scarcely improved. A United Nations report on the country described it simply, and accurately, as 'decomposed'. On the island of Fernando Po plantations were overgrown and the cocoa crop lay rotting and unharvested while people starved in the streets. Poverty and demoralisation were all around. Simon and I spent most of our fortnight there sleeping on warehouse floors and dining on bananas and stewed rat.

It was a relief to get back to civilisation, though soon after reaching London, at a dinner party with Laraine, I started feeling very strange, very sick and – after one glass of wine – very drunk. She took me to the local hospital, where they diagnosed a stomach upset and sent me home. It was only due to Laraine's persistence I didn't die from cerebral malaria. Eventually she got me into the Tropical Diseases hospital, where they diagnosed and treated the real condition. At the same time Simon Winchester was in the isolation wing of a hospital in Oxford, suffering from the same revenge of Fernando Po.

When I was well enough to get my bearings again, Andrew Neil was in the fourth month of his reign at the *Sunday Times*. Distinct parallels with Equatorial Guinea were emerging. Demoralisation was widespread. Heads rolled. Reporters complained of their copy being axed, or rewritten; political lines were enforced; photographers moaned about cut-backs.

Redundancies were on offer and many rushed to take them as a retreat from what they saw as a bullying regime. Each day would see another person clearing his desk. It was obvious that Neil had an open cheque to clear out the old Harry Evans hierarchy and replace it with his own loyalists, more amenable to Murdoch's way of thinking.

I had no personal quarrel with the editor. I saw a lot of people I'd worked with closely departing even before Neil's pogrom. James Fox and Francis Wyndham had left to write books, Phil Jacobson and David King had gone freelance, Alex Mitchell departed to become the cutting edge of British Trotskyism, while Murray Sayle had gone to Tokyo to start a family at the age of fifty. I was well used to people going while I stayed in the same place. Yet I was also of an earlier era which the new management seemed to find abhorrent. And I was not what you might call a Company man. On the whole I do my own thing, which previously had been the paper's own thing also, in a very committed – some would say over-committed – way. Hitherto I'd been seen as an advantage to the paper. I didn't see why that should change. I didn't see myself as a threat to Neil, or why he should so view me. Running the newspaper wasn't my job, though like all news-papermen of my length of experience I would put in a word if things went badly astray. But the new order was really not interested in anything the old had to say.

For a while the polite forms were preserved between us. Neil and I would exchange strained rictuses in the corridor. I did not find him an attractive character but I never thought that was a necessary quality in an editor. It did not count for much if the man was running a great newspaper. But I began to have my doubts on that score, particularly in my own area. Great events would be taking place around the world and I would not be sent. I put up ideas of my own – to cover the famine in Ethiopia, the turmoil in South Africa – and again I would not be sent.

The work did not dry up by accident. At an early stage Neil gathered the magazine staff around him to describe the way ahead. A friend who was at the meeting summed up its message for me when I returned from abroad: no more starving Third World babies; more successful businessmen around their weekend barbecues. And that was the direction things took.

When I began as a photographer, I believed that my work would suffer if I allowed it to become political. In the event it turned out to be nothing but political for I consistently took the side of the underdog and the under-privileged. It had now become so political that I found myself having to fight merely to be allowed to take my pictures – and I was losing that fight.

I grew deeply unhappy. I was not doing the work for which I was known and which I had the ability to do. I was just drifting round the office, loitering without intent, very fed up.

One night I met up with a friend of mine, an American called Bill Buford who ran Cambridge University's magazine, *Granta*. We found ourselves in a little Italian restaurant in Soho, sloshing back pasta and glasses of rough red wine. He wanted to run an interview with me, and a lot of my pictures.

I unloaded my feelings about the *Sunday Times*. I told him that I thought my working life was finished. They were going exclusively for a Leisure and Lifestyles magazine. All I was doing now was standing around in a safari jacket while the safari itself never took place.

In due course the following appeared:

I still work for the *Sunday Times*, but they don't use me. I stand around in the office, and don't know why I'm there. The paper has completely changed: it's not a newspaper, it's a consumer magazine, really no different from a mail-order catalogue. And what do I do, model safari suits? Cover some Women's Institute reception? Someone in the office said recently that I should think up new approaches to my work: 'You ought to learn how to use strobe lighting, because we don't want to use any more of those photos of . . .' People are starting to reject, or at least turn their backs on, my sort. They seem happy with the way the press is developing. They certainly don't need me to show them nasty pictures. I should wise up: what is the point of killing yourself for a newspaper proprietor who wouldn't bat an eyelid on hearing you'd died?

A few days after *Granta* came out, the story about my disenchantment was picked up by the *Guardian* diary column. Michael Rand phoned me in Somerset.

'I think you should get on the train and come up. Neil's seen that piece, and he's hopping mad.'

'Do you think it's curtains?' I asked.

'Well, it might be,' he replied.

I arrived at the *Sunday Times* and went straight to see the editor's secretary, Joan Thomas, and said, 'I believe Andrew wants to see me.' I was asked to hang around for some minutes until he was ready. Then it was, 'Hello Don, will you sit down please.'

Neil said something about it being time to roll up my sleeves, which I thought was a slightly unfortunate choice of words, but I responded politely. I mentioned ideas that I had put up which made good journalistic sense but which had been vetoed. It was a conversation going nowhere because I picked up right away that Neil was not really interested in having a discussion. He wanted me out. He wanted me out because I was an irritation, an embarrassment, someone like Sir Walter Raleigh, who had been left over from the previous century, and had to be executed to tidy things up.

He just wanted to manoeuvre the dialogue so things would come out the way he planned. I knew this for sure when he asked a junior executive on the magazine to join our icy deliberations. Had he really wanted a 'roll up your sleeves' talk about what I could do for the magazine he would have called in Mike Rand, who was the best art director in the country, who had handled my pictures for twenty years, and who was just twenty paces down the corridor.

This three-handed game was played for a while, with me saying I thought the magazine needed revitalising, and Neil rejoining with – oh, we're not doing that, it's no longer that sort of magazine, and that's not what we want any more.

We were not getting anywhere. I said, 'Well, I don't want to be dragged into your office every six months and bollocked for not doing well.'

Neil then worked up the bottle to tell me what he had intended all along. 'I want to say one thing about you. I don't like people who take the money and criticise the newspaper. So I think you should leave.'

He looked across at the junior executive and back came the echo – 'Yes, I think Don should leave.'

I stood up. 'That's fair enough with me,' I said, and I turned my back on him and walked out of the room. I went straight to Mike Rand and said, 'Well, that's it.'

I walked out for good from the paper I had served for eighteen years.

39

HEART OF DARKNESS

I WENT OUT into a chilly and uncertain world, a middle-aged out-of-work photo-journalist without prospects.

There was a kind of shock wave going through Fleet Street – and not only Fleet Street, but the whole of the magazine world. It was the unofficial announcement of the end of photo-journalism. These were the monetarist-sharp Eighties and they didn't want any more shocking pictures of war, horror and famine. They wanted style. They wanted to go for consumer images. No marketing operation wanted its products advertised alongside a dying child in Ethiopia or Beirut. Now they didn't have to worry any more. The newspapers were on their side.

Domestic marketing could hardly be the driving force of what I understood by journalism. Nor after all my wars and journeys did I want to be back at Square One, snapping garden parties and celebrities, to be phoned up by a picture editor at any time of the day or night to be told – 'Don, could you go from A to B and photograph C' – and be off like one of those messenger boys who ride motorbikes around town.

Bleak times lay ahead. I tried to meet them with a semblance of the surface confidence which had carried me through dangerous times before. Inside I was a man losing his identity. My whole training had been to look out, to scan the horizon for new stories to tell. Suddenly I was forced to look inwards. In there lurked old darkness, and a new guilt from my marriage break-up.

I tried a television version of *Homecoming*, but my still

276

black and white pictures, which had such force on a page, did not transfer well to a small screen demanding movement. My thoughts – at this moment of flux – wouldn't coalesce into commentary. Besides, this *Homecoming* path was one I had trodden before. It is never wise, in a mechanical way, to retrace old ground. I felt like that clockwork toy on General Aoun's desk – wound up to do my act.

At first, and for some while, life with Laraine was an idyll. But though we did astonishing things together, I wasn't achieving much. I was lurking around the flat in Notting Hill, waiting for the breadwinner to come home. I went adrift once those *Sunday Times* days were over. I had no commitment. I was lonely. Two households mopped up a lot of redundancy money. I was hard up, and though Laraine's generosity stretched beyond all imagining, there's nothing worse for a man like me than someone else paying the bills. I am old-fashioned. I don't feel comfortable in the receiving role. I made a point of paying in restaurants, though without regular income it was a lifestyle I found impossible to sustain.

At the same time I was being polished up beyond recognition. I had been happy as that shadowy figure jumping on to aeroplanes with army gear, kitbags, helmets and boots, and wading through mud. I was that man of action. I wanted to be that man. Now I was being groomed into something else. I was persuaded to buy a dinner jacket. We were at a party, and someone said you could get one at Hackett, but whatever you do, don't buy the dead man's shoes. Because Hackett's is a posh second-hand shop, where rich old girls take their old men's gear when they pop off.

So now I am walking round in a dead man's dinner suit. I don't know why it's different from wearing, as I did in Vietnam, a dead soldier's flak jacket, but it is. When I go to these expensive dos at night, it's another person in that dinner jacket. It's not old Don McCullin. I am just airing it for this dead man. Keeping his image alive.

My real self sneaked off somewhere else. I found a new peace exploring landscape. I found it healing; the blunt side of the knife. You can run your hands down it, and they are not injured. You can touch it, and there is no blood. I found another peace in exploring distant places – travelling with my friend Mark Shand, going off to live with primitive tribes, sleeping rough and wading through rivers, losing the rubbish from my mind. I found greater peace working in our house in Somerset with Laraine. We eventually had a small elf of a son whom I totally adore. We called him Claude.

But all this took money, and I needed work. With supreme irony I found the readiest projects from the enemy that had driven me out of journalism – advertising itself. The pay was quite startling. I could earn in one day more than I earned in two months running across battlefields for the *Sunday Times*.

They wanted me there because, bizarrely, while reality was fleeing from newspapers, it was creeping back into ads. They call it pseudo-realism. It is the surface style, not the essence they are after. They order a touch of realism just as they order a touch of nostalgia; just as post-modernist architecture uses a touch of classical porch.

I give of my best with this advertising work, as I did with journalism, and sometimes – especially when I do public service advertising – I feel it's worthwhile. But sometimes I find I'm obliged to set up, with actors, for the purpose of artistic effect, the kind of scene I've waded through in blood in real life. It is not what I am about.

Essentially I'm still a newspaper animal, confronted with a lot of work I don't particularly like. I now have the most beautiful house in the world but I leave it to take pictures I often find ludicrous. If you ask me deep down what spiritual satisfaction there is in the work, I have to say almost entirely none. For that I flee to landscape in Somerset, and to foreign parts.

All this has little to do with the real reason for the shadow on my mind. That comes from something different, something utterly dreadful. Something that told me fate had really turned her face on me. I am not a dead man now. I am an insomniac, not sleeping, not eating. I feel wild. I am angry, actually. I am angry. Because my last two years must go down in my small history, in all the dreadful years, as the worst of all.

It began on a lovely July day in 1987. I was working in my dark room in Somerset, when the phone rang. I had a premonition. I mean, a telephone is just a telephone yet it can destroy you with one ring. As I left the dark room to pick up the phone, I thought, Shit, I've got to go out into the light.

I don't like going out into the light when I'm in the dark room. I like the consistency of the dark. It keeps me safe. The dark room is a very good place to be. It's a womb. I feel I have everything there that I need. My mind, my emotions, my passions, my chemicals, my papers. My negatives. And my direction. In the dark room I am totally together.

I emerged into a lovely day to answer the phone. It was my daughter Jessica.

'I'm afraid I've got some bad news for you. Mum's leg has gone funny. It's sort of paralysed. It happened in the garden at home yesterday. Something has gone badly wrong with her. She can't walk and she's gone to see the doctor.'

She sounded very worried. When I called back she said. 'Mum's arm has gone funny now.' I put down that phone after my daughter's conversation and went into the dark room. And it died for me, the dark room, that day. I just switched on all the lights. I threw away all the chemicals. I made a cup of tea and walked ceaselessly round the house, trying hard not to put two and two together or think of all the brain injuries I had seen in all those wars.

40

OF LOVE AND DEATH

CHRISTINE HAD THE support of a friend called Michael, who was an educated and charming man. He rang me to say, 'I'm afraid things are very bad. We've seen a specialist in Harley Street. He's told Christine he's afraid it's a brain tumour. She collapsed in the surgery. We took her straight to Barts.'

I drove to London. Laraine took me to St Bartholomew's hospital and waited outside. I saw my wife's mass of blonde hair as she sat on the edge of the bed.

I said, 'I'm here.'

'Michael's coming too,' she said. 'Back from Cambridge.'

We talked. She asked me to help her to the end of the ward. Suddenly I saw she was a cripple. Overnight this lovely young woman I married twenty-two years ago had become a cripple. She was dragging her leg, and her arm was stiff and useless. She was virtually paralysed all down one side. My beautiful Christine had become a hemiplegic.

My feelings were so strong I had to leave the ward. I went back to Laraine sitting in the car. I felt utterly numb. I could hardly handle myself.

I talked to the consultant. In these circumstances, you don't take much in. It could be a progressive sort of thing or not, I gathered. It could have a poor prognosis. But there were astonishing cures. They had identified the tumour. When it was possible, they would operate to remove it, though it was a very large-scale operation. Much had to be done. Many tests were needed. Many investigations, many scans . . . It all took time. We should try to focus on normal life. I had been planning to take my son Alexander to Sumatra in September: should we, I asked, go now?

'Nothing at all can be predicted,' the consultant said, 'nor at what precise time we can operate. My advice is always go ahead as planned.'

I focused on this journey to stabilise the turbulence now overwhelming my brain. Alexander hadn't been told, at Christine's request, how bad things were.

We left London, worried and tense. The last stage in the journey to the Mentawei Islands, off the west coast of Sumatra, was a sixty-mile sea crossing in what looked like a most unseaworthy local boat. People said don't worry, they're the best sailors in the world in these parts. It struck me that a lot of the best sailors in the world are at the bottom of the sea.

Halfway across, at two in the morning, we hit a Force 10 electric storm. It started with lightning and got worse and worse. The seas were climbing and forming great canyons. Like the circumstances now of Christine and our family, they had grotesque and gothic scale. Looking behind, I saw, in lightning, a wall of sea about sixty feet high. Our forty-foot boat was dwarfed as we plunged into the yawning trough. There were women and children below decks and they were wailing as we tossed. I looked for the captain and found he had abandoned his post and taken shelter from his lack of courage and lack of knowledge. He was unconscious, or fast asleep, on deck. We rolled into him to revive him. As the storm went on through the night I began to believe I had brought my son here to die. I prayed, sincerely.

We limped into the islands in the morning eight hours later than scheduled, more or less alive. My son, in the quiet aftermath, caught a fish the size of a settee. I told him how bad I felt, putting him through such dangers. He looked up and said, 'I thought it was great.'

There was a sort of grey glass between me and the sights we saw on our journeying river. The hibiscus and the orchids, and the fishing tribesmen went by like a glazed moving film. I said one morning, 'I wish we could telephone home.'

Our Indonesian guide startled me by saying, 'You can telephone. From Mentawei town. There is radio bounce. Radio bounce to Padang, Padang bounce to Jakarta, Jakarta to London.'

We made the journey by dug-out canoe to the little port that had this radio communication. Three and a half hours later, to my astonishment, because much dealing and money had been involved, they said that London was on the line. I could see Alexander outside the booth. He looked scared. I heard Laraine's voice.

'How is she?' I said straight off.

'She's fine. They've done the operation. And it's going to be all right.'

I came out of the booth and I could have embraced my son. I could have embraced the world. I said, 'Alexander, she's going to be all right. Your mother's going to be all right!' A smile spread on his face, and the tears sprang in his eyes. From there on we were like two smiling chimpanzees. We joked our way through everything, the rats, the sea storms, everything.

We went straight to the hospital when we got back to London. The doctor intercepted me before we reached the ward.

'You've got to prepare yourself for a shock.' The blood left my head. 'No. It's not what you think,' he said. 'It's just that she won't look like the woman you saw here before.'

It had been an eight-hour operation to remove her tumour.

I went in, tentative and alarmed. I approached and could see first of all . . . something like a sock where her forehead was. Her hair had all gone.

For a moment I saw a little hunched up old man. Then I drew closer. She was dozing. When her eyes opened, I thought she still looked beautiful. We talked gently. Our son was there. I left.

I did strange, distraught, unhelpful things after seeing Christine. I walked in a frantic sort of state round the wig department of Selfridges. I looked at the women in the shopping crowds. I looked at their hair. I got angry, thinking why are all these women here, with flowing hair, walking and laughing.

As I was leaving the hospital the doctor had come up to me and said, 'Can I talk to you, Mr McCullin?'

Now there's a funny thing about doctors. They won't tell you what you need to know. They skirt round it. It's a new thing with them – they don't actually hit the nail on the head. They keep on hitting your fingers with the hammer instead of the nail.

I said, 'I'd very much like to talk. What is going on?'

'It's not good news. I'm sorry.'

I went cold. 'What are you trying to tell me?'

'I'm not trying to tell you anything,' he said. 'Only that it's not good news.'

After a moment's silence I said, 'I'm totally confused. I don't find that helpful. Please, doctor, what is going on?'

'Well, we've removed the tumour,' he said, 'but I'm afraid there is a mischievous tumour somewhere else in the body and we can't locate it. She's had all the tests that anyone could have.'

I found myself floundering helplessly in a situation that was too bewildering to face.

My confidence started dying with Christine. I realised you could shoot photographs until the cows came home but they have nothing to do with real humanity, real memories, real feelings. I started a sort of non-stop analysis of my life, who I was and what I had done. It went on for twenty-four hours a day in my head, as I did futile and hopeless things that weren't any use to Christine. I didn't know the danger I was to myself and to Laraine too. I had become unwittingly, unknowingly, a danger to our relationship. Like the women in Oxford Street, I resented her. I resented her privileged health. For a year and a half of Christine's life-and-death struggle, Laraine had to struggle against my resentment and inchoate actions, until she became resentful herself at this treatment. It became our daily bread.

I went to visit Christine in Bishop's Stortford. She was on a blood-thinning drug, so she was always chilly, even in summer. She wore a wig. Her hair didn't grow again.

For a while it looked as if she was holding on, reviving even, carrying on, despite her disabilities, as normally as possible.

But the day came when she had a fit. She was rushed to hospital. A scan found another tumour. I was with her and Michael when the consultant told her: 'I'm afraid I have to tell you you've only a short time to live.'

It was like a shattering blow. It pole-axed her. She collapsed in his surgery and vomited.

I phoned my elder son Paul in Australia. The tacit agreement had been that the state of things shouldn't blight the children's lives so hard too soon. Now there was nothing for it.

Before I could tell him my news, he confided his. 'Dad, you must all come out here. I'm going to get married.'

I had to tell him. 'If you don't come home right away, you might miss your last chance to see your mother.'

He came thundering back. Months later Paul was still at his mother's side. By now the condition had altered Christine's gentle character. Her personality had changed, though she was still bravely doing her best to keep up an ordinary life. She told me once, 'Whatever you do, don't show your grief before the children.'

Paul, trying to do his best, struggled to reconcile love and death. He would move the wedding from his girl's Australian home. He would give his mother the greatest pleasure he could before her time. He would have the wedding where his mother could attend, in England.

No one felt that the smallest gaiety could be raised at Bishop's Stortford. My son asked if the wedding could be held at our beautiful Somerset village. It seemed the only solution.

I put the hardest of questions to Laraine – could we bring Christine here? Could we hold the wedding reception in our house and garden?

Laraine looked sad as she said generously, 'Of course we can.' She threw herself into organising marquees, getting the catering done. It was a most difficult situation that she was facing.

Christine was taken by Michael to buy a new outfit. She was holding on, and holding out for this wedding.

Two weeks before the day, she had another relapse. She was being eaten away by cancer. Her doctor said she couldn't survive the journey or be moved. Frantically arrangements were cancelled and rearranged again. A small wedding would take place at Bishop's Stortford. We would gather there in the living-room for the reception, so that she could be with her son on his wedding day.

Christine survived until the morning of the wedding but did not see her son married. The undertakers came to the house to collect her before we set off for the church. It was at this terrible moment that we decided to go ahead, to honour her, as if nothing had happened.

For a while I went through something like madness, never quite going over the edge.

Soon after Christine died, Laraine and I separated. Paul and his wife are also far away. My son Alexander sometimes stays with me, but mostly I'm alone in my house in Somerset. The ghosts in my filing cabinets sometimes seem to shock me – the ghosts of all those dead in all those wars, especially that little Biafran boy. Now, since that last head-on collision with life, there are also the ghosts of my loves.

With this book, perhaps they will be set free.

INDEX

Israel 219–20; Beirut bombing 264; Six Day War (1967) 82–8, 99, 145–6, 189, 191, 217; Yom Kippur battle (1973) 188–91

Jack, Ian 242
Jackson, Peter 258–9
Jacobson, Philip 191, 247, 250, 254, 272
Japan 194
Jerome's, Holloway Road 22
Jerusalem 84–8
Jeunesse see Simbas
Jihad, Abu 219
Johnson, President Lyndon 70
Jordan 144–9, 228; Palestinians 144, 217–19
Julio (Paraguayan teacher) 195–6

Kadiweus, the 151, 152
Kamairos, the 153
Kampala, Uganda 167–78
Kan Tow, Vietnam 68–9
Kano, Nigeria 108, 109–10
Kashmir 124–5
Kennedy, Father 118
Kenya: national service 26–7
Khartoum: national service 28
Khashoggi, Adnan 204
Khashoggi, Soraya 204–5
Khe Sanh, Vietnam 70, 95, 104–5

Khmer Rouge 134, 135, 136, 137, 139–41, 186, 201–2
Khomeini, Ayatollah 229, 232, 235
King, David 77, 80, 272
Kinshasa (Leopoldville) 55–6
Knightley, Phillip 82–3, 259
Ku Klux Klan 78
Kurds 233, 234
Ky, Marshal 139

Larkins, W.M. (animation studio) 21–2, 23, 30, 33, 36
Law, Roger 77
Lebanon: Christians/Christian Falange 205, 207–11, 213–14, 263, 268; Palestinians 205–6, 208, 213, 216–22, 264–7; see also Beirut
Le Carré, John (David Cornwell) 227–8; The Honourable Schoolboy 227; The Little Drummer Girl 219, 228
Leese, General Sir Oliver 91, 92
Lennon, John 80
Leopoldville, Congo 55–6, 59
Le Reynier, Jacques 220
Leroy, Catherine 106
Lewis, Norman 150–2, 153–5, 194–200, 268

Press Council 242–3
Prey Veng, Cambodia
135–6, 138–9
Provos see IRA, Provisional
Puerto Barrios 155
Pyramids, the 24

Qom, Iran 230
Quang Tri, Vietnam 182,
185, 203
Quarantina, Beirut 208–14,
216
Quartet Books 216
Quick magazine 56, 70

Ramlan massacre 220
Rand, Michael 77, 80, 89,
90, 157, 257, 258, 259,
273, 274, 275
Reagan, President Ronald
246
Red Cross, International 65,
201, 220
Rolleicord camera 28–9, 38,
40
Royal Airforce: national
service 23, 24–9
Royal Anglian regiment 162
Royal Ulster Constabulary
161
Russian occupation of
Afghanistan 236–40

Sabra (Palestinian camp)
264–6, 267
Sachs, Peter 22
Sahara desert 127–8, 130,
132

Saigon, Vietnam 67–8, 94,
134; blacklist 202–3
St Jorré, John 65
San Salvador 246–7
Sardinia 123–4
Savak (Iranian secret police)
230, 232
Sayle, Murray 83, 84, 144,
145–9, 272
Schramme, Colonel Jean
'Black Jack' 65
Shand, Mark 278
Shattila (Palestinian camp)
264
Shawcross, William 183
Shirley, John 261
Sigal, Clancy 34
Sihanouk, Prince Norodom
134–5
Simbas (Jeunesse) 59, 60,
61–2, 63
Simpson, Colin 83–5, 88
Six Day War (1967) 82–8,
99, 145–6, 189, 191, 217
Smith, Colin 127, 128
Smith, Godfrey 79–80, 193
Snowdon, Lord see
Armstrong-Jones,
Anthony
Soames, Sally 189
Soviet occupation of
Afghanistan 236–40
Sri Lanka 242
Stanleyville, Congo 55, 56,
58–60, 63
Stein, Abner 227
Stern gang 220
Stern magazine 190, 191

www.randomhouse.co.uk/vintage